BOUNDLESS HORIZONS

MARIE CLAY'S SEARCH FOR THE
POSSIBLE IN CHILDREN'S LITERACY

BOUNDLESS HORIZONS

MARIE CLAY'S SEARCH FOR THE POSSIBLE IN CHILDREN'S LITERACY

EDITORS: BARBARA WATSON AND BILLIE ASKEW

Rārangi maunga, tū tonu, tū tonu.

Rārangi tangata, ngaro noa, ngaro noa.

You have gone

But your mountain

Is everlasting.

www.pearsoned.co.nz

Your comments on this book are welcome at
feedback@pearsoned.co.nz

Pearson Education New Zealand
a division of Pearson New Zealand Ltd
67 Apollo Drive, Rosedale, North Shore 0632, New Zealand

Associated companies throughout the world

First published by Pearson Education New Zealand 2009

NZ ISBN 978-1-4425-1845-2

Cover design: Helen Andrewes
Cover image: iStockphoto
Back cover image of Marie Clay: Reading Recovery Council of North America
Text design and production: Springfield West
Produced by Pearson Education New Zealand
Printed in Malaysia via Pearson Education Malaysia (CTP-VVP)

Library of Congress Cataloguing-in-Publication Data

Boundless horizons : Marie Clay's search for the possible in children's
literacy / Billie Askew and Barbara Watson, editors.
    p. cm.
Includes bibliographical references.
ISBN-13: 978-0-325-02676-3 (pbk. : alk. paper)
ISBN-10: 0-325-02676-9 (pbk. : alk. paper)
1. Language arts (Early childhood) 2. Reading--Remedial teaching.
3. Clay, Marie M. I. Askew, Billie J. II. Watson, Barbara.
LB1139.5.L35B68 2009
372.6--dc22
                         2009005962

The dedication to this book is reprinted (with permission) from *Earth, Sea,
Sky* by Patricia and Waiariki Grace, Photographs by Craig Potton, Published by
Huia Publishers and Craig Potton Publishing.

Contents

Introduction

Boundless Horizons traces Marie Clay's pursuit of an idea that started with her research question, 'What is possible for children with reading problems?' It tells the story of Reading Recovery, the early literacy intervention that has enabled young children around the world to overcome their initial difficulties to become independent readers and writers. That remarkable international phenomenon had its origin in Marie Clay's search for the highest possibilities in children's literacy.

Our original intent was to reprint Marie Clay's early research reports, documenting the eight projects integral to the development and trialling of Reading Recovery in schools. Because these reports no longer seemed contemporary, they were not included in her 2005 publication *Literacy Lessons Designed for Individuals*. Yet we were concerned that this vital historical research record might be inaccessible to researchers, educators, and theorists. We were particularly aware of Marie Clay's caution:

> Reviews of material for articles generally go back no more than twenty years, so in the near future the early research base and rationale for Reading Recovery is likely to be lost.

When we encouraged Marie to make the research reports available in some other format she challenged us to create a new kind of publication, one that would place the reports within the broader scope of international research and evaluation.

This book responds to that challenge. It has grown to be much more than simply a reprint of the original research studies. Recognizing Marie's ongoing quest for yet unrealized possibilities just beyond the horizon, we honour the research question that motivated and guided her life's work: 'What is possible?' We have given prominence to her exceptional scientific methodology. International contributions demonstrate the strength of Marie Clay's influence on subsequent research on Reading Recovery as an evidence-based, early literacy intervention.

Part One, *Breaking the Bonds of the Ordinary*, explains the historical New Zealand educational environment in which Marie Clay studied and worked, including events leading to her early exploration of what is possible for children experiencing initial difficulties. A reprint of the original research reports follows, providing the cornerstone for this volume. The focus then shifts to an examination of her use of an *unusual lens*. She recalls:

> How early could one see the process of learning to read moving off-course? I asked. The obvious way to approach the problem was to use the strategy of biological science in studying unplotted territory, and that was to observe and record exactly what occurred in the natural setting.

Marie Clay's inspired choice of that unconventional methodology made her search possible and legitimized the unusual lens of carefully controlled, sensitive observation for subsequent research into the behaviour of young literacy learners.

From the mid-1980s, the demand for Reading Recovery in other countries extended the research horizons further. Marie Clay accepted each new implementation challenge as a problem to be worked through, its solution a possibility to be found. Research efforts continued around the world. In Part Two, *Continuing the Search for Possibilities*, three chapters highlight research on Reading Recovery outcomes for children in New Zealand, Australia, Canada, the United States, and the United Kingdom and Ireland. The consistency of independent findings on the effectiveness of Reading Recovery in very dissimilar settings offers compelling evidence that Reading Recovery accomplishes its goals no matter how different the children or how diverse the educational systems in which they are schooled.

In a parallel response to the growing demand for Reading Recovery overseas, Marie Clay worked closely with local educators and administrators to investigate the practicalities of replication in other educational settings. In Part Three, *The Capacity to Reach Beyond*, we hear Marie Clay's voice as she shared processes for guiding the implementation of Reading Recovery within an education system. The chapter draws on five of her publications detailing implementation issues in global settings. Integral to the success of any implementation is accountability for outcomes of all children. 'Every Child Counted' describes ways in which each country currently operating Reading Recovery collects, analyses, and reports data on outcomes for every child receiving a series of individual literacy lessons. Such scrupulous monitoring is a unique and remarkable feature of Reading Recovery everywhere.

Marie Clay continually looked forward, always envisaging possibilities for the future. Her work was never static. From the beginning, Reading Recovery had an in-built responsiveness to change with commitment to tentativeness when working with a dynamically changing theory, receptiveness to the discourse of new research and theory, and flexibility in problem-solving a systemic intervention. And there were always new questions that needed answers. In Part Four, *Envisioning the Way Forward*, the final chapter celebrates our commitment to her vision of the future for children, for teachers, for schools and systems, and for society.

This book conveys only part of the incalculable legacy left by Marie Clay. Surrounding her early research reports with supporting material for a new, twenty-first century audience has been a fascinating task. Even harder would have been the task of conveying the sheer exhilaration of those original teachers and Tutors/Teacher Leaders when, for the first time, they experienced the joy of helping young children move from incipient literacy failure to being confident, independent, successful readers and writers with previously unheard-of acceleration. But we need not be troubled on that score because, of course, that experience is replicated daily by thousands of committed Reading Recovery teachers in countless schools across the globe. Speak to one who works in a school near you and hear the success stories of the children. That is the essence of Reading Recovery: it is above all Marie's gift for children.

We join all the contributing authors and reviewers in celebrating every aspect of Marie Clay's magnificent legacy. We honour a brilliant, single-minded scientist and innovator who, by her lifelong dedication, has made such a difference for those children in each of our countries who find reading and writing so troublesome. Truly her work broke the bonds of the ordinary, influencing researchers, teachers, administrators, and indeed all educators who work to prevent literacy failure for young children everywhere. Thanks to her unwavering vision, we too can raise our eyes to boundless horizons.

Barbara Watson and Billie Askew

Part One

Breaking the Bonds
of the Ordinary

1

Research Origins:
The Historical Context

Ann Ballantyne

Reading Recovery is an extraordinarily long-lived and successful innovation. By focusing on the 30 years that preceded the development and implementation of Reading Recovery in New Zealand, a context is provided for publication of the early New Zealand research reports reprinted in Chapter 2 of this volume. The story begins in 1946 when Marie Clay began graduate studies for a Master of Education degree at Victoria College in Wellington, New Zealand and ends with the development of the early literacy intervention in the late 1970s. More generally, this chapter offers an exploration of the intellectual and educational wellsprings of an early intervention/prevention approach to struggling readers and writers. It attempts to capture the ways that the 'pre-existing organization' (Clay, 1987, p. 38) of literacy instruction in her home country shaped Marie Clay's research choices and interests at the same time she worked with colleagues to inform, enhance, and change aspects of that instruction. This account draws on material gathered as part of a policy study of Reading Recovery in New Zealand (Ballantyne, 2009).

Overview

Several features of the New Zealand education system provided a consistent and stable background to the developments described in this chapter. Prior to a major restructuring of educational administration in 1989, the system of governance in this country was multilayered and administratively complex. The central Department of Education provided policy advice to the Minister, designed the curriculum, graded teachers, inspected and advised schools, organized and funded teacher training and professional development, and regulated all aspects of the education system. Regional Education Boards employed teachers, disbursed funding and resources to schools, and served as a base for an important regional presence of the Department — the School Inspectorate and Advisory Services.

At the school level, principals and teachers had considerable discretion within the framework of a national curriculum while parent and community representatives contributed to the work of operating schools through school committees but had little say over policy or practice. The Department of Education engaged in extensive consultation with community and educational groups including the influential organization representing primary teachers, the New Zealand Educational Institute (NZEI). Despite their opposing roles at the negotiating table, the Department and Institute had a long history of shared purposes, projects, and personnel (Simmonds, 1983). Department officials worked closely with teacher representatives to develop and update national curriculum statements, to prepare teaching guidelines and resources, and to plan in-service programmes for teachers. Any new educational initiative in the primary school would have been unlikely to flourish without the support of the NZEI.

These features of the education system remained constant throughout the period covered in this chapter, but in other respects the capacities and priorities of the service changed greatly. During the years 1946 to 1976, we can distinguish three phases of development in primary education, each of which relates in some distinctive way to Marie Clay's academic career and to the eventual development of Reading Recovery.

In the late 1940s, when Marie Clay (née Irwin) completed primary teacher training and began graduate studies at the local university college, the education system was struggling to meet rapid post-war growth in the school population with limited resources and an acute shortage of teachers. Despite 20 years of progressive leadership by esteemed educator Dr Clarence Beeby, issues of quantity rather than quality dominated the policy agenda. By the early 1960s, however, the challenges of supplying teachers and buildings were beginning to be resolved and more attention could be paid to the quality of instruction and to training and support for teachers. Training of primary teachers was extended to three years and advisory and support services were greatly increased. When a new series of early readers was introduced in primary schools in 1963, the same year that Marie Clay began her seminal study of emergent reading behaviour, specialist advisers were newly available to support the innovation.

The 1970s ushered in a period of excitement and creativity in school language and literacy programmes generally. Academics, teachers, and advisers collaborated to establish the International Reading Association (IRA) in their districts and to mount annual reading conferences. When New Zealand children scored higher than any other country on international evaluation studies of reading literacy and comprehension in 1970–1971 (Thorndike, 1973), literacy educators from around the world began to pay attention to pedagogical developments in this country.

At the same time there was a sharper focus on children who were not succeeding at school, including many from minority and new immigrant families. Beginning in the mid-1970s, an innovative in-service training programme was made available to teachers of Junior Classes (years 1–3 in New Zealand) throughout the country. Teachers were sensitized to the plight of young children for whom literacy learning was difficult but found it hard to cater for such children in the classroom setting. The Reading Recovery Project was initiated in 1976 in response to calls for assistance with junior children who were struggling with literacy learning. It was a new initiative, but one that was rooted in 30 years of research, critique, and advocacy.

An historical perspective on reading and reading difficulties in New Zealand

The progressive educational ideas of John Dewey, Susan Isaacs, Percy Nunn, and others disseminated through the New Educational Fellowship (NEF) attracted attention in many Western nations during the 1920s. NEF branches were not established in New Zealand until the late 1930s, but individual educators subscribed to the *New Era* magazine and progressive ideas were promoted in the teachers' colleges and in the NZEI journal, *National Education* (Abbiss, 1998). Several New Zealand educators who were active in the NEF later held influential positions in New Zealand education (Middleton & May, 1997). Foremost amongst them was Clarence Beeby who was appointed to lead the newly formed New Zealand Council for Educational Research (NZCER) in 1934 and became Director General (DG) for the Department of Education in 1940. Beeby had been introduced to the British infant school 'discovery-learning' approach while a student at Canterbury Teachers' College (New Zealand) in the early 1920s and remained a strong proponent of active child-centred pedagogies throughout his 20 years as Director General (Beeby, 1992). NZCER, with the support of the Minister of Education, Department of Education, and NZEI, arranged for NEF supporters to pay an extended visit to New Zealand in 1937. Schools in the main centres were closed, conference sessions were broadcast, and an estimated 21,000 people took part in activities related to the visit (Abbiss, 1998).

The call for more activity in the curriculum and classroom and a shift away from the formal methods of the time struck a chord with New Zealand educators. Child-centred, discovery-learning approaches were established as the *ideal* model for Junior Class teaching in this country. Closer ties with North America from the late 1940s brought an influx of resources and guidebooks for teachers and a new emphasis on 'scientific' methods and assessments (Soler, 1998) but did not displace the child-centred tradition in Junior Classes. When the Department introduced the *Janet and John* reading series in 1949 (the series was published in Britain, but modelled on an American basal series), New Zealand teachers were encouraged to see the benefits of a careful gradient of difficulty while retaining a child-centred language and meaning focus.

> If . . . the accepted principles of 'modern' teaching practice are incorporated in the text-books, the teacher's work is greatly simplified: she will have more time to consider the primary aims of reading and the children will have at every stage a feeling of confidence and pleasure in their increasing ability. (Simpson, 1949, p. 2)

Departmental publications characterized reading as one of the 'language arts,' along with writing, speaking, and listening, and promoted a view of reading instruction in which children would learn to read in a natural and happy way under the guidance of teachers who were responsive to the instructional needs of individual children. This stance expressed an attitude of trust in classroom teachers, but it also placed a heavy responsibility on relatively untrained infant teachers, working with large classes, often in relatively isolated country schools. There can be little doubt that the reality of classroom instruction frequently fell short of the ideal and that many children failed to learn to read and write under these conditions. Such failures caused less consternation and controversy than they would today, in part for practical reasons; a fast-growing post-war economy based on labour-intensive primary production ensured that there was a continuing high demand for unskilled and semiskilled labour. But it also had to do with ideas and beliefs. The progressive and egalitarian ideals of the period aspired to equal *opportunity* rather than equal educational *outcomes* and were underpinned by assumptions that would later be recognized as problematic. It was assumed, for example, that heredity set fixed limits to what children could be expected to learn, so some were expected to fail; and there was a firm conviction that it was harmful to try to teach children to read before they reached a particular 'mental age,' and were 'ready' to read (Department of Education, 1961, p. 64). Marie Clay's research and theorizing would lead her to challenge both these assumptions and to advocate early intervention as an alternative approach; but it would be some time before this critique was heard.

An early challenge

Marie Irwin, as she was then, completed her teacher training and BA degree at Victoria College,[1] Wellington, in 1946 and started teaching children in special education classes while studying for a Master of Arts degree. She found that she was able to teach the children in her classes to read despite their low scores on intelligence tests, and reported on this in a Master's thesis entitled *Teaching of Reading to Special Class Children* (Irwin, 1948). The overseas literature suggested that children of low intelligence would often learn to read above their 'mental age' but an extensive survey of children entering special classes revealed that these levels of achievement rarely occurred in New Zealand, particularly for children at the upper end of the special class mental abilities range. Irwin's survey revealed that the typical student entering a New Zealand special class in 1947 was 10 years old, had experienced 5 years of failure in mainstream classes, and had a further 5 years of compulsory schooling in which to be 'retrained academically and socially' (Irwin, 1948, p. 112).

The young researcher wrote critically of New Zealand practices, noting (a) the late referral of these children out of mainstream programmes where little attention had been paid to their special needs; (b) the scarcity of information that was passed on to their new teachers; (c) inadequate training for special class teachers who worked in isolation, in widely dispersed settings; and (d) confusion about instructional methods and a lack of experience with carefully graded, scientifically designed reading materials (Irwin, 1948). From her reading of the literature, Marie Irwin concluded that reading instruction for special class children should be largely individual, should focus on prevention rather than correction, and should aim to build confidence and motivation. She argued that a suitable programme would adopt a whole word and meaning emphasis from the start, make use of language experience and graded readers, and foster visual discrimination skills that would become increasingly analytic over time.

> It is desirable to use [the student's mental energy] as economically as possible and not to divert it into efforts which are unproductive ... Reading instruction should follow the methods most suited to his psychological nature and the earlier such teaching is begun the less effort will be wasted relearning. (Irwin, 1948, p. 52)

This research was conducted 30 years before the development of

---

1 Victoria College, Wellington, was at that time a campus of the University of New Zealand. The Teachers Training College was a separate institution.

Reading Recovery, with a different school population and at a time when educational concerns and priorities were very different, but it foreshadowed Marie Clay's later work in several distinctive ways. Here was the characteristic sense of urgency about improving access for children for whom literacy learning is difficult; here, too, was the careful critique of existing provisions and a clear statement about need for an economical, early intervention/prevention approach.

Meagre support for struggling readers

The Master's research built on an earlier survey of special education provisions conducted by Marie Irwin's supervisor and later colleague at the University of Auckland, Professor Ralph Winterbourn (1944). While both reviews focused on special class children, they reflected a more general lack of resources and services for children for whom literacy learning was difficult.

In an oral history interview Ruth Trevor, one of the first (and very few) reading clinicians in New Zealand in the 1940s and 50s, recalled the tremendous opposition in those days to the idea of clinical help for struggling children. When she and fellow clinician Yvonne Chapman-Taylor (née Malcolm) visited reading clinics in the United States during the late 1950s, they were impressed by the opportunities American teachers had to gain specialized knowledge in the field of reading difficulties (Openshaw, 1991). Back in New Zealand, however, they gave their support to the long-standing Department of Education position that 'it was more important to try to modify the sort of teaching of reading that went on in the classroom . . . so that these children could by and large be handled in the school' (Trevor in Openshaw, 1991, p. 57). Both educators became Reading Advisers when these services expanded in the 1960s.

Reluctance to provide extensive clinical and remedial services for struggling readers remained a distinctive part of the official approach to literacy teaching in New Zealand throughout the period covered here and was an important feature of the context for the development of Reading Recovery.[2] It was a policy stance that had both positive and negative effects. On the positive side it ensured that intellectual energy and expertise was focused on developing approaches to classroom instruction that were sensitive to the needs of individuals rather than searching for organic causes and labels for literacy difficulties. On the

---

2 Also surprising given that several distinguished and influential New Zealand educators, among them Clarence Beeby, Marie Clay, Don Holdaway, Myrtle Simpson, and Ruth Trevor, were reading clinicians at some point in their careers.

other hand it resulted in a lack of recognition of and scarcity of services for children who struggled with literacy learning and ensured that little effort was made to develop expertise in teaching them.

Of course, classroom teachers were less easily convinced that all children could be taught to read without specialist help. They knew first hand how difficult it could be to provide suitable support in the classroom for children who were struggling with literacy learning and the teacher organizations regularly called for more accessible reading material for older failing readers, more reading clinics, and extended psychological services.

Insights from various sources

Marie Clay became aware of the lack of support for children who were struggling with literacy learning early in her educational career. After completing her MA in 1948 she worked for a period as an assistant psychologist for the Department of Education and was responsible for assessing the children whom schools referred for possible special class placement. She and other colleagues who carried out this work (Openshaw, 1991) found that many of the children referred for assessment were of normal intelligence but severely behind in reading.

> One out of ten would be suitable for special class and the other nine would be having difficulty but would not be recommended for special class. So I knew that there were a lot of children out there that needed help in the literacy area — because I had tested so many of them. (Clay, 2000)

About this time Marie Clay's interest in learning difficulties led her to consider post-graduate study with Fred Schonell at the University of London (Clay, 1997, 2007). But that door closed when Schonell left London to work at the University of Queensland, Australia. Happily, a Fulbright Scholarship provided her with an alternative opportunity to study at the University of Minnesota. Finding when she arrived that the special education courses she intended to take were not available, she studied developmental psychology and clinical child development at the university's Institute of Child Welfare. This programme broadened her knowledge base and interest in the study of child development generally, and in particular alerted her to the importance of observing atypical development *in the context of normal progress.* (Clay, 2000)

On her return from the United States, Marie Clay taught older primary children in the coastal North Island town of Wanganui where she gained a reputation for being able to teach 'tricky' children to read and write. Hers must have been a challenging class to take over when she moved with her family to Auckland in the mid-1950s! There she worked part-time as an educational psychologist and, while at home with her own young children, tutored some older struggling readers. Insights gained from this tutoring provided a reference point for later theorizing about the end-point of early literacy instruction. It was very hard work, she said, for both children and teacher but she found that the children eventually reached a point where they took over the learning for themselves. 'I don't know what happened, but after we'd worked for a period ... they eventually seemed to take off and I didn't feel responsible for the take-off ... none of the reading theories I knew about could explain that.' (Clay, 2000)

An emphasis on instruction and expertise

In the early 1960s, the government initiated a major public review of the compulsory education sector. The report of the New Zealand Commission on Education was released in the same year that Marie Clay began the pilot study for her doctoral research and provides some insights into the state of literacy instruction in New Zealand schools at the time. The enquiry was prompted by public controversy over the progressive teaching methods promoted by the Department of Education and referred to in the media as 'playway' and 'Beebyism.' The Department acknowledged that some children were having difficulty learning to read but defended the child-centred progressive approach, claiming that 'the skill of reading is taught and used freely and naturally in schools' (Ewing, 1961, p. 67).

Given the volume of submissions from the Department and teacher organizations (Scott, 1996), it was perhaps not surprising that the report endorsed the progressive teaching methods advocated by the Department, finding that they were underpinned by 'a body of educational theory that is firmly based and consistent' (Commission on Education in New Zealand, 1962, p. 32). The Commission also endorsed the Department's view that improved classroom teaching would provide the best defence against reading failure:

> The solution of the problem does not lie in the appointment of large numbers of specialist staff but is essentially a matter for the general classroom teacher. It requires more and better trained teachers with a sounder knowledge of how to teach reading properly throughout the school. (Commission on Education, 1962)

But the Commission noted that current school practices fell far short of the ideals aspired to, and criticized the Department of Education for failing to communicate effectively with parents and teachers about its aims and methods. Concern about the quality of teaching (and teachers) was evident in recommendations calling for (a) a radical reform of teacher training; (b) continuing curriculum revision; (c) the use of standardized tests in the basic subjects to be followed by remedial teaching where necessary; and (d) the establishment of a Curriculum Development Unit, which would enable the Department to keep up to date with overseas developments in an organized and timely way. The Commission recommended, as a matter or urgency, the appointment of an itinerant reading adviser 'in each of the new educational districts' (Commission on Education, 1962, p. 473).

Implementation of the Commission's recommendations over the next 5 to 7 years led to a significant strengthening of the curriculum leadership capacity of the Department of Education and a marked increase in the availability of in-service training, advice, and guidance for teachers. Where there was only one national Reading Adviser (Ruth Trevor) in 1957, there were an additional 10 regionally based Advisers by 1964. Where there had been a solitary Curriculum Officer there was, by 1964, a Curriculum Development Unit (later 'Division') staffed with around eight experienced and respected educationalists.

The Clay doctoral research:
What really happens for children?

When Marie Clay gained a position in the Department of Education at the University of Auckland in the early 1960s, she began to think about a focus for PhD research. She was aware of the research of Sam Kirk and Barbara Bateman at the University of Illinois, directed towards identifying underlying cognitive and/or language disorders in children who were achieving poorly at school despite average intelligence and opportunity. But she found herself in disagreement with the theoretical ideas and assessments associated with the new concept of learning disorders (Clay, 1972c). A developmental perspective led her to expect variety and complexity in young children's responses to early literacy instruction, and she decided to explore this diversity using observational methodologies that were being used at the time to study oral language development. Two questions guided the initial design of the project:

Is there anything worth studying in the first year of reading instruction that can throw light on reading progress? Are there individual differences which could lead to reading failures observable in the first year of learning to read? (Clay, 1966, pp. 89–90)

Parents and teachers of new entrant children assisted with a pilot study which confirmed that children respond very differently to their first encounters with school, and uncovered self-correction as an important sign of early reading progress.

Although her research methodology called for a descriptive approach to data collection, Marie Clay's interest went beyond the description and explanation of reading difficulties. From the outset, she sought to find ways to prevent difficulties from occurring. Her assumption was that prevention would involve a two-step process. First, in order to develop better ways of 'observing and diagnosing inadequate learning' (Clay, 1966, p. 9), it would be necessary to observe the full range of children's responses to early literacy instruction, especially the responses of high progress children. The second step would require schools to provide 'differential treatments . . . to smaller groups of children who fail to make good progress for different reasons' (Clay, 1966, p. 8).

For the main project, weekly observations were made of the reading and writing behaviour of 139 new entrants in five classrooms located in five city schools — two in 1963 and three more in 1964. The schools were selected to represent different student populations and a range of teaching quality that was generally above average. The children in the sample entered school in the first weeks of the school year and were followed throughout their first year of school. Every week Marie Clay collected samples of the children's written language (or drawings) and recorded their oral reading of texts that had been introduced to them by their teacher (Clay, 1966, p. 24). The observational data together with standardized tests administered at 5.0, 5.6 and 6.0 years identified some children who made rapid progress in literacy learning and others who struggled, went off-track, became confused or passive, and made very little progress.

In her doctoral dissertation and the academic publications which followed, Marie Clay reported the progress of 100 children who remained available for the research throughout the year and whose only home language was English. The children's progress and associated behaviours were analysed in terms of quartile groups — high, high-middle, low-middle, and low achieving children — formed on the basis of a standardized word reading test at 6 years. This analysis revealed marked differences in patterns of behaviour, learning opportunities, and outcomes for the four groups. The frequent first-hand observations provided detailed information about the different ways that children's literacy learning could go off-course during their first year at school (Clay, 1967a). Records showed that the teachers had delayed the introduction of graded reading material for low progress children and that these children moved slowly up through text levels and read far fewer words, with lower accuracy rates, and little evidence of self-correction. She concluded that '*a quartile group of children with reading problems was created in the first year more by failure to start than by handicapping methods of instruction or inappropriate reading behaviour*' (Clay, 1968, p. 59, emphasis in original).

Marie Clay found some correlations between general intelligence and reading readiness scores and later reading achievement but judged that these were insufficient to justify the practice of delaying reading instruction for children who seemed poorly prepared for literacy learning. Instead she recommended closer observation, more attention, and 're-teaching' as the appropriate teaching response for children who were making slow progress (Clay, 1966, p. 115).

Research tools and findings

The measurement tools that were available when Marie Clay began her doctoral project were not sensitive enough to capture early reading behaviour or to accurately identify children having difficulty. During the course of the project she developed and validated several novel assessment tasks and observation techniques. Some of these would become a standard part of Junior Class assessment practice in New Zealand schools (the 'running record' of oral reading behaviour on continuous text, the 'Letter Identification Test,' the 'Clay Word Test,' and a 'conventions of written language' measure that was a precursor of 'Concepts about Print' (Clay, 1979). Later versions of the two language tasks, morpheme completion and sentence repetition, were published for general school use as *Record of Oral Language and Biks and Gutches* (Clay, Gill, Glynn, McNaughton, & Salmon, 1983). Other tasks such as those used to assess children's response to inverted and degraded print information were primarily research tools.

Administration of specially designed, age-appropriate tasks at the beginning, middle, and end of the children's first year at school enabled Marie Clay to explore correlations between a range of variables related to language and literacy achievement. The speed with which the gap opened between high and low scoring children in language and literacy tasks was striking. All the children scored poorly on measures of print perception when they started school close to their fifth birthday but by 6 years of age the low progress group had barely reached the point where the high progress children were at school entry. This pattern was also marked for the language assessments — at 6 years of age the low progress group had still not caught up with where the high progress group was at 5. Clay was surprised to find that 25% of the children in the monolingual research sample made minimal gains in the language assessments across the first year of school, and even more surprised when she discovered that these children were as disadvantaged in terms of language skills as a mixed-language group from the same communities that had been excluded from the main analyses.

The progress of four language groups

The relationships between oral language skills and reading achievement suggested that differences in oral language skills might contribute to success or failure in reading (Clay, 1966, p. 176), and soon after the first study was completed Clay set out to explore these relationships in a longitudinal study of four language groups in the first 2 years of school. The social and educational context for this study was a marked increase in the numbers of both Maori and Pacific Island children in Auckland city schools. Maori urban migration had accelerated significantly between 1956 and 1966 and immigration from Pacific Island nations was encouraged to fill job shortages in New Zealand. Funding for the study came from a foundation established in the wake of a government report that highlighted educational underachievement among Maori children (Hunn, 1961).

The project involved weekly observation of 360 children from four different language backgrounds: one Maori, one Samoan, and two mono-lingual English language groups, one of which was designed to be an 'optimum-English' group with at least one professional parent. An innovative cross-lagged design was used to produce longitudinal data in an economical time frame by following four groups of children of different ages over the same 6-month period. Two independent samples within each age/language grouping allowed for simultaneous replication of findings (Clay, 1982).

English language skills (including sentence repetition and morpheme completion), visual perception of print, and progress in reading were assessed at the beginning and end of the 6-month observation period. The results for the language variables showed that all language groups progressed in a developmentally appropriate way with the optimal English group retaining an initial advantage over the 'other-English,' Maori, and Samoan groups which were ranked in that order at all test points. An unexpected finding, replicated across both samples, was that the Maori groups performed less well on reading than the other three groups *despite* their continuing language advantage over the Samoan children, 75%

of whom spoke English as their second language. Scores on tests of the visual perception of print were highly correlated with reading progress for all four language groups after 1 year of instruction, and the relative placement of the ethnic groups on the visual perception measures was the same as for the reading tests. It seemed that the visual perception of print was a decisive set of learning for the first year at school and that language variables played a greater part in distinguishing between groups in the second year. This finding challenged the prevailing assumption that the slower progress of Maori children was attributable to language background variables (Clay, 1982, p. 101), and focused attention on skills that were learned at school rather than home background.

The study also reinforced the earlier finding that children's progress at 6 years of age was highly predictive of later achievement. Marie Clay spoke about this study at the International Reading Association World Congress in Sydney in 1970 and published several articles covering different aspects of the research (Clay, 1970a, 1971a and b, 1974, 1975), but the full report was considered sensitive at the time and was not published (Clay, 2000).

The impact of Clay's descriptive research

The two longitudinal studies would seem to have important implications for literacy instruction in New Zealand schools. A new series of Department-supplied readers and instructional guidelines had been introduced in primary schools just as Marie Clay started her doctoral research. The *Ready to Read* series of graded readers[3] was the first to be developed by the Department's own publishing branch and broke from the earlier reading series in a number of ways that both reflected and contributed to shifts in classroom teaching of reading in New Zealand. The new series was developed through a process of extensive consultation and trialling involving Junior Class teachers, Reading Advisers, teachers' college and university lecturers, and the NZEI (Simpson, 1962). Like the previous *Janet and John* series, *Ready to Read* provided a careful gradient of difficulty, but the vocabulary was less tightly controlled and the language was more like what young children might be expected to hear and use. The accompanying handbook called for a shift away from the word-learning emphasis of *Janet and John* and placed more emphasis on preparing children to understand the situations, words, and language used in the texts and to draw on many sources of information in their reading. Children would learn to recognize high frequency words through frequent

---

3 The small 'child-sized' format and short, single narrative of each of the readers led them to be known as the 'little books'.

exposure in natural language contexts rather than by separate teaching. Between entering school and being introduced to the *Ready to Read* books, children had many reading experiences including language experience stories based around a centre of interest, recorded as wall stories or on large charts, and reading of descriptive labels on the nature table.

Marie Clay did not have Department backing, or even approval,[4] for the doctoral research project and did not set out to evaluate the new approach, but as the schools in her doctoral study were using the new books she was well placed to observe how the teachers managed the materials and how the children responded. In her dissertation, she expressed measured approval for the instructional approach along with some important cautions. She noted, for example, that the visual discrimination of print 'tends to develop <u>unduly slowly</u> over the first year of instruction' (Clay, 1966, p. 299, underlined in original) and also cautioned that a method of instruction which emphasized whole sentences and stories was likely to present problems for children with low language skills (Clay 1966, p. 169). Moreover, the doctoral study provided clear evidence that a significant number of children were not learning to read in the 'natural and happy' way advocated in curriculum statements — indeed, were not learning to read at all in their first year at school. This evidence presented a strong challenge to the traditional 'wait and see' approach to early reading difficulties. Follow-up data collected 1 and 2 years after the end of the study demonstrated that paths of progress established in the first year of school predicted where children would be 2 and 3 years later (Clay, 1967b).

Marie Clay was well aware of the significance of her findings. She quickly prepared articles for publication in local and overseas journals and took every opportunity to speak to educators and administrators about the research. An invitation to address the Auckland Headmasters' Association[5] as part of a series of Extension Course lectures provided an opportunity to share her findings with people who were in a position to make the organizational changes that were needed, and she spoke out strongly.

> We have a school system which allows the good readers to get better and the poor readers to drop further and further behind the average for three years before significant action is taken. (Clay, 1967b, p. 29)

---

4 The Department did not reply to Marie Clay's letter advising of her proposed research and she sensed suspicion and distrust of her project (Clay, 2007).

5 This meeting was reported in the NZEI publication *National Education* and later published by the Association (Clay, 1967b).

She called for the school leaders to provide more continuity in the staffing of first-year classrooms, to end the practice of delaying reading instruction for children who were considered 'unready,' and to arrange for close observation and extra teaching time for children who were falling behind during the first year at school.

Marie Clay's research challenged assumptions about readiness and produced observation techniques and tasks that made it possible to detect children having difficulties well before standardized tests would provide reliable information. But Department officers showed little interest in her findings at this time. When the National Reading Adviser, Ruth Trevor, presented a paper on beginning reading at the 1968 World Congress in Copenhagen (Trevor, 1970), she made no reference to Clay's research. Marie Clay was not invited to contribute to broader discussions on classroom literacy programmes at the time and perceived that later interest in her work was focused less on its implications for classroom programmes than on the monitoring and assessment techniques (Clay, 1979, 2007).

A degree of complacency and unconcern about reading difficulties continued throughout the 1960s; clinical services for children who struggled with literacy learning remained scarce and there was no specialist training for remedial teachers. This lack of urgency was evident in an address given by the Director of Primary Education, Bryan Pinder, to parent representatives at a New Zealand School Committees' Federation conference in 1967. Pinder acknowledged that reading difficulties were a major problem and *'one that would always be with us'* (my italics), and went on to say:

> There are fifty different reasons why it is difficult for a child to learn to read. Circumstances in the home play an important part, especially pressure from parents. Primary schools in NZ have been doing a tremendous job with this for the last 20 years. They haven't always succeeded and now secondary schools have to face the problem. NZ teaching standards are very good by world standards. (Pinder, 1967)

In other words, 'we're doing our bit; teachers do their best; parents aren't always helpful; and some children probably won't learn to read.' Children having difficulty were recognized as a management problem *for teachers*, but there was little acknowledgement of the personal or social cost of reading failure for children and their families, and the close relationship between the Department and teacher organizations seemed to leave little space for parents' concerns to be heard. This stance would change quite radically during the 1970s and the remaining sections in this chapter examine factors that contributed to the change.

A changing educational environment

The early 1970s saw a blossoming of interest, excitement, and confidence amongst literacy educators in New Zealand. Building on the government-supplied *Ready to Read* series of 'little story books,' and with active leadership from Reading Advisers, Inspectors, and teachers' college lecturers, New Zealand teachers were developing a distinctive approach to early literacy instruction. It combined child-centred, language experience traditions with attention to a gradient of difficulty in natural language texts and flexible grouping of children with similar needs. The approach was creative, eclectic, and largely home grown, although links were made to the work of overseas theorists such as Ken Goodman (1967) and Frank Smith (1971). Reading and writing were viewed as meaning-oriented activities and visitors from America were struck by the absence of skills teaching and workbooks.

In Auckland the work of Don Holdaway — teacher, clinician, Reading Adviser, and later Auckland Teachers' College lecturer — was hugely influential. Holdaway emphasized the critical role of language, communication, and motivation in literacy development. Over several years in the 1960s and early 1970s, he worked in local Auckland schools to develop and trial the Shared Book Experience approach in which teacher and children shared repeated readings of high interest books in enlarged format. And he was the prime mover in the development of an innovative professional development programme, the Early Reading In-service Course (ERIC), designed to prevent reading failure in culturally diverse classrooms.

Other factors served to heighten the interest in literacy instruction. A new activism had arisen amongst literacy educators and parents, evident in greater involvement of professionals with the International Reading Association (IRA), international evaluative studies, and ERIC, and of parents in the formation of the parent advocacy group, Association for Children with Specific Learning Disabilities (SPELD). In this changing environment, the recognition of reading difficulties as an important social problem was preparing the way for Reading Recovery to be seen as an appropriate solution.

In 1970–1971, New Zealand participated for the first time in international studies of literacy achievement conducted by the International Evaluation Association (IEA). New Zealand educators were encouraged to find that 14- and 17-year-old children in this country achieved the highest mean scores in both the literacy and comprehension assessments (Purves, 1973; Thorndike, 1973). Involvement in the IEA studies and New Zealand's high scores contributed to increased attention and interaction with literacy educators abroad.

The first council of the International Reading Association had been established in Auckland in 1963 and by the end of the decade the Association had become an important national source of ideas and networking for literacy educators, bringing numbers of visiting academics and educators to New Zealand. Many came to praise but some were critical of the limited preparation of teachers and teacher trainers for the teaching of reading and the Education Department's perceived neglect of children's reading difficulties.[6]

Precursors of change

The Early Reading In-service Course (ERIC)

In 1971, a committee convened by the Auckland District Senior Inspector (DSI) initiated a long-term, research-based project that aligned well with the Department's orientation towards preventing reading difficulties through improved classroom practices and Adviser-led in-service training. The aim of this 'Early Reading Project' (later to be known as the Early Reading In-service Course, or ERIC) was 'to bring together and to disseminate a reliable body of insights in a practical form which would efficiently modify patterns in teaching and set in motion a movement among teachers which would result in a high level of awareness and commitment centred upon preventing failure in the early years of schooling' (Holdaway & Penton, 1973).

The Early Reading In-service Course (ERIC) was an immediate and important precursor of the Reading Recovery project. It was a product of the combined energies of local educators and administrators — a local initiative that was adopted and implemented nationally in a short space of time. Its focus was on the early detection and prevention of reading difficulties. The course design reflected a trust in teachers' professionalism and created a role for experienced teachers with additional training to support and guide the innovation in schools. Marie Clay was a member of the development committee and a consultant for the project. Her research provided the basis for several components of the course. As teachers learned to administer the 'Diagnostic Survey' and to observe young readers more closely, they asked for more help with the children who were struggling.

---

6 *National Education*, 1 August 1973.

A changed angle of vision

While the 1970s brought increasing confidence and sense of direction in the teaching of literacy in New Zealand, these positive attitudes were accompanied by a sharpened awareness of the economic and human costs of failure to learn to read and write. A sense of urgency to provide assistance for children having difficulty created a climate of opinion highly receptive to the development and adoption of an early literacy intervention. In his opening address to the 1978 Reading Association Conference, Director General of Education Bill Renwick referred to 'a fundamental change in the angle of vision from which failure is viewed' (Renwick, 1979, p. 3). The burden of responsibility had shifted, he said, from the individual to the institution, from personal psychology to sociology. 'Whereas Johnny's failure to learn to read was once a regrettable problem, but his own, it was now acknowledged to be a problem of and for the education system' (Renwick, 1979, p. 3).

Renwick referred to the mounting evidence of unequal education outcomes for Maori children, the continuing influx of second language learners from Pacific nations, and increasing evidence that children from a range of backgrounds were struggling with literacy learning. In a worsening economic climate, with unemployment rising for the first time in 40 years, children having difficulty learning to read could no longer be ignored.

> Literacy and numeracy are now linked with employability in ways they have never been before in this country. People who until quite recently could make their way in life, despite inadequate reading are now at risk. And the question that is being asked is: What is society and, in particular the education system, doing about it? (Renwick, 1979, p. 3)

Renwick's address highlighted the changing economic circumstances arising from the sharp rise in oil prices and Britain's decision to join the European common market, two factors that created serious problems for an economy highly dependent on export of primary produce. Renwick also identified a growing dissatisfaction with equal educational opportunity as a guiding principle in the context of markedly unequal outcomes for some children. Changing expectations had been evident in the different principles adopted by a major public review of education conducted in the early 1970s. The Education Development Council recognized then that to achieve equal educational outcomes, resources would have to be redistributed and increased.

> Equity as a principle of educational provision is appropriate for the last quarter of this century just as the provision of equality of educational opportunity has guided educational development since the last quarter of the nineteenth century. (Advisory Council on Educational Planning, 1974, p. 18)

This Working Party report also noted that 'parental agitation and teacher dissatisfactions' (p. 206) suggest that there was inadequate provision for children having reading difficulties and called for greater attention to remedial teaching in pre-service training and for the appointment of more remedial specialists in schools.

Parental and community agitation

Another force shaping the discourse around learning difficulties during the 1970s was the newly formed Association for Children with Specific Learning Difficulties or SPELD (Buchanan, 1996). This parent and community group lobbied the Department of Education to provide specialist help for children (and adults) who struggled to read and write and whose literacy difficulties were presumed to arise from organic dysfunction. SPELD was able to persuade the Minister of Education of the need for a national survey to determine the incidence of reading difficulties. Speaking to the sixth New Zealand reading conference in 1976,[7] Director General Bill Renwick acknowledged that some children's problems remain intractable, and that SPELD had been effective in 'urging the adoption of policies aimed at assisting them' (Renwick, 1976, p. 12), beginning with the 'identification and description of the target group of children who have specific reading difficulties' (Renwick, 1976, p. 12).[8]

A 1978 report described 'Project Child,' as the survey was called, as 'an ambitious project for which the incidence survey was only one part; the larger objective was to develop an early identification and prevention treatment for 6–6½-year-olds considered at risk of developing educational handicaps' (Walsh, 1978, p. 6). But the $84,000 incidence survey did little more than confirm what was already known, that around 7% of 11-year-old children were reading 2 or more years behind expectations for their age. The proposed 'Early Intervention Study' dropped from view, no doubt because a different early intervention project was already under way.

---

7   It is interesting to note that 6 out of the 12 published papers from this conference referred specifically to reading difficulties, failure, or remediation (Waikato Council of the International Reading Association, 1976).

8   Clay declined to join the advisory committee for this project which included university and college of education lecturers, Department, NZCER and SPELD representatives (Clay, 1980).

The genesis and development of Reading Recovery

The idea of recovery

Throughout the early 1970s, Marie Clay was playing an active part in changing attitudes towards literacy and literacy difficulties. A wave of publications made her ideas and research findings available to New Zealand teachers. Articles in the Department publication *Education* (Clay, 1970b, 1970c) encouraged teachers to observe the direction and pace of change in early reading behaviours and introduced the observation techniques that would soon be published as *The Early Detection of Reading Difficulties: A Diagnostic Survey* (Clay, 1972b), along with the test booklet needed for the administration of the 'Concepts about Print' assessment. In the accompanying text *Reading: The Patterning of Complex Behaviour*, Marie Clay (1972a) elaborated the theoretical and practical implications of her research and spelt out four steps that schools should take in order to prevent reading failure: (a) monitor and record progress in the first-year programme; (b) check each child's progress across a range of literacy tasks as they reached their sixth birthday; (c) provide 're-teaching' for low progress children in their second year; and (d) attend to the staffing of early classes (Clay, 1972a, p. 110). The recommendation with respect to 're-teaching' was very specific.

> A flexible and experienced teacher, well versed in individualised teaching techniques, and especially qualified in a wide variety of approaches to reading instruction, must be available for intensive and sustained re-teaching of low progress children in their second year of school on the basis of the results of this diagnostic survey. (Clay, 1972a, p. 110)

Marie Clay was actively involved with the International Reading Association (IRA) at home and abroad. From 1970, the annual reading conferences provided an important forum for sharing research findings and advocating measures to prevent reading failure. In an address to the second New Zealand conference, she first used the term 'recovery' in relation to early intervention (Clay, 1972d). The title of her paper, 'Can we reduce reading failure to two percent?' referred to the work of Swedish researcher Eve Malmquist who had demonstrated that it was possible to reduce reading failure to 1 or 2% using a test, teach, test, re-teach approach. Clay argued that attention to the quality of programmes, materials, and teacher training would not reduce the failure rate significantly below 10–20%; what was needed for the remaining children was an individualized *recovery* approach. 'We acknowledge the need for individual programmes in remedial reading which is a recovery procedure. But prevention procedures must [also] be individualized' (Clay, 1972a, p. 26).

Addressing the fifth annual New Zealand reading conference in 1974, Marie Clay took up the issue of specialist training for reading teachers, linking it to an earlier address by Christchurch Teachers' College lecturer David Doake (1973). Doake had argued that inadequate preparation in the teaching of reading had created a self-fulfilling prophecy whereby reading retardation was accepted 'as a normal condition for a number of children' and the remedial reading teacher had become 'an expected part of the school staffing schedule' (Doake, 1973). He called for better pre-service, in-service, and specialist training for the teaching of reading and, in the longer term, advanced degree courses, reading clinics on university and teachers' college campuses, and the release of teaching staff to conduct in-depth research. Recalling Doake's address, Marie Clay claimed that New Zealand was swimming against an international tide that emphasized specialist training: in 1960 most New Zealand universities taught courses about remedial reading and by 1970 most did not (Clay, 1976).

> . . . letting our clinical services run down by not providing for the training to replace the current clinicians is not an appropriate response to Doake's criticism about our expecting to have a remedial population in every school. Removing the tail from the low side of the normal distribution of reading achievement may call for a great deal more clinical know-how than we have at present. (Clay, 1976, p. 100)

She argued that the Department's focus on raising the standard of class-room instruction and the lack of a university component meant that the preparation of reading specialists had become trapped in a teach-yourself-on-the job model of training.

> When you leave a gaping need in society without a source of informed opinion, 'fools rush in' — with earnest, well-meaning attempts to meet the need. But training and planned solutions are needed rather than backyard industry in an activity as complex as remedial reading. (Clay, 1976, p. 103)

Marie Clay called for an injection of high level, high quality training courses for consultant specialists and teacher educators and referred in passing to one group of teachers who would need specialist training, that is, 'special acceleration teachers for the children caught in the six year survey' (Clay, 1976, p. 103). This reference to *special training* for 'recovery' teachers was made before the initial development of the Reading Recovery teaching procedures and more than 2 years before a professional training for Reading Recovery teachers was established.

The Reading Recovery Research Project 1976–1977

Marie Clay had taught classes in educational psychology and child development at the University of Auckland since 1960. At the beginning of 1975, she was appointed Professor and Head of Department. A year later she began a small project that set out to explore the ways that an experienced teacher might work in a one-to-one setting with young children who had not made a good start with learning to read. This project was funded over 2 years by an annual grant of $500 from a discretionary 'innovations' budget administered by the Auckland District Senior Inspector (Clay, 1977a). The grant paid for graduate assistant Susan (now Sarah) Robinson to work for the project for a few hours each week. Robinson, a skilled teacher who had completed in 1973 a Master of Education thesis on early writing, taught two children individually behind a one-way viewing screen in an old building at the university while Marie Clay observed. A two-way sound system allowed her to hear the lesson and make suggestions for teaching moves to the teacher through ear phones. She talked with the parents who had brought their children in for lessons while they both watched and listened, a practice that would become integral to Reading Recovery teacher training.

By the latter part of 1976, a set of teaching procedures had been developed that were based on what seemed to be the most useful teaching interactions with children as they worked on text reading and writing tasks. At the beginning of 1977, Marie Clay, wishing to observe a wide range of teachers working with children individually, invited a group of Supervising Teachers of Junior Classes, Reading Advisers, and itinerant reading teachers to join the development team. The eight members agreed to give individual lessons to two 6-year-old children two or three times a week and to teach behind the one-way viewing screen and discuss progress at fortnightly meetings.

During the 2-year development phase, many techniques were tried, observed, and debated. The process of refinement continued on successive drafts of the teaching procedures as the teachers discussed, trialled, and edited each teaching move and decision. The procedures were derived from the practice of experienced teachers using their knowledge of successful processing to work with children finding early literacy learning troublesome, but were rigorously analysed in relation to current theories of the reading process. Thus, many were discarded (Clay, 1979, 1987; Clay & Watson, 1982). At the end of this development phase, Marie Clay had identified five areas that would need to be attended to in the next stage of the project: (a) more frequent teaching of children; (b) articulation of the most effective procedures to provide better guidance for teachers; (c) a focus on instructional economy including decisions *not* to do certain things with particular children; (d) conceptualizing the goal in terms of independence — that is, of the young reader developing a self-extending system of strategies for working on text; and (e) attention to the timing and process of discontinuing tuition to ensure the child's continued progress in classroom instruction when individual lessons were withdrawn (Clay, 1987).

Field trials and replication 1978–1979

Towards the end of 1977, Marie Clay prepared a report for District Senior Inspector Terry Walbran, a very perceptive administrator who held a Master of Education in reading. The report detailed the progress of each of the 30 children who had been tutored and contrasted Reading Recovery with two other ways of approaching the issue of reading difficulties:

— a *survey* approach would identify children who were falling behind but not until they were at least 7 years old and would not provide guidance about how to teach the failing children;

— a *specialist testing* approach would identify children with unusual profiles as 'learning disabled' but would predict failure rather than inform instruction.

By contrast Reading Recovery aimed to achieve satisfactory progress by addressing the child's strengths and weakness in reading behaviours (Clay, 1977a). In the letter accompanying the report, Marie Clay sought permission to trial the intervention in schools and asked for continued funding for a part-time experienced teacher for up to 15 hours per week.

I am rather excited by the possibility of school-based trials. We are close to recommending an early attack on reading difficulties that arises from a theory of the reading process in normal children. If we can make it work in four different schools, and ideally have almost all children leaving the infant department reading to our criteria, we may have made a significant assault on reading difficulty. (Clay, 1977b)

Marie Clay was not aware that the Department had an excess of teachers (in those days, teachers were trained on salary at the state's expense) and was surprised to be offered full-time release for five experienced teachers to work on the project. Her initial response was to decline the offer. Persuaded to accept, she selected five schools, varying in size, type of organization, population and location, in which to trial the intervention (Clay, 1982). The school principals were asked to release an experienced Junior Class teacher willing to train for this early intervention teaching, to administer a Diagnostic Survey to all children as they turned 6, and to ensure that the individual tuition was not interrupted for any reason.

Because Susan Robinson was no longer available, Barbara Watson, another member of the development team, was invited to work for the project, initially part-time. She was an expert teacher of reading and had experience with teacher professional development both as a Supervising Teacher of Junior Classes and trainer for the ERIC resource teachers. During 1978 and 1979, she trained close to 100 teachers in Reading Recovery procedures, supervised the implementation of Reading Recovery in schools, collected the research data, and began to prepare the Tutors who would be needed to train teachers in different regions across New Zealand as the intervention expanded.

Reading Recovery had been launched. Over the next 3 decades it would reach out to embrace different school systems, continents, and languages. The excitement emanating from the first five Auckland schools to trial this new educational intervention has continued to grow and more than 2 million children around the world have been given a second chance to become literate.

References

Abbiss, J. (1998). The 'New Education Fellowship' in New Zealand: Its activities and influence in the 1930s and 40s. *New Zealand Journal of Educational Studies, 33*(1), 81–93.

Advisory Council on Educational Planning (1974). *Directions for Educational Development: Report of the Working Party on improving teaching and learning.* Wellington, NZ: Government Printer.

Ballantyne, A. (2009). *Beating the odds: Causes and conditions of policy persistence in the case of Reading Recovery.* Unpublished doctoral thesis. Auckland: The University of Auckland.

Beeby, C. E. (1992). *The biography of an idea: Beeby on Education.* Wellington, NZ: New Zealand Council for Educational Research.

Buchanan, P. (1996). *Breaking down the barriers: Aspects of the first 25 years of SPELD in New Zealand.* Wellington, NZ: SPELD NZ Inc.

Clay, M. M. (1966). *Emergent reading behaviour.* Unpublished doctoral thesis. Auckland: The University of Auckland.

Clay, M. M. (1967a). The reading behaviour of five-year-old children: A research report. *New Zealand Journal of Educational Research, 2*(1), 11–31.

Clay, M. M. (1967b). A challenge to some educational concepts from recent research on Auckland school entrants. Extension Course Lectures. Auckland: Headmasters Association.

Clay, M. M. (1968). A syntactical analysis of reading errors. *Visible Language, 8*(3), 275–282.

Clay, M. M. (1970a). An increasing effect of disorientation on the discrimination of print: A developmental study. *Journal of Experimental Child Psychology, 9*, 297–306.

Clay, M. M. (1970b). Early reading behaviour: A guide to sensitive observation. *Education, 19*(1).

Clay, M. M. (1970c). The early detection of reading difficulties: Some investigatory techniques. *Education, 19*(5), 26–31.

Clay, M. M. (1971a). Sentence repetition: Elicited imitation of a controlled set of syntactic structures for four language groups. *Monographs of the society for research in child development.* Serial No. 143.

Clay, M. M. (1971b). The Polynesian language skills of Maori and Samoan school entrants. *International Journal of Psychology, 6*(2), 131–145.

Clay, M. M. (1972a). *Reading: The patterning of complex behaviour* (1st ed.). Auckland: Heinemann.

Clay, M. M. (1972b). *The early detection of reading difficulties: A diagnostic survey* (1st ed.). Auckland: Heinemann.

Clay, M. M. (1972c). Learning disorders. In S. J. Harvill & D. R. Mitchell (Eds.), *Issues in special education* (pp. 231–243). New Zealand: Hodder & Stoughton.

Clay, M. M. (1972d). Can we reduce reading failure to two percent? In *Proceedings of the Second New Zealand Reading Conference.* Auckland: Auckland Reading Association.

Clay, M. M. (1974). The spatial characteristics of the open book. *Visible Language, 8*(3), 275–262.

Clay, M. M. (1976). Teaching of reading: A future orientation. *The revolution in reading: Proceedings of the 6th New Zealand conference on reading.* Hamilton: Waikato Council of the International Reading Association.

Clay, M. M. (1977a). *The Reading Recovery project.* Report to the District Senior Inspector. Auckland: National Reading Recovery files.

Clay, M. M. (1977b). Letter addressed to the District Senior Inspector, Terry Walbran. Auckland: National Reading Recovery files.

Clay, M. M. (1979). Theoretical research and instructional change: A case study. In L. Resnick & P. A. Weaver (Eds.), *Theory and practice in early reading.* New Jersey: Lawrence Erlbaum.

Clay, M. M. (1980). Reading and public concern. Paper presented at the 10th Conference on Reading, Auckland Council of the International Reading Association, Auckland, NZ.

Clay, M. M. (1982). *Observing young readers.* Exeter, NH: Heinemann.

Clay, M. M. (1987). Implementing Reading Recovery: Systemic adaptations to an educational innovation. *New Zealand Journal of Educational Studies, 22*(1), 35–57.

Clay, M. M. (1997). International perspectives on the Reading Recovery program. In J. Flood, S. B. Heath, & D. Lapp (Eds.), *Handbook of research on teaching literacy through the communicative and visual arts* (pp. 655–667). New York: Macmillan Library Reference USA (a project of the International Reading Association). (Reprinted in *Journal of Reading Recovery,* Fall 2007.)

Clay, M. M. (2000). Personal communication.

Clay, M. M. (2007). Simply by sailing in a new direction you could enlarge the world. *Journal of Reading Recovery, 7*(1), 7–12. [Reprinted from C. M. Fairbanks, J. Worthy, B. Maloch, J. V. Hoffman, & D. L. Schallert (Eds.). (2004). *Fifty-third yearbook of the National Reading Conference* (pp. 60–66). Oak Creek, WI: National Reading Conference.]

Clay, M. M., Gill, M., Glynn, T., McNaughton, T., & Salmon, K. (1983). *Record of oral language and biks and gutches.* Auckland: Heinemann.

Clay, M. M., & Watson, B. (1982). An inservice programme for Reading Recovery Teachers. In M. M. Clay, *Observing young readers.* Exeter, NH: Heinemann.

Commission on Education in New Zealand (1962). *Report.* Wellington, NZ: Government Printer.

Department of Education (1961). *Language in the primary school.* Wellington, NZ: Government Printer.

Doake, D. B. (1973). Teacher education in the field of reading. In *Proceedings of the Third New Zealand Reading Conference.* Auckland NZ: Auckland Reading Association.

Ewing, J. L. (1961, March). Extract from a submission to the Commission on Education, presented by the Chief Inspector of Primary Schools. *National Education, 43,* 65–68.

Goodman, K. (1967). Reading: A psycholinguistic guessing game. *Journal of the Reading Specialist, 6*(4), 126–135.

Holdaway, R. D., & Penton, J. M. (1973). Detection and prevention of failure in the early stages of reading: Report on the project as of October 1973. New Zealand: Unpublished report for the District Senior Inspector's Standing Committee on Reading.

Hunn, J. K. (1961). *Report on the Department of Maori Affairs.* Wellington, NZ: Government Printer.

Irwin, M. M. (1948). *Teaching of reading to special class children.* Unpublished master's thesis. Wellington: Victoria College, The University of New Zealand.

Middleton, S., & May, H. (1997). *Teachers talking teaching 1915–1995: Early childhood schools and teachers colleges.* Palmerston North, NZ: Dunmore Press.

Openshaw, R. (1991). Schooling in the 40s and 50s: An oral history: Social studies, reading, mathematics. Palmerston North, NZ: Education Research and Development Centre, Massey University.

New Zealand Educational Institute (1973, 1 August). *National Education.* Wellington, NZ: New Zealand Educational Institute.

Pinder, B. (1967, June). Address by Director of Primary Education to New Zealand School Committees Federation annual conference. Reported in *National Education, 49,* 225.

Purves, A. (1973). *Literature education in ten countries.* Stockholm: Almquist & Wiksell.

Renwick, W. L. (1976). Perspective on the teaching of reading in New Zealand today. *The revolution in reading: Proceedings of the 6th New Zealand conference on reading* (pp. 1–6). Hamilton, NZ: Waikato Council of the International Reading Association.

Renwick, W. L. (1979). The way ahead in reading. Address to the New Zealand Reading Association Conference, August 1978. *Education 3*(38), 2–10.

Scott, D. J. (1996). The Currie Commission and report on New Zealand Education 1960–62. Unpublished doctoral thesis. Auckland: University of Auckland.

Simmonds, E. J. (1983). *NZEI 100: An account of the New Zealand Educational Institute 1883–1983.* Wellington, NZ: New Zealand Educational Institute.

Simpson, M. M. (1949). *Reading in the infant room.* Wellington, NZ: Department of Education.

Smith, F. (1971). *Understanding reading.* New York: Holt, Rinehart and Winston.

Soler, J. (1998). The politics of learning to read: 1960s debates over literacy instruction in the New Zealand primary school. *New Zealand Journal of Educational Studies, 33*(2), 155–166.

Thorndike, R. L. (1973). *Reading comprehension education in fifteen countries.* Stockhom: Almquist and Wiksell.

Trevor, R. (1970). Beginning reading. *Education, 19*(4), 14–19.

Walsh, D. F. (1978). *Project child: Incidence survey; A report on the incidence of specific learning difficulties in form 1 pupils in New Zealand primary and intermediate schools.* Wellington, NZ: New Zealand Council for Educational Research.

Winterbourn, R. (1944). *Educating backward children in New Zealand.* Christchurch, NZ: Whitcomb & Tombs.

2

The Reading Recovery Research Reports

Marie M. Clay

These research reports are reprinted as in the original. Minor editing changes have been made to ensure clarity for readers in the international community. As appropriate, terminology, style, and references have been updated. The term 'programme' is not used frequently nowadays but it has been retained here, as in the original.

The first reports were first published in The Early Detection of Reading Difficulties with Recovery Procedures *(1979a). They describe the early research base and rationale for Reading Recovery. Additional reports were added in* Reading Recovery: A Guidebook for Teachers in Training *(1993a).*

Many changes have taken place in the operation of this early literacy intervention, and the material reported here does not provide guidance for implementing Reading Recovery in education systems. For such information, see Literacy Lessons Designed for Individuals: Part Two: Teaching Procedures *(Clay, 2005).*

A research programme was undertaken to explore the extent to which it was possible to undercut reading and writing failure in an education system by a programme of early intervention. Eight projects in this research programme are reported here in somewhat abbreviated form for teachers and administrators.

The research question for all of these studies was 'What is possible?' It was not possible in New Zealand at that time to ask how well this programme worked compared with competing programmes since none existed. The only realistic comparison was with a) children unable to be given the programme or b) other children in the same age cohort and in classroom programmes. After the first year's success, the first alternative was judged to be unethical. The second alternative required an unconventional research design that allowed for three aspects of the treatment that other researchers have found to be problematical.

1. Children spend varying lengths of time in treatment, according to need, and new children enter the programme throughout the year. Analysis of results for a particular school year catches up a group who have had less than the required treatment and whose results cannot be 'added to' those who have been in the programme the required time for them.

2. Children who enter Reading Recovery are the lowest achievers in their age cohort in their own school. As the programme aims to bring those children to average levels of achievement, it is necessary to test whether this is achieved by having a research design which allows comparison with the age cohort in that school.

3. Several 'relative' criteria are used in Reading Recovery. The children selected are the lowest achievers in their school, and that level may vary from school to school. Similarly, the children cease to receive individual tuition when they have reached average achievement for their age cohort in their school and are able to survive in their class-rooms and maintain their progress. Such criteria work well for self-managed schools, and despite the variability between schools found in education systems, but they present some problems for traditional research designs.

Reading Recovery is an intervention designed to function effectively in an education system so these research projects sought answers to questions about what would be possible if one delivered instruction in a different way and the appropriate comparison was to compare the end result with that of ordinary classroom instruction.

Studies reported here are these.

1 The development project, 1976–1977

2 The field trial research in 1978

3 The one-year follow-up research, 1979

4 The replication study, 1979

5 The analysis of lesson content, 1978

6 The three-year follow-up, 1981

7 National monitoring, 1984–1988

8 The Reading Recovery subgroups study, 1991

1   The development project

Marie M. Clay

The aim of the project was to record how teachers worked with children having marked difficulty learning to read and write in a one-to-one teaching situation. We aimed to describe the range and variability of reading and writing behaviours shown by the children and the range and variability of the teaching responses made by the teachers. The children had completed their first year at school. (In New Zealand, children start school on their fifth birthday).

The project began in 1976 with a year of detailed observation and record-keeping as I worked with one teacher, and continued in the second year with practitioners, a team of six people — teachers, supervising teachers, reading advisers, and senior University students. They agreed to find time to teach two children individually. They agreed to meet once every two weeks to observe each other and to discuss procedures and assumptions. Procedures were evolved for observing the teachers at work, using a one-way screen. At these sessions the team would discuss pupil and teacher responses as they occurred, and following the lesson they would challenge the teachers who had demonstrated to explain why they chose a technique, a particular book, or a specific progression. They were asked:

- What contributed to a teaching decision?

- How could they justify it?

- What other difficulties or achievements were the procedures related to?

- Why did the children react in this or that way?

- Why did they not move the child more quickly?

During such discussions the implicit assumptions of the teacher had to be explained verbally rather than remaining intuitive hunches. The process of articulating the basis for a teaching decision was always difficult.

A large number of techniques were piloted, observed, discussed, argued over, related to theory, analysed, written up, modified, and tried out in various ways, and, most important, many were discarded. Carefully graded sequences within each technique were described. Thus the procedures were derived from the responses of experienced teachers to children as they tried to read and write. The process of refinement continued over the next three years, as several drafts of the teaching procedures were written, discussed, and edited by the teachers. The procedures were derived from the practice of teachers who were working with failing children but they were discussed and analysed in relation to current theories of the reading process. Revision of rationales and procedures continues as 'current theories' change and the balance of research evidence shifts.

The 6-year-old children who were referred to the programme were diverse in their response to print. No two children had quite the same problems. Children on the same level of text varied in their profiles of test scores. One may conclude therefore that these children read texts of similar difficulty with skills of different strengths. It followed from this that each child's Reading Recovery programme must be designed to suit the responses in his repertoire and so programmes differed from child to child.

Critical evaluation of the results of the development project at the end of 1977 suggested that the five most important areas to receive attention in the next stage of our project would be:

1. **Organisation**   Children probably needed more intensive programmes than two or three lessons each week if they were to move quickly at accelerated rates of progress.

2. **Teaching**   The most effective teaching procedures from our records should be gathered together and articulated to provide better guidance for teachers.

3. **Efficient choices**   If effective teaching is to occur, sound choices must be made about appropriate procedures. It follows that certain procedures are de-emphasized or eliminated from some children's programmes. Decisions not to do certain things in recovery programmes may be very important. This is a somewhat novel concept in the area of reading difficulties. It relates to economical use of the child's learning time.

4. **Conceptualizing the goal**   The goal of teaching should be a self-extending system, a set of behaviours which lead the child to control more difficult texts merely because he reads them. The important components of a self-extending system are the in-the-head strategies which the child initiates to capture information in the visual and verbal features of the text, or to detect an error that has been made and to find some way of self-correcting it, using past knowledge to solve a novel problem. Teachers in our next stage of developing the treatment should deliberately focus the child's attention on such processing strategies.

5. **Transfer or generalization**   We must think clearly about the process of discontinuing children from tutoring and the ways in which we could ensure continuing progress back in classrooms. It is not a contradiction to say that we needed to become specific about such generalization.

2   The field trial research
Marie M. Clay

The Field Trial research (1978) was an exploratory study to find out what kinds of outcomes were possible.

This study reports the results of the first year of working in schools, the first year of developing the teacher training, and the teaching being done by teachers who were in training. We had observed good teachers of problem readers working in one-to-one situations, and we had observed the children. We had articulated what we thought were some of the children's problems, and what seemed to be efficient and economical teaching procedures.

The next step was to demonstrate that these procedures worked and that children made progress. However, if an early intervention programme were to be adopted in schools, we also had to demonstrate that our procedures could work in different school settings. Such evidence would be most important for New Zealand educators who are traditionally very sceptical about the contribution that academics and researchers can make to effective teaching. In addition we would somehow have to find convincing evidence to support the argument for one-to-one teaching, for which there was no precedent in the system.

The research questions in 1978

1. The practical questions concerned how the programme could be implemented in schools.

   - Could experienced teachers without specialist training use the procedures effectively?

   - How would the programmes need to vary from school to school?

The plan of operation must allow for teachers to differ, for schools to differ, and the children in different schools to differ. How teachers worked, how many children they took each day, and what timetables they derived were not predetermined. Teachers discussed their ideas on these matters with the research staff. Consultation, not prescription, was the key word. We wanted to see what organization teachers would evolve for mounting the programme in their schools.

2. The other questions concerned what reading progress could be made.

- To what extent could the poorest readers be helped by individual tutoring?

- How many could be helped?

- What were the outcomes of the programme for the tutored children in comparison with the untutored?

- Could the gains made in tutoring be sustained after withdrawal of the supplementary tutoring?

The schools

The schools were different in size, in type of organization,[1] in population and location. All were in the suburbs of a large metropolitan area. School A was a small school in an older state-housing area with some solo parents. School B was in a mixed working- and middle-class suburb. School C was on the edge of both a middle-class and a working-class new housing area and was the biggest school. In School D the children were predominantly from working-class backgrounds with much movement in and out of the school. School E was a larger school in a newer state-housing area with 60% of the children having solo parents. Auckland schools have high proportions of Maori and Pacific Island children.

The teachers

Principals in those five schools were asked to use the allocated extra teacher to release an experienced teacher of beginning reading who volunteered to do this Reading Recovery training. The teachers released had from 5 to 12 years' experience. Academic background was not a requirement. All the teachers had been trained in Teachers' Colleges and did not have University diplomas or degrees. The conditions of a school's participation in the research study were:

---

1 Two were open-plan and three had single-cell classrooms.

- that the teacher be allowed to test *every 6-year-old* within two weeks of his/her birthday

- that she arrange a programme of individual tutoring for suitable children

- that her participation in this programme would not be interrupted for any reason (such as relieving, sports duties, and school trips).

Testing every child after one year of instruction

To allow for comparison of the children who received help with their classmates who did not, the total age cohort was tested in the five schools. The dates of testing, linked to sixth birthdays, were scattered throughout the year for children whose birthdays fell between 1 September 1977 and 30 September 1978. The mean age of the 291 children at initial testing was 6 years 1.5 months because testing which began in February 1978 included children born in the previous September. Children who transferred into the schools later in the year were tested if they belonged to the same age cohort.

Who was tutored?

From the 291 children in the age cohort in five schools, 122 were given special help.

How children were distributed on the reading books after 1 year of school differed markedly from school to school. Two main reasons for this were a) that the children entering schools differed in background experience and ability from school to school and b) that schools paced the introduction of the reading programme differently. Some schools began book reading early and pushed ahead rather rapidly. Others took a longer time to establish foundation skills. Therefore, children selected for individual tutoring were not chosen by setting a particular attainment level. *They were selected by the relative criterion of being the lowest scorers on text reading in that particular school.* The lowest scorers in School C might have scores as high as the average scorers in School E. It was not the point of this study to raise all children's performance above a particular level. The teacher available in each school was trying to *raise the performance of the low-progress readers in that school.*

The working hours of the teacher set limits to how many children she could take into her programme. The responsiveness of children to individual teaching determined the number of weeks a child remained in the study. Factors which tended to lengthen time in the programme were language problems, family mobility, unsettled family circumstances, sickness and/or absence, general retardation, and unusual learning problems.

The proportion of the age cohort who were individually tutored in this field trial year differed from school to school because each school, irrespective of size, was allocated a full-time teacher.

The tutoring programme

Children received individual daily teaching by selected teachers who were undergoing a year's inservice training. Training sessions were held every 2 weeks. This allowed quality control over the teaching on the one hand, but, on the other hand, the teachers were apprentices, learning how to implement the programme and coming to grips with the decision-making it called for.

The teacher who had completed an Observation Survey Summary Sheet Report[2] had on hand an analysis of behaviours which should relate directly to her teaching programme.

A typical teaching session included a particular set of activities. These placed the emphasis on using text for most of the lesson. As the goal of the programme was to return children to average reading groups in their classrooms, it was necessary to accelerate their progress to achieve this. Accelerated progress would be most likely to be achieved if:

- the child had many opportunities to read and write

- the tasks were the same as the ones on which improvement was required, i.e., reading messages and writing sentences

- the child was building a complex, flexible system of alternative responses (Clay, 1991).

When skills are taught in isolation, more time must be spent in learning to combine these, and more difficulty is experienced with switching to alternative responses. This slows down learning.

The teacher arranged to see children on a timetable that suited her and the school. Sometimes this was once a day and sometimes twice a day for two sessions (see Table 1).

---

2 At the time of this research the *Diagnostic Survey* was used (Clay, 1979a). This was renamed *An Observation Survey of Early Literacy Achievement* (Clay, 1993, 2002, 2006).

The teacher training

The teachers were being trained throughout the year. At first the teachers were encouraged to draw on their past experience. Gradually Reading Recovery procedures were introduced and demonstrated, and teachers were encouraged to change their concept of the task. Every two weeks one of the five teachers would demonstrate by teaching one of her pupils while the other teachers observed and discussed the procedures on the other side of a one-way screen.

Topics raised by the teachers in these discussions seemed to suggest that their attention to the reading process was shifting:

- from teaching for items of knowledge (letters known, words remembered) and getting the child to habituate a skill or memorize a new element

- to developing in the child the willingness to use a variety of text-solving strategies.

Another feature of the shift was away from having the 'poor reader' dependent on the teacher and towards teaching in such a way that the child had many opportunities to teach himself something.

Records

Teachers were encouraged to keep a diary or log book as a personal history of the year's work. Personal reactions and queries were to be dated and entered on both teacher behaviours and perceptions, and child behaviours. In addition each teacher kept the following records on individual pupils.

- An Observation Survey Summary Report was prepared for each child when he was accepted into the project.

- A Lesson Record was kept for each session with the child, detailing at what point in the teaching sequence the teacher was working and how the child responded. This provided a record of the small step gains, and of the progressions which the teacher selected from the teachers' handbook.

- One Running Record of text reading was usually taken in each session.

- A graph of progress by Book Level was plotted from one Running Record each week.

Contact with parents

We hoped schools would feel free to approach parents in whatever would be their normal procedure. In fact, contacts during this first year were minimal.

The discontinuing of tutoring

When the teachers judged from the children's work that they would be able to work with and survive in an appropriate group in their classroom and maintain their progress, they recommended discontinuing the tutoring. At this point, to provide an objective check on the teacher's estimate of progress, an independent tester re-administered the Observation Survey. In most cases when a comparison was made with the entry test scores, progress in all tests and on text reading was noted and individual tutoring was discontinued. Sometimes a recommendation was made to continue intermittent lessons to support a child or give further instruction in specific areas of weakness. Occasionally a child was not ready to be discontinued. In most cases the teachers were conservative in their recommendations for discontinuing and had carried the children for longer and to higher levels than we had expected. New children entered individual tutoring throughout the year as lessons were discontinued for others.

Testing at the end of 1978

In the last 2 months of 1978 all children in the age cohort in the five schools were retested by two independent testers. Book Level and Reading Vocabulary were used as two measures of general reading progress.

Book Level (Running Records)

The most relevant measure for demonstrating progress was Book Level because it assessed the child's management of problem-solving on continuous text. A scale of difficulty was provided by two Caption Book steps, 24 steps for the basic reading series[3] plus three paragraphs (2, 3 and 4) from the Neale Analysis of Reading Ability (1958), making 29 steps. The highest level on the scale that a child could attempt with 90% (or above) accuracy determined his score. This type of measure had proved to be a valid and reliable test of reading progress in other research (Clay, 1966; Robinson, 1973; Wade, 1978). It is not an equal interval scale.

---

3   The original New Zealand 'Ready to Read' series (1963).

Reading Vocabulary

A standardized test was also used. Previous research with children of this age in New Zealand schools (Clay, 1966) had shown that low-progress children could be given the Word Test and high-progress children could be given the Schonell R1 test and that a satisfactory measure *for research purposes* was obtained by combining these two scores. This procedure was used again in this study and the combined scores for Reading Vocabulary yielded a normal distribution. A Word Test score provides only a sign or indicator of reading progress because the test behaviour that is scored does not involve management of the behaviours needed to read continuous text.

The other tests used were from the Observation Survey: Concepts About Print (CAP), Letter Identification (LI), Writing Vocabulary (WV), Dictation Test (DIC) [renamed Hearing and Recording Sounds in Words, 1993] (Clay, 1979a; see also Clay, 1993b, 2002, 2006).

Scores on these tests were interpreted as indicators of some component reading skills covering directional and visual discrimination learning (CAP), letter identity (LI), a writing vocabulary of words known in every detail (WV), and sound-to-letter association (DIC) [HRSW].

Results: Organizational factors

How did teachers adapt this opportunity for individual instruction to the setting of their particular school?

Numbers and sex of children

The number of children who received tuition from teachers ranged from 20 to 30 per teacher per year working full-time (Table 1). Sixty-one percent of the children tutored were boys and 39% were girls.

Weeks in programme

Table 1 shows the average pattern, and individual school averages, for time in tuition. There was an average lag of 3 to 5 weeks between sixth birthday and entry to the programme for a variety of unavoidable reasons such as vacations, a full tutoring roll, a need for testing to be scheduled, and/or absences.

The average length of individual programmes was 13 to 14 weeks. It should be stressed that this was an average length of time in tuition; individual children needed more time in the programme.

Length of lessons

The arrangements that teachers made for lessons varied from child to child and from teacher to teacher. Three teachers used a 40-minute lesson most of the time and others used a short and a long lesson, one of 30 minutes and a second of 10 minutes later in the day (Table 1).

Table 1: **Organisation Differences in Five Schools**

	Number of children tutored	Mean weeks in programme		Mean length of lessons (in minutes)	Mean number of lessons
		Discontinued	Not Discontinued (End of school year)		
A[a]	22	15.1	12.0	40.5	27.6
B[b]	28	11.3	11.8	40.0	21.8
C	22	11.6	13.0	35.9	33.8
D	29	13.2	13.8	26.7[c]	33.3
E[a], E[b]	21	16.2	15.1	40.0	26.4
Average		14.0	13.1		

a These schools had women principals, the others had men.

b These schools had open plan organization for junior (elementary) classes.

c Mean length of lesson was affected by some use of shared instruction.

Results: progress of the children

The progress of the three groups will be reported — the Control group, the Discontinued group, and the Not Discontinued group. Readers will recall that new children entered the programme throughout the year.[4]

Control group The 160 children not selected for tutoring (who were of the same age group, attended the same schools, and had higher initial attainment) were used as a reference group for the tutored children (Table 2).

Discontinued Children who were tutored and discontinued during the school year had been back in the class programme for an average of 12 weeks (N = 53). Another discontinued group were those who were receiving tuition up until the time of final testing and who met the criteria used to discontinue children (N = 27). These two subgroups make up the Discontinued group.

Not Discontinued These were children who were receiving tuition at the time of final testing (the end of school year) and needed further instruction (N = 42). They had entered the programme as others left it and their programmes were incomplete.

---

4 On the average five teachers taught and discontinued eight children each, then taught and discontinued another eight, and then admitted a further seven children who had incomplete programmes at the end of the school year.

Table 2: **Initial and Final Test Scores**

Test	Group	Test time	N	Mean	SD	Sm	t-test[a] of differences	Correlation of Initial and Final Test
Book Level	Discontinued	1	80	6.33	3.67	0.41	25.80	0.53*
		2	80	18.53	3.96	0.44		
	Not Discontinued	1	42	2.48	1.61	0.25	15.12	0.48*
		2	42	8.21	2.76	0.43		
	Control[b]	1	160	12.54	5.86	0.46	22.12	0.64*
		2	160	20.86	5.47	0.43		
Reading Vocabulary	Discontinued	1	80	9.25	9.32	1.04	4.09	0.42*
		2	80	27.63	6.46	0.72		
	Not Discontinued	1	42	4.76	2.96*	0.46	12.28	0.47*
		2	42	14.76	5.20	0.80		
	Control	1	160	24.03	16.78	1.33	19.18	0.74*
		2	160	33.53	11.51	0.91		
Concepts About Print	Discontinued	1	80	13.86	2.78	0.31	18.14	0.35*
		2	80	19.79	2.34	0.26		
	Not Discontinued	1	42	10.90	2.89	0.45	16.05	0.71*
		2	42	16.00	2.45	0.38		
	Control	1	160	16.83	3.43	0.27	5.73	0.64*
		2	160	17.41	3.77	0.30		
Letter Identification	Discontinued	1	80	37.20	13.52	1.51	9.92	0.14
		2	80	51.55	3.20	0.36		
	Not Discontinued	1	42	23.67	14.39	2.22	12.78	0.72*
		2	42	43.29	9.59	1.48		
	Control	1	160	49.86	8.67	0.69	3.91	0.55*
		2	160	50.74	6.30	0.50		
Writing Vocabulary	Discontinued	1	80	10.38	5.80	0.65	17.67	0.18
		2	80	45.69	12.24	1.59		
	Not Discontinued	1	42	5.64	2.90	0.45	14.92	0.47*
		2	42	24.05	9.21	1.42		
	Control	1		(Not administered)				
		2	160	48.19	21.76	1.72		
Dictation [HRSW]	Discontinued	1	80	15.44	7.83	0.88	21.39	0.31*
		2	80	33.24	2.97	0.33		
	Not Discontinued	1	42	8.29	7.31	1.13	17.31	0.62*
		2	42	24.52	6.53	1.01		
	Control	1	160	27.70	8.59	0.68	6.50	0.65*
		2	160	32.96	5.82	0.46		

a   All t-tests are above 2.69 and are significant.

b   This should be called a comparison or reference group because it was not a randomly assigned group. It was a group deliberately chosen to show the outcome achievements of the treated group in relation to their average and better peers.

*   Correlations that were significantly above zero at the $p < .01$ level.

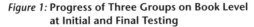

Figure 1: Progress of Three Groups on Book Level
at Initial and Final Testing

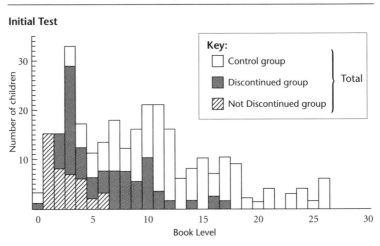

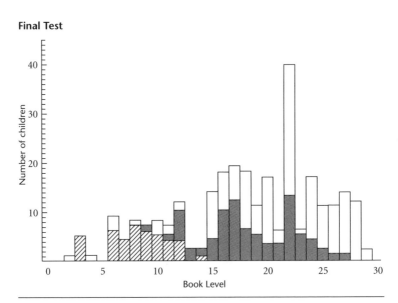

Within-group changes

The mean test scores of all three groups (Discontinued, Not Discontinued, and Control) increased from initial to final testing on Book Level, Reading Vocabulary, Concepts About Print, Dictation [HRSW], and Letter Identification so that statistically significant differences were recorded (see Table 2). Writing Vocabulary was not administered initially to the Control group, but significant differences were found for both tutored groups.

Figure 1 shows the progress of the three groups on Book Level at initial and final testing. The Reading Vocabulary Test graph (not shown) plotted a similar shift. Despite the very different nature of these measures, one measuring accuracy on text and the other word reading in isolation, the type of change for each group was similar.

The movement of the Discontinued group from low-level scoring to average levels is visually apparent and the fact that the Not Discontinued group need further tuition can also be noted.

A third way of reporting the progress was with the gains in Stanine scores. These are reported in Table 3 and Figure 2.

Table 3: Gains in Stanine Scores for All Measures
(with t-tests for significant differences between groups)

Test	Group	N	Mean	SD	SE_m	t_1
Book Level	Discontinued	80	2.84	1.13	0.13	4.62*
	Not Discontinued	42	2.00	0.80	0.22	0.29
	Control	160	2.06	1.20	1.11	
Reading Vocabulary	Discontinued	80	2.76	1.01	0.11	5.30*
	Not Discontinued	42	1.69	0.87	0.13	0.94
	Control	160	1.89	1.23	0.11	
Concepts About Print	Discontinued	80	2.99	1.51	0.17	9.65*
	Not Discontinued	42	2.14	1.00	0.15	4.83*
	Control	160	1.19	1.14	0.13	
Letter Identification	Discontinued	80	2.33	1.36	0.15	5.47*
	Not Discontinued	42	1.83	0.93	0.14	2.45
	Control	160	1.34	1.17	0.11	
Writing Vocabulary	Discontinued	80	4.15	1.28	0.14	9.06*
	Not Discontinued	42	2.00	1.17	0.18	
	Control		(Not administered)			
Dictation [HRSW]	Discontinued	80	2.71	1.14	0.13	8.29*
	Not Discontinued	42	2.14	0.95	0.15	3.99*
	Control	160	1.38	1.11	0.10	

* t-test indicates a significant difference between groups.

Figure 2: Gains in Stanine Scores in Discontinued, Not Discontinued, and Control Groups

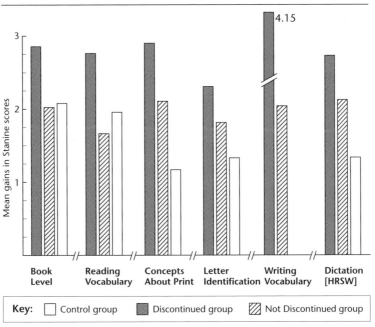

The pupils who received individual tuition made gains which equalled or exceeded the gain scores made by their classmates who showed initially the higher achievement. The following statements refer to *the number of Stanines gained* but they do not imply that the groups were scoring at the same level on the tests.

a The Discontinued group made higher and significantly different gains from the Control group in all tests. (Writing Vocabulary was not administered initially to the Control group.) (See Table 3 and Figure 2.)

b The Not Discontinued group made gains that were not significantly lower than those of the Control group on Book Level, Reading Vocabulary, and Letter Identification. They were significantly higher on Concepts About Print and Dictation [HRSW].

c The Discontinued group made significantly higher gains than the Not Discontinued pupils on Writing Vocabulary.

The only children in the age cohort (282) for whom the programme was insufficient or unsuitable, were:

- four Pacific Island children with insufficient English to understand the instructions of the Observation Survey (and presumably the instructional programmes). Many Pacific Island children made satisfactory progress in the programme.

- one Indian child with flaccid cerebral palsy who made little progress and who was referred to the Psychological Service.

- two children who were helped in the programme but were also seen by the Psychological Service as possibly needing placement in special classes for children of low intelligence.

The Field Trial study results surprised us. High numbers of children were discontinued, the third intake of children had incomplete programmes, and only 7 children had to be referred for specialist reports and continuing help. Further comment on the Field Trial phase has been made in the 1-year follow-up research (next section).

3 The one-year follow-up research
Marie M. Clay

One year later the progress of all the children in the Field Trial Research was reassessed. Many things could have upset any trends established by tutoring in the previous year. Control children might forge ahead at a faster rate once the early skills had been mastered as they profited from wide-ranging individual reading. Discontinued children might be unable to build on their gains and so slip back. Not Discontinued children might have slipped further behind or they might have been able to accelerate their progress. No further individual help had been provided during this year.

The research questions

Questions for the one-year follow-up study were:

- What gains were made in 1979?

- Was the relative status of the groups maintained?

- Were gains made during tutoring sufficient to allow children to progress with their average classmates?

51

- Were the gains made better than those predicted by the statistical phenomenon of regression to the mean?

The research phases

This description of phases is necessary for the interpretation of the tables and figures in this section.

The children entered school on their fifth birthdays and were tested one year later, on their sixth birthdays. As this birthday occurred anywhere between September 1977 and September 1978 the first phase began for individual children at variable dates throughout the year.

The tutoring phase (Phase 1) The tutoring phase began soon after a child's sixth birthday and continued as long as necessary to meet preset criteria of performance based on reading strategies. On average a period of 13 to 14 weeks was needed. Children were discharged from tutoring when they demonstrated a set of behaviours thought to be related to surviving in the ordinary classroom programme. If children did not demonstrate these behaviours they continued in the programme. Of necessity the tutoring phase ended for all children at the end of the school year, December 1978.

Back-in-class phase (Phase 2) The decisions about discontinuing tutoring and the staggered timing of the children's entry into the tutoring phase created a group of children who had a period back in their classroom after tutoring and before the end of the school year.

The follow-up phase (Phase 3) No contact was made with the children during 1979. Some moved to new schools. In December 1979 all children who could be located in the Auckland area were retested by trained testers not associated with the programme. Of the 291 children originally tested in five schools at 6 years, 282 were retested in December 1978 (97%) and 270 in December 1979 (93%). Numbers in the groups at follow-up were Control 153 (160), Discontinued 76 (80), Not Discontinued 41 (42). The losses were low in number and spread across the groups.

Results

Table 4 and Figures 3 and 4 summarize the comparisons at Initial (age 6.0), Final, and Follow-up testing for the total group and each subgroup. Mean scores rose during Reading Recovery instruction for tutored groups and gains continued in the following year at a satisfactory level.

Table 4: **Mean Scores for Research Groups on Book Level and Reading Vocabulary**

Test	Group	Mean 6:0	Mean 1978[a]	Mean 1979[a]	SD 6:0	SD 1978[a]	SD 1979[a]
Book Level	Total	9.40	18.51	24.39	6.22	6.42	4.92
	Control	12.54	20.86	26.36	5.86	5.47	3.29
	Discontinued	6.33	18.53	24.66	3.67	3.96	3.10
	Not Discounted	2.48	8.21	16.23	1.61	2.76	4.75
Reading Vocabulary	Total	16.20	28.86	41.52	10.40	11.29	13.13
	Control	24.03	33.53	47.07	16.78	11.51	12.11
	Discontinued	9.25	27.63	39.09	9.32	6.46	7.36
	Not Discounted	4.76	14.76	24.59	2.96	5.20	8.99

a   End of school year.

*   Differences are significant at $p < .01$ level.

Figure 3: **Mean Scores for Reading Vocabulary at Initial, Discontinuing, Final, and Follow-up Testing for Control, Discontinued, and Not Discontinued Groups**

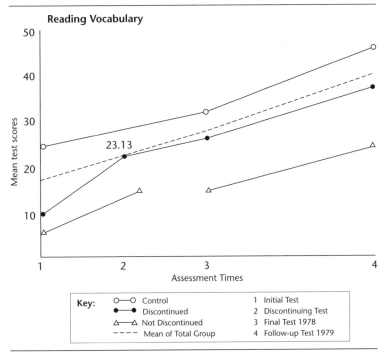

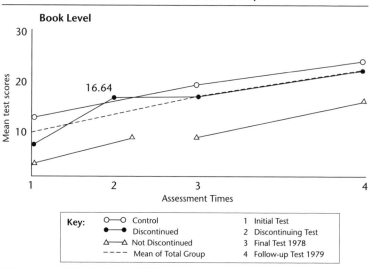

Figure 4: Mean Scores for Book Level at Initial, Discontinuing, Final, and Follow-up Testing for Control, Discontinued, and Not Discontinued Groups

Key:		
O—O Control	1	Initial Test
●—● Discontinued	2	Discontinuing Test
△—△ Not Discontinued	3	Final Test 1978
– – – Mean of Total Group	4	Follow-up Test 1979

The Control group scored above the mean of the total group at each of three testing times (Initial, Final, and Follow-up) on two test variables, Book Level and Reading Vocabulary.

The Discontinued group of children had low Initial scores. Final scores were well within one standard deviation of the Control group's Final means, and they retained that position at Follow-up testing. It would be reasonable to claim that children in that position should be able to profit from the usual classroom instruction. This applied to both the Book Level and Reading Vocabulary measures.

For the Discontinued group the correlations of Initial Scores with Final and Follow-up scores were lower, as one would predict following this intervention programme (Table 5).

For the Not Discontinued group the correlations of Initial scores with Final and Follow-up scores were higher than for the Discontinued group (they were not so influenced by the programme) but lower than those of the Control group (Table 5).

Table 5: Correlations between Initial Scores and Final Scores
(3–11 Months) and Follow-up Scores (15–23 Months)

		Time	Control	Discontinued	Not Discontinued	Total
Book Level	Final		0.64	0.54	0.48	
	Follow-up		0.50	0.30	0.48	0.61
Reading Vocabulary	Final		0.74	0.42	0.47	
	Follow-up		0.63	0.20	0.50	0.71

Do Initial scores predict Final and Follow-up scores?

To answer this question steps were taken that would take account of a regression to the mean effect. Pupils who score lowest tend to make the greatest gains on a second testing. It was necessary to show that any movement of the children with low reading attainment towards the mean of the group was greater than would be predicted by a regression effect. The correlation between two sets of scores for the total group was used to establish a predicted Final, and a predicted Follow-up score for each value in the scale of scores. For every child a difference score was calculated between a) the predicted Final and the actual Final score and b) the predicted Follow-up and the actual Follow-up score. Mean difference scores for Control, Discontinued, and Not Discontinued groups were compared by t-tests.

The results in Table 6 show that for Book Level and Reading Vocabulary the Control group were close to predicted scores on each variable, and on both occasions. The Discontinued children were consistently higher than would be predicted, i.e., their gains were greater than would be predicted by regression effects on each variable and on both occasions. The Not Discontinued children were consistently lower than would be predicted on each variable and on both occasions.

Table 6: Mean Difference Scores between Predicted N^1 and Follow-up N^2 Scores for Book Level and Reading Vocabulary**

			Book Level		Reading Vocabulary	
Group	N^1	N^2	Final	Follow-up	Final	Follow-up
Control	160	153	0.14	0.44	0.94	0.45
Discontinued	80	76	2.34	1.66	2.26	2.33
Not Discounted	42	41	-5.02	-4.84	-6.56	-6.36

* t-tests yield significant differences at the $p < .01$ level.

** A difference score of 0.00 represents no difference from the predicted score. Plus scores are higher than predicted; minus scores are lower.

The results of the t-tests between the mean difference scores for groups show that the Discontinued group made significantly better progress than the Control group relative to their Initial scores, and this trend was maintained at Follow-up. The Discontinued group made significantly better progress than the Not Discontinued group relative to their Initial scores and this trend was maintained at Follow-up.

In summary, the results support the interpretation that the children who were tutored until it was judged that they could survive in their classrooms were at Follow-up one year later scoring above predicted scores while the children with incomplete programmes who were judged not to be ready for the termination of their individual tutoring programme were in every comparison below predicted scores. This is taken to be support for two theoretical arguments. The first is that the operational criteria used for judging that children were using certain processing strategies while reading were successful in separating out two groups of children. The second is that the theory upon which the instructional programme was based (that gains in reading can be described in terms of operations carried out by children rather than items of knowledge gained) has received endorsement since discontinuing judgements were made on the evidence of strategic behaviour.

The need to complete Reading Recovery programmes in the following school year for the incomplete group was now clearly evident because after their incomplete programmes these children did not spontaneously shift into the average group.

Table 7: **Follow-up Test Scores for Children Who Transferred into Research Schools**

	N	Book Level	Reading Vocabulary
Control	153	26.36	47.07
Discontinued	76	24.66	39.09
Not Discontinued	41	16.44	24.59
Transfers*	36	21.44	36.11
Total (without transfers)	270	24.39	41.52

* Supplementary analysis: the transfer group

Note: During the Follow-up Phase when no Reading Recovery programme was available to the schools, 36 children of the same age cohort transferred into the research schools. They were tested at Follow-up as a group who had not been in contact with the Reading Recovery programme. Their scores on four test variables were significantly lower than those of the total group, and lower than the Discontinued group (see Table 7) but higher than those of the Not Discontinued group. The gains of the Discontinued group showed a level of achievement one year later, higher than that of all children who had changed schools, a group which would include competent, average and poor achievement children.

4 The replication study

Marie M. Clay

An in-service course in 1979 trained new teachers in the operation of Reading Recovery programmes in 48 schools. These teachers worked at individual teaching for 10 hours a week, a considerable reduction on the 25 hours available in the 1978 field trial schools. Consequently the 1979 teachers taught and discontinued fewer children per teacher and lesson time was reduced from 40 to 30 minutes. Because they taught fewer children and yet selected the poorest in their schools, the children were, as a group, more challenging and difficult than those taught in the field trials. A class teacher in each school was trained to carry out the final testing to provide for independent assessment.

The research question

The research question was 'Under such changed conditions how well would three new groups of teachers perform in comparison with the five field trial teachers in 1978?'

Could the results of the first year be replicated by a large number of teachers in a large number of schools?

Procedures

The 48 schools which had teachers in training in 1979 were listed alphabetically and divided into three groups (B, C, D) providing three replication samples. The average levels of scoring for the 1979 groups (B, C, D) were compared with the 1978 field trials results (called Group A).

Results

In Table 8, 'Dis' refers to children discontinued with time in their class-rooms after tutoring before the end of the year (phase 2), 'Dd' refers to children discontinued without a period of time in their classrooms after tutoring (no phase 2), and 'Not Dis' refers to those not ready to be discontinued because of less than complete programmes (end of school year).

Table 8: Comparison of the 1978 Sample (A) with Three Replication Samples in 1979 (B, C, D) on Initial and Final Scores

		Initial			Final		
		Dis	Dd[a]	Not Dis	Dis	Dd[a]	Not Dis
Reading Vocabulary	A	11.79	8.15	4.76	29.54	22.19	14.76
	B	8.39	9.53	5.85	29.98	22.42	13.73
	C	8.71	9.50	4.62	28.52	24.65	11.90
	D	8.65	6.71	4.38	28.29	23.13	12.16
	F ratios	3.87*	1.22	0.92	0.74	1.16	1.68
Book Level	A	6.94	5.07	2.48	20.17	15.04	8.21
	B	4.69	6.78	4.02	20.52	16.89	9.31
	C	5.19	7.15	2.82	19.29	17.15	8.03
	D	5.14	4.13	2.25	19.51	15.00	7.75
	F ratios	3.46*	2.91	4.67**	1.59	3.34*	1.12
Writing Vocabulary	A	11.02	9.11	5.64	51.02	39.96	24.05
	B	8.63	10.26	7.05	49.56	38.74	25.07
	C	9.08	11.55	5.15	48.10	39.10	18.77
	D	8.67	7.88	5.43	42.79	35.21	16.66
	F ratios	2.09	1.38	1.48	2.87*	0.81	4.62**
Dictation [HRSW]	A	16.25	13.89	8.29	34.38	31.07	24.52
	B	11.58	12.74	9.33	33.73	33.63	25.40
	C	12.65	14.90	5.61	33.63	32.85	20.72
	D	13.00	11.29	6.50	33.65	32.96	21.81
	F ratios	3.19*	0.61	2.71	0.68	2.91	2.59

a Discontinued without phase 2

* Differences significant at the $p < .05$ level.

** Differences significant at the $p < .01$ level.

The Initial and Final scores for the four samples in Table 8 cluster within a narrow range. Results for Concepts About Print and Letter Identification tests yielded similar results. It is possible to conclude that teachers guided by a year-long inservice course were able to replicate the results of the 1978 field trials in regard to the level of most scores although they were not working full-time and therefore helped fewer children.

F-tests for each set of scores suggest the following qualifications to the above conclusion (Table 8).

Children taken into the programme in 1979 (samples B, C, D) had lower scores on entry in Reading Vocabulary and Book Level but similar final scores compared with the 1978 sample. Teachers presumably retained them in the programme until they reached satisfactory levels of performance.

Final Writing Vocabulary scores tended to be lower for the 1979 groups. There is a strong possibility that teachers in 1979 with less tutoring time available gave less time to writing.

Overall the results in 1979 fairly replicated the field trials of 1978 and variations between samples were small. Time for tutoring emerged as an important variable and lower entry scores imply more individual tutoring time.

5   The analysis of lesson content
Marie M. Clay and Barbara Watson

It is important for policy-makers and researchers to know whether a programme can be delivered as designed.

In November 1981 the New Zealand Department of Education approved a research grant for the retrospective analysis of records of children who were in the Reading Recovery trials in 1978. Teachers had been required to keep notes of exactly what occurred in each individual lesson. An evaluation of the programmes delivered was made from the analysis of those records.

Finding the children

The 122 children taught during the field trials of the Reading Recovery project in 1978 were traced in December 1981. A letter to each school brought quick returns listing the children still attending or providing the name of the next school attended. All the children were traced. Six were not available for retesting as they had left the Auckland area. This was a high retention rate after 3 years.

Ethnic group membership

In 1978 we did not know what ethnic groups the Reading Recovery children belonged to. In December 1981 a research assistant visited each school to make detailed enquiries about ethnic group membership. Teaching, clerical, nursing, caretaking staff, and parent helpers supplied information and the children themselves or siblings were occasionally consulted. The information included:

- all the information about the ethnic group membership of any one child, allowing for one, two, or more than two group affiliations

- the kind of evidence that informants were using to arrive at their judgements

- the roles of people providing the information.

Decisions were made about the quality of this information and a classification of 'Not Known' was used if these sources produced inconsistent, unreliable, or insufficient information. An approach to the children's parents did not seem justified for what was a case-file reanalysis study, although we recognized that the parents would provide the most valid information.

On this information we excluded 5 of the 52 Maori or Pacific Island children (three children for whom we had insufficient evidence, one part-Maori child with a very high proportion of European ancestry, and one adopted child). The six children who now lived outside the Auckland District were all Polynesian (Maori or Pacific Island children), and one further child from these groups was absent from school throughout the retesting period. This reduced the available sample of Polynesian children to 40. Children who had fewer than 15 lessons were also excluded because it was decided to set a lower limit to the time spent in the programme. This resulted in the loss of a further six children, reducing the number of Maori and Pacific Island children to 34 (24 Maori and 10 Pacific Island children).

The research samples

Of the 122 children from Discontinued and Not Discontinued groups who had received Reading Recovery tuition in 1978, 68 were selected for the present study. No exclusions were made on the basis of achievement: the reasons for exclusion were ethnic group membership not clear (five cases), non-availability (six cases), insufficient time in the programme (six cases), absent during testing (one case), majority group excluded by matching (36 cases). There were six samples, shown in Table 9.

Table 9: **Study Samples**

	Polynesian		European[a]
Maori			
1	12 with 2 Maori parents	1 E	matched to 1 on entry testing
2	12 with 1 Maori and 1 European parent	2 E	matched to 2 on entry testing
Pacific Island			
3	10 with 2 parents from the same island group	3 E	matched to 3 on entry testing
Total	34		34

a European refers to white children from English-speaking homes, also referred to by the Maori term 'Pakeha'.

Results

Lessons per week

Daily lessons are a requirement in the Reading Recovery programme. The present analysis has shown that in the field trials this ideal condition was a long way from realisation. In the six subgroups the average number of lessons per week ranged from 1.47 to 1.96 (Table 10) although five per week were scheduled. Sickness, weekday holidays, absenteeism for other than health reasons, and not being able to arrange for the lessons because of other school activities are the probable reasons for the low averages. They are not accounted for by teachers having to relieve in other classes or to take on other responsibilities, and the school holidays were excluded from the calculations. There was a much lower rate of instruction than the programme called for, and this points to the need for Reading Recovery teachers to be active in reducing interference with daily lessons.

Table 10: **Lesson Analysis – Reading**

Group	Sample	Lessons per week	Books read per lesson	New books per lesson	Books reread (mean accuracy)
Maori	1	1.47	2.50	1.23	94.97
Maori-European	2	1.59	2.07	1.12	94.34
Pacific Island	3	1.52	2.51	1.17	95.08
European	1 E	1.59	2.16	1.21	95.57
European	2 E	1.58	2.15	1.13	95.63
European	3 E	1.96	2.06	1.22	96.47

Average number of lessons for each group

The average number of lessons for each group ranged from 22.50 to 25.33. The lowest time was given to Pacific Island children and the highest time to Maori children. The differences are not important as the variability from child to child within the groups was very great.

Number of books per lesson

The children read between two and three books per lesson, the range of the six subgroups being 2.06 to 2.51 (Table 10). This implements the recommendations for teaching. It was suggested that the children should begin the lesson by reading one or two easy stories (books) and that later in the lesson a new book would be introduced by the teacher and then tried by the child. At least half of this reading was rereading texts previously read successfully.

New books per lesson

What was the rate at which new books were introduced? The averages ranged from 1.12 to 1.23 books per lesson (Table 10). The teachers exceeded the requirement to try to introduce a new book per lesson. The teacher was skilfully selecting books to suit the particular child's language, concept, and reading development which the teacher was acutely aware of, and she was working individually with each child which meant that careful selection was possible. A new book meant a book which had not previously been worked on; it did not necessarily mean a step-up in difficulty level. Sometimes this occurred; at other times the child read at the same level of difficulty. The teachers aimed to move children as rapidly as possible through the various levels of the graded readers while allowing for two other things — quantities of easy reading and the use of many different reading series and story books. The number of new books read is consistent with these aims.

The measure of difficulty of the texts

Running Records of the child's responses (correct responses, errors, and self-corrections) taken on the second reading of a new book allowed for a calculation of the accuracy with which a child read a book. Teachers usually took a Running Record before moving the child to another book, to obtain a quantitative check on the quality of the child's reading. The mean accuracy level of the six subgroups ranged from 94.34 to 96.47, implying that the children were managing to read the texts in effective ways.

Stories written

The teaching procedures required the teachers to have a story-writing section in every lesson. The records show that they did not achieve this. The average number of stories written each week ranged from 0.86 to 1.05, never matching the number of lessons for any group (Table 11).

The average number of stories per session ranged from 0.55 to 0.69 (Table 11).

Table 11: **Lesson Analysis – Writing**

Group	Sample	Lessons per week	Stories per week	Stories per session
Maori	1	1.47	1.02	0.66
Maori-European	2	1.59	0.86	0.55
Pacific Island	3	1.52	1.00	0.68
European	1 E	1.59	0.99	0.66
European	2 E	1.58	1.05	0.69
European	3 E	1.96	0.96	0.56

Summary of the lesson analyses

There is a similarity across groups in the average number of sessions, the new books per lesson, the books read per lesson, and the mean accuracy levels. There is also similarity in the writing activities. At this level of analysis, differences between ethnic groups in the way the programme was implemented were minimal. *Differences between the recommendations for teaching and what occurred were pronounced. The good results achieved were gained on the risky foundation of a partial implementation of the recommended programme.* Reading Recovery teachers should monitor how well they are implementing the programme so that the feedback can alert them to the areas which need closer attention.

On the basis of these data it is not possible to estimate what would happen if the recommended programme of intensive instruction were to be implemented. One might predict faster progress and a shorter intervention period. On the other hand, the shifts demanded of these children were radical compared with classroom progressions. It may be that this present rate is as fast as such children can move. No amount of guessing or argument at this stage will answer this question. Further data from a fully implemented programme would be required.

Undoubtedly, absences from school interfered with full implementation of the programme. This may indicate that when the programme is introduced, parents need to be consulted and a verbal contract to maximise the opportunity for the child should be entered into by both the home and school.

It may not be realistic to expect the average number of lessons to equal the number of days available for teaching but it is quite possible to make 'Stories Written' equal the number of lessons.

6   The three-year follow-up

Marie M. Clay and Barbara Watson

The research questions

Two questions were raised by educators in relation to long-term outcomes of the Reading Recovery programme.

- Were the children who had Reading Recovery programmes in 1978 continuing to progress with the average groups in their classes in December 1981?

- Was the Reading Recovery programme suitable for Maori children?

The Reading Recovery programme undertook a difficult task. Children with the poorest performance in reading at 6:0 were selected. It was against normal expectations that such children from the low end of the achievement distribution could be brought to average levels of attainment in as little time as 13 to 14 school weeks in both reading and writing. Above-average levels of attainment would not be expected. It would be against normal expectations for many children to retain average placements 3 years later given the ups and downs of school instruction and of child health and family circumstances. With a partially implemented programme in which children who entered school in Term 3 could not receive a full programme because it was only funded for a calendar year (the New Zealand school year), significant results would not be predicted, *yet these Not Discontinued children were included in the three-year follow-up samples.*

The subjects

The ethnic subgroups described in Section 5 were used. There was a total of 68 children, 34 Polynesian and 34 European in six subgroups (see Table 9).

Results from earlier studies

Results were extracted from the studies reported in Sections 2 and 3 for these three ethnic groups (Maori, Pacific Island, and European). Tests of achievement were available for:

a Entry to the programme   Initial

b End of the programme   Discontinuing

c December 1978   Final

d December 1979   Follow-up

For some children b and c were the same time as their tuition was discontinued at the end of the school year (final), not during the year (see page 46).

The original 'Ready to Read' series of graded readers (plus some graded paragraphs from the Neale analysis [1958]) have been used in several research reports as an ordinal scale of 29 unequal steps used to indicate reading progress (see page 44). The highest level of book read at 90% accuracy or above can be used to calculate a mean book level for a group. Table 12 shows similar trends for all subgroups on mean book level with the Maori and Pacific Island groups slightly lower than the Europeans at a, b, and c and increasingly so at d.

Table 12: Mean Book Levels on Four Occasions

Group	Sample	N	Entry	Discontinuing	End of 1978	End of 1979
			a	b	c	d
Maori	1	12	4.42	12.42	13.75	19.91
Maori-European	2	12	5.83	14.58	16.42	21.75
Pacific Island	3	10	3.00	11.50	12.50	19.90
European	1 E	12	4.58	14.58	15.92	23.83
European	2 E	12	5.75	14.92	16.92	23.18
European	3 E	10	3.90	13.20	14.20	22.60

Schonell R1, a word reading test, was used at the same testing points. Raw scores from this test are given in Table 13. The reader will note:

- the exceedingly low scores of all groups at entry to the programme

- comparable gains but low test scores at the end of the programme (Discontinuing) and at the end of 1978 because this test was unable to capture the magnitude and variety of the changes in reading behaviours that occurred at this level

- more or less equivalent status of the groups in December 1979 when the test provided a more reliable and valid estimate of reading level.

Table 13: Mean Schonell R1 Raw Scores on Four Occasions

Group	Sample	N	Entry	Discontinuing	End of 1978	End of 1979
			a	b	c	d
Maori	1	12	1.75	6.58	8.50	18.45
Maori-European	2	12	2.08	7.42	10.92	20.00
Pacific Island	3	10	1.00	5.90	8.10	20.10
European	1 E	12	1.17	8.25	9.42	20.83
European	2 E	12	2.75	7.67	10.25	20.27
European	3 E	10	0.70	4.60	7.40	20.50

Follow-up after three years

Class placements

The 6-year-olds in 1978 were about 9 years old by December 1981. They were therefore suitably placed after 4 years at school in either Standard 2 or 3 (8 to 9 years old) under the promotion policies of New Zealand schools. There are three educational reasons why some might be located in Standard 2.

- They had entered school in the second half of 1977 and had 3 or more years in the Junior Classes 1 to 3.

- They entered school early in 1977 and being slower learners or through life circumstances (for example, illness, changes of school, family events) they required three years or more in the Junior classes 1 to 3.

- They were in schools where promotion rates were slower than average because of the entry characteristics of the total population of the school.

Every ex-Reading Recovery child was either in Standard 2 or 3 when this follow-up study was complete. Table 14 reports the number of children at or above class level for age at 1 January 1981 for the Total group and the subgroups.

It is clear that schools placed the ex-Reading Recovery children according to age for class in almost all cases.

Table 14: **Class Placements by Age at 1 January 1981 (percentages)**

Age	Group	Below S2	S2	Above S2
8:0 – 8:11	Total	0	38	5
	Polynesian[a]	0	16	2
	European	0	22	3

Age	Group	Below S3	S3	Above S3
9:0 – 9:11	Total	1	24	0
	Polynesian[a]	0	16	0
	European	1	8	0

a See Table 9.

Follow-up test results

Time available between the signing of the contract for this research and the end of the school year determined the selection of tests.

- The Burt Word Reading Vocabulary Test (New Zealand Council for Educational Research, 1981) was used because it provided norms for New Zealand children.

- The Schonell Word Reading Vocabulary Test (Schonell R1) was used because it provided a check with earlier Reading Recovery assessments (Table 13).

- Peters Word Spelling Test (Peters, 1970) was used to capture control over writing vocabulary.

Text reading could not be assessed because of the time constraints. Tests were administered by a team of five independent trained testers.

These test results allow an evaluation to be made of one of the major claims for the Reading Recovery programme. Children are kept in the programme until they can rejoin an average group in their class and the aim has been to equip them with independent learning strategies that will enable them to maintain that position. Had this been achieved?

Table 15 reports achievement ages for the Total group and two ethnic subgroups in December 1981 when the children were completing Standard 2 or 3. Group means for reading and spelling were at expected levels for class placement. For the purpose of these analyses it has been assumed that a child in Standard 2 with an achievement age of 8:0 to 9:0 years should find the class programme within his ability. The range of Standard 3 was taken as 9:0 to 10:0 years. *This does not take time of year into account.*

Table 15: Schonell and Peters Achievement Ages for the Total Group and Ethnic Subgroups in S2 and S3 (December 1981)

Group	N	Schonell R1		Peters Spelling	
		M	SD	M	SD
Total	68	9.04	1.36	9.28	1.79
Polynesian	34	9.28	1.34	9.31	1.50
European	34	8.80	1.37	9.25	2.06

Table 16 shows the mean achievement ages according to class placement for each ethnic subgroup. At the end of 1981 children were making the following progress.

- For the European and Pacific Island group in Standard 2 (N = 28) mean test scores were within the age band for class placement.

- For the European and Pacific Island groups in Standard 3 (N = 16) mean test scores were within the age band for class placement.

- For Maori children in Standard 2 (N = 10) mean reading scores were at or just below the lower limit defined as satisfactory for class level in this study but the mean spelling score was above this limit.

- For Maori children in Standard 3 (N = 14) mean reading scores were at the lower limit defined as satisfactory for class level in this study but the mean spelling score was above this level.

Table 16: **Mean Achievement Ages of Each Ethnic Subgroup by Class (December 1981)**

Class	Group	N	Burt (NZ)[a]	Schonell R1	Peters Spelling
S2	Maori	10	7:5 – 8:0	8:1	8:5
	European	15	9:1 – 9:6	9:0	8:8
	Pacific Island	6	8:8 – 9:3	9:2	9:1
	European	7	9:5 – 10:0	9:5	9:0
S3	Maori	14	8:8 – 9:3	9:0	9:5
	European	9	10:1 – 10:6	9:7	10:1
	Pacific Island	4	10:5 – 11:0	10:0	11:0
	European	3	11:4 – 11:9	10:9	11:5

a The New Zealand revision of the Burt test gives score equivalents in age bands.

In an analysis which avoided the reading age bands of the Burt test by using raw scores of the Burt, Schonell, and Peters tests, Maori groups had scores which were lower than Pacific Island or European children in every instance but the levels of scoring were satisfactory for class levels (Table 17).

Table 17: Raw Scores on Burt, Schonell, and Peters Tests for
All Subgroups, December 1981 (Ages 8:0 – 9:11)

Group	Sample	N	Burt (NZ)		Schonell R1		Peters	
			M	SD	M	SD	M	SD
Maori	1	12	46.42	17.15	33.67	13.94	28.58	11.12
Maori-European	2	12	48.00	14.24	41.42	13.99	29.27	8.95
Pacific Island	3	10	59.00	16.01	45.40	13.24	33.10	9.40
European	1 E	12	58.17	15.85	43.63	11.37	32.25	5.74
European	2 E	12	57.67	15.66	36.18	13.47	31.58	6.68
European	3 E	10	63.70	15.31	49.20	13.19	33.40	5.48

Table 18 reports the lowest and highest scores of each subgroup. The
ranges of scores were 2 to 3 years above and below the means.

Table 18: Lowest, Highest, and Mean Achievement Age
Scores for Subgroups (Ages 8:0 – 9:11)

	Lowest		Mean		Highest	
Group	Maori	European	Maori	European	Maori	European
Burt (NZ)	6.1 – 7.6	7.0 – 7.5	8.1 – 8.6	9.1 – 9.6	12.3 – 12.8*	12.3 – 12.8*
Schonell R1	6.3	7.2	8.6	9.3	11.1	12.1
Peters Spelling	6.1	7.1	9.1	9.3	12.4	12.7

Ethnic Group	Pacific Is.	European	Pacific Is.	European	Pacific Is.	European
European	7.1 – 7.6	6.6 – 7.0	9.3 – 9.8	10.0 – 10.5	12.3 – 128*	12.3 – 12.8*
European	7.5	7.5	9.5	9.9	11.6	12.1
European	6.6	7.6	9.9	9.8	12.7	12.3

* Ceiling level of New Zealand norms on test.

7 National monitoring[5]

Marie M. Clay

Annual surveys were carried out by the Department of Education from the beginning of the expansion of Reading Recovery (1982–1984) to national coverage in 1988. The feasibility of national implementation of such a strategy is of considerable interest both within and beyond New Zealand.

Reading Recovery went through 3 years of development and 4 years of researched trials in various parts of the country (1976–1983) before the Department of Education adopted a policy to slowly expand the programme to give it national coverage. In the 1984 school year the programme reached over 3000 children, and despite a change of Government the expansion policy continued.

Each year, from 1984 to 1988, the Department of Education called for returns on the delivery of the programme in the following way. The central office of the Department approved a data collection form which was distributed through the Liaison Inspector in each Education Board area to Reading Recovery Tutors who checked that each school running a programme filed a return recording the outcome of their year's operation. These forms were analysed by the Department annually as an accountability check on the operation of the programme.

Who needs a Reading Recovery programme?

We know from much recent research that preschool children pay attention to stories and to print and have some ideas about what reading and writing are. This has been called 'emerging literacy,' an apt term. (Strickland & Morrow, 1989).

In their first year of school, children should have rich opportunities to learn more about literacy in a good classroom programme because most will be able to move successfully into literacy learning in reading and writing. I have described this as a transition period when children translate their previous competencies into ways of responding which work within the demands and opportunities of that classroom programme (Clay, 1991). Most children's responses to literacy instruction show fluctuation and variance in the first months of school, but by the end of the first year

---

5 While the data collection and analysis are not something I can take credit for, I appreciate being given permission by the New Zealand Department of Education to publish this report and acknowledge the vast amount of work contributed to this report by many teachers, Tutors, and administrators. This report was first published in the *New Zealand Journal of Educational Studies*, Vol. 25, No. 1, 1990, pp. 61–70. Reprinted with permission.

it is possible to distinguish those who are having some trouble making the transition and those who are clearly falling behind the large group of children who are succeeding. Some of these children have been sick and absent for long periods, others seem to be confused by the complexities of literacy, and still others take longer to learn. Reading Recovery offers such children supplementary help to make the transition to being effective literacy learners. What they now need is to learn at an accelerated rate to catch up with their classmates.

Many critics have not understood that the teaching procedures used in Reading Recovery are not recommended for the majority of children; they are able to succeed in a variety of classroom programmes. The few children who need Reading Recovery are those who find it hard to develop effective processing for reading, or for writing, in their school's programme. *The aspects of the complex learning that are most troublesome will vary from child to child.* This is one reason why no classroom programme in the first year of instruction will be adequate for all children: those who fail have problem diagnoses which differ one from another. It is also why each teaching programme must be individually designed for each child.

The Reading Recovery programme fits into the first 2 years of any education system in this way. Children are offered a sound classroom programme in the first year of school and then, if need be, a second chance to make a satisfactory transition once it can be established reliably that such extra help is needed. Results from research studies in three countries (Clay, 1985; Pinnell, DeFord, & Lyons, 1988; Wheeler, 1986) lead to the conclusion that most children *will* be able to make the transition if they receive the supplementary help offered in Reading Recovery from specially trained teachers in a short-term intervention. The goal is to alter the trajectory of each child's progress, and bring as many low-achieving children as possible up to the average band of performance in their classes with sufficient independence to continue to work at or beyond this level of achievement in reading and writing. Such a goal runs counter to the expectations of many educators but it has been reached by a high proportion of Reading Recovery children.

All prevention programmes are likely to deliver treatments to individuals who may not have needed them. (The immunisation of infants against whooping cough provides one example.) Early intervention programmes involve a prediction about future risk, of sickness in the medical field, or in the present case, of educational failure. Such predictions involve the system in making judgements about how much risk they are prepared to take, and those judgements determine the limits that are placed on the availability of the treatment. (Recent arguments about who should get into Reading Recovery focus on this issue, e.g. Glynn et al., 1989; Nicholson, 1989.)

There are, therefore, two different problems for an education system to solve; first, how to deliver good first instruction in literacy, and second, what kind of supplementary opportunity of an intensive kind to provide for individuals who are low-achieving in that good instruction programme. Beginner instruction cannot be all things to all children, and a second opportunity programme should be available to children with unsatisfactory learning histories in the first year of school.

Organizational issues

The following discussion relates to some aspects of the implementation plan for Reading Recovery.

The programme is an intervention delivered in the 'real world' of schools, by good classroom teachers with special training. The instruction must be varied to meet individual differences and it is delivered during individual lessons for variable periods but always for the shortest necessary period.

A school decides whether to adopt the programme and whether to have one or more experienced junior class (children 5 to 8 years of age) teachers trained. Then the programme becomes available to the lowest-achieving children who have been at school one year not excluding any category of children in normal classrooms for any reason.

This basis of selection overcomes several possible problems.

- It avoids categorising children on the basis of problem diagnoses because it selects children who are not progressing in achievement in relation to the progress of their classmates.

- It avoids trying to identify which children are at-risk before they have even been given a fair chance to succeed in a good classroom programme.

- It avoids some of the errors that teachers might make if they tried to select children earlier.

- Chances of wrong identification are further reduced because teachers have to select the extreme cases, who are relatively easy to identify, and the criteria of selection are performance in those day-to-day literacy activities which teachers know about.

When resources are in short supply principals have sometimes suggested that children with the greatest need could be excluded from the programme in favour of children whose problems are less extreme and who are more likely to respond to treatment. If this step is taken, the programme becomes one aimed at improving performance but not aimed at the prevention of reading and writing difficulties in the education system. It would be a case of selecting children into the programme who were most likely to succeed without it, and excluding from the programme the children least likely to succeed without it. It becomes a programme based on discrimination against a group of children compared with a programme based on equity principles. If teaching time is available, and children with the greatest need have not been excluded, schools may wish to include children whose problems are less extreme. There is no reason why this individual instruction will not be facilitating and helpful to any child, since the instruction is individually designed to meet the pupil's needs.

The percentage of children reached in this strategy to reduce literary failure depends, then, on the resources available. Selection is made from the poorest achievers, and an education system might reach 5, 10 or even 20% of children in the age group. Some schools in affluent districts in the USA have decided to help the lowest 30% of their children. It must be remembered that there is a spin-off effect from having a Reading Recovery programme in the school. When the classroom teacher knows that her two or three lowest achievers are working individually with the Reading Recovery teacher she has more time to give to the lower achievers in her class who will not be getting individual help.

The prevention strategy already operates in very different education systems, following on from very different first-year instruction programmes. It allows for the assumption that different causative factors will be operating for different individuals. It addresses the need to provide different sequences of instruction to meet individual needs and for those programmes to vary in length, short for some and up to about 20 weeks for others. It respects the fact that school and education systems are of very different sizes and types, and that their intake populations differ. As a general preventive strategy it seems to have been able to be adapted to most settings, although the problems of remoteness and very small schools present the most difficulties.

Children entering the programme reach criteria for being discontinued in 12 to about 20 weeks of daily, 30-minute lessons, individually designed and individually delivered. The criteria require those discontinued from the programme to have become independent learners within the average band of the classroom to which they belong and to be able to survive in that classroom 'with a not-noticing teacher' — the most risky scenario. High success rates obtained in a short time are needed to make the programme cost-effective and a high-quality programme based on sound training of the teachers is required to achieve these outcomes.

The cut-off time of around 20 weeks is arbitrary but is part of the planning to make the prevention programme cost effective, for otherwise it would be in danger of accumulating a clientele who need long-term help. Then help would not be available to the continuing flow of low-achieving children finishing their first year at school who need short-term help. Again, a school or system with ample resources could set the upper limit of time in the programme at some other level, but it is likely that the few children who have not accelerated in their progress within that period need a different kind of help and should in any case be referred for a specialist report and special needs programming after about 20 weeks in Reading Recovery.

So the actual percentages of all school children helped by such an early intervention strategy as Reading Recovery will depend on the resources an education system is prepared to allocate, the quality of staff training, the effectiveness with which the programme is implemented, and the success of professionals in explaining the benefits of the early intervention strategy for the learners and for the education system (Clay, 1987).

The programme currently operates nationally in New Zealand, in parts of Australia, in the state of Ohio and other parts of the USA (Clay, 1987), and in England. As education systems differ, differences in the management of the programme have been necessary affecting age of entry, time spent in the programme, and criteria for entry and for discontinuing.

Five years of operation in New Zealand

Table 19 presents numbers for the following:

- children in the New Zealand birth cohort (Column 1)

- children admitted to the programme (Column 2)

- children discontinued within 20 weeks at average band levels for their classroom; full programme (Column 3)

- children entering the programme late in the school year, having incomplete programmes of under 20 weeks who will continue in the following year (Column 4) (see Section 8)

- children leaving the school (Column 5)

- children referred for special reports and special needs programmes (Column 6) (see Section 8).

Table 19: **Status of Children Leaving Reading Recovery over Five Years in New Zealand: Numbers and Percentages**

Year	Birth cohort 1	In RR N 2	Full RR N 3	Incomplete N 4	Left RR N 5	Refer on N 6
1984	49574	3200	2036	867	176	128
1985	51211[a]	5323	3093	1615	357	238
1986	49044	7468	4536	2097	475	360
1987	49789	9240	5904	2509	512	313
1988	49482	10511	6494	2976	648	390
	%	%	%	%	%	%
1984	100	6.45	4.11	1.75	0.35	0.26
1985	100	10.39	6.04	3.15	0.70	0.46
1986	100	15.23	9.25	4.27	0.96	0.73
1987	100	18.56	11.86	5.04	1.03	0.63
1988	100	21.24	13.12	6.01	1.31	0.80

a 1984 6-year-old population.

Note: Figures in the top half of Table 19 are those given in the End of Year Summary Tables of the Department of Education.

In the second part of Table 19 the numbers are expressed as percentages of the New Zealand birth cohort.

1. Changes between 1984 and 1988 are consistent with the policy of expansion of the programme, and its infrastructure (for training and support), to an increasing percentage of low-achieving children (Column 2).

2. About two-thirds of the annual intake are discontinued during the calendar year in New Zealand (Column 3) and in each country where it has been tried. Because children spend variable time in the programme, no longer than necessary, and because each teaching place in the programme has typically been filled by two-and-a-half children in a calendar year, about one-third of the children receive an incomplete programme (Column 4). (The reason these children's lessons have not been discontinued is that they have only been in the programme a few weeks and have not yet reached the required

discontinuing criteria for independent processing and a high chance of survival back in the classroom.) So in New Zealand in each calendar year, one-third of the children must be expected to enter the programme late in the year and continue in the programme in the following year. The actual number of children carried over from the previous year was only recorded in the national returns in this form in 1987 and 1988.

3. The percentage of children leaving the school (Column 5) occurs through mobility of families, and while every effort is made to include them in a Reading Recovery programme in their new schools, there are no data on this group.

4. Column 6 reports the low percentages of children judged by the school team not to meet the discontinuing criteria of Reading Recovery, not predicted to succeed within the average band in their classrooms in both reading and writing with a 'not-noticing teacher,' and referred for a specialist report and recommendations for programming for a longer period.

The figures in Table 20 are confirmatory, showing that the same levels of results were being obtained in each of 10 Education Board districts across New Zealand. These figures are not proportions: they are percentages, showing that very rarely has the percentage of children referred to specialists reached the 1% level.

Table 20: **Children Referred for Further Help as a Percentage of the District Birth Cohort[a]**

	1	2	3	4	5	6	7	8	9	10
1984	0.21	0.27	0.59	0.27	0.57	0.68	0.03	0.91	0.80	0.77
1985	0.44	0.32	0.33	0.32	0.08	0.52	0.30	0.44	0.54	0.51
1986	1.03	0.78	1.09	0.71	0.91	0.11	1.20	0.47	0.76	0.55
1987	0.74	0.76	0.95	0.55	0.57	0.23	1.45	0.47	0.53	0.43
1988	0.99	0.95	0.75	1.09	0.83	0.36	0.60	0.57	0.72	0.40

a Derived from the End of Year Summary Tables of the Department of Education: 50 returns from 10 New Zealand Education Boards, 1984–1988.

It was predicted that the number of children referred for specialist reports would rise because of the increasing willingness of schools to refer children as early as 6-and-a-half and the psychological services recognizing the importance of their role in making this early intervention strategy work. There is still a residual reluctance in schools to refer children and in the psychological services to see such children at 6-and-a-half years, despite the availability of detailed records of their response to individual efforts to teach them over about a 20-week period. This may result from optimistic hope that things will come right, or priority rating on urgent cases in waiting lists. If such reluctance were overcome, and preventive action given more weight, one would expect the percentage of children referred for specialist reports to continue to increase, towards and above 1%.

There is a less positive reason why these percentages might increase. Reading Recovery is a programme which calls for high effort: the changes in children who are struggling are hard-won, so continued quality of programme implementation is needed to keep the percentage of children who need to be referred for further help as low as possible. If the quality of the programme should drop, if teachers expect the changes to occur without the immense effort that has been invested by teachers to this point, the success of a prevention programme and its acceptability could result in lowered effort or quality and fewer children would be discontinued.

National implementation has been possible

The figures in Table 19 indicate that the programme has sustained its promise of providing a second chance to learn literacy for many children while at the same time expanding to national coverage. To date, the training and organizational support arrangements have maintained its quality as indicated by the operational figures. A small national coordination team of Trainers, and local Tutors training teachers and managing the local district running of the programme have proved to be effective support for the expansion. The teacher training is an in-service programme, with the Reading Recovery trainees working as 'apprentices' under tuition and supervision during their first year of operation. To allow for expansion and replacement of staff who leave for various reasons it has been necessary to train a group of Tutors every 2 years as the programme has expanded.

Current issues

The quality of the data

These results report only the functioning of the children at the time of discontinuing from Reading Recovery or at the end of the school year, or at referral for specialist reports. And they are careful but 'in-house' assessments by the teachers delivering the programme, rather than the result of independent surveys. Two research studies have shown that 3 years later most children retain their gains and continue to function within the average band of their classes (Clay & Watson, 1982; Pinnell et al., 1988).

Participation of schools

Expansion of the programme depends, in part, upon the willingness of schools to opt into the programme and to find resources to mount it and expand it in their schools. Participation increased from 409 to 1107 schools in 1988. One might conclude that schools place value on having these children helped to make the transition into literacy and work within the average band of their classrooms.

Reading Recovery under 'Tomorrow's Schools'[6]

In many ways this programme was ahead of the administrative reforms in New Zealand. Ideally the decision to mount a Reading Recovery programme should be made by an individual school, after considering that school's needs. The goal of having an early intervention programme was to improve literacy learning within that school and reduce strains on the upper-primary (9–12 years) classes by having fewer literacy problems in the upper-primary school. A team of teachers, often the principal, the senior teacher in the junior (5–8 years) school, and the selected Reading Recovery teachers make the decisions about how many children and teachers they need to meet their particular goals. The national constraints have been in the advice to make the programme efficient and effective by selecting the poorest achievers not excepting anyone, and setting the about a 20-week limit for time in the programme. (Even that is flexible because if the school has the resources they are free to take in children for longer periods. They may also admit mainstreamed children with special needs reports, as long as they are not excluding children for whom the programme was designed. This means providing for extra teaching time.) Decisions about the programme within a school should be made by the school's team in the interests of the needs of that school. That fits well with the 'Tomorrow's Schools' model.

---

6 Major administration reforms shifted schools from district control to local school management by October 1989.

Criticism of the entry criteria

A critique of the programme's research (Nicholson, 1989) and the Reading Recovery in Context report (Glynn et al., 1989) claim that children may be entering the programme for whom it is unnecessary. I accept that this is inherent in a prevention strategy. The Reading Recovery in Context report recommends a conservative approach to such a risk in the form of fixed criteria for entry, set low and based only on text reading level. This issue deserves a detailed response that does not belong here but schools should bear three arguments in mind.

- Establishing a cut-off limit for entry to the programme in terms of text reading alone (compared with the six evaluation measures available) increases the possibility of selection errors and increases the risk of the prevention strategy incurring high failure rates.

- A conservative cut-off point for entry into a prevention programme increases the risk that there will be children not included in the programme who subsequently fail. Such selection errors reduce the chances of the programme being seen as viable and therefore being funded. Making too many selection errors will threaten the survival of a programme.

- A child may be able to read text tolerably well but may not be developing a writing vocabulary. In the profile of measurements used with Reading Recovery children this is regarded as an indication of help needed. The Reading Recovery in Context research paid no attention to the writing side of literacy.

Overview of the achievements

The spread to near-national coverage and the results of Reading Recovery in numbers of children discontinued show that this is a programme which schools and teachers have been able to mount and deliver. They have seen a high proportion of the children who have immense difficulty making the transition into formal literacy brought to a fair measure of independence in classroom work in a relatively short period of time. The results challenge much accumulated wisdom about literacy problems; clearly they are alterable variables for many children.[7]

---

7 The Research and Statistics Division of the New Zealand Ministry of Education, Wellington, has published summaries of Reading Recovery data for 1989, 1990, 1991, and 1992. Latest figures show that the programme is reaching 24% of children and more rural schools have been involved.

8 The Reading Recovery subgroups study

Bryan Tuck and Marie M. Clay

Although the percentage of children who need longer-term help is low, they are a group about which we need more information. The research division of the New Zealand Ministry of Education funded a research project directed to this problem.

As people become familiar with the Reading Recovery programme and notice the consistency with which it can bring high numbers of children to average band performance in their classrooms, the next questions to be asked are about the unsuccessful subgroup, the children who do not meet this criterion. Questioners are concerned about the policy in Reading Recovery that these children be referred for a specialist report around the twentieth week of the programme, and what happens to these children after they leave Reading Recovery. The erroneous assumption is often made that these children have failed to make progress on the programme; that is not so. Although they have failed to achieve the average level for their classes, they may be making steady but slow progress.

This report deals with information on three Reading Recovery subgroups, and one of those subgroups consisted of children who were referred out of the programme for a specialist report. The study confirms the current implementation practices but suggests implications for fine-tuning the delivery of further services to children who cannot be successfully discontinued in a Reading Recovery intervention. The results of this research have implications for the policies and provisions of the Ministry of Education and the practices of schools.

The research design

The samples

An analysis was made of detailed records kept by Reading Recovery teachers for three groups of children (N = 420) taught in New Zealand in 1988. The analysis compared change over time in the achievements of children who reached average-band performance for their classes, with children who did not reach this criterion level and required specialist reports. Also studied were a group of children who entered the programme late in the school year and whose programmes were continued after the long summer vacation.

Random samples were drawn from national returns of a) all children in Reading Recovery in December 1988 who had successfully completed their programmes (i.e., they were Discontinued), and b) all children who entered late in 1988 and whose programmes were to be completed in 1989 (i.e., To Be Continued). We called for complete lesson and programme records for 988 Discontinued children, and 906 To Be Continued children.

Every child who was unable to successfully complete the programme (390 children out of a total of 9860) made up the third research group. They were called the Referred group because the appropriate next move for these children was that they should be referred for a specialist report.

Teachers returned the records as requested but full records were available only for a proportion of the randomly selected children. From those children with full records we selected all the Referred children (140) and matched them with Discontinued (140) and To Be Continued children (140) to form triplet sets, controlling for school and teacher difference. Other approaches to sampling would have produced an impossibly small Referred group since it is known to be about 1% of the age cohort (Clay, 1990) and the main thrust of this project was to investigate child outcomes and policy implications for this group.

However, because of these sampling procedures generalization from these samples to the total population of children who enter Reading Recovery must be tentative. There was one Referred child in the research sample for every three such children in the national programme; there was one To Be Continued child in the sample for 21 such children in the national programme, and there was one Discontinued child in the sample for 46 such children in the national programme. Table 21 sets out sampling details.

Table 21: Details of Sampling

Group A	In Reading Recovery 1988	Records requested	Records returned	Full records returned	Final sample	Final as % (of column 1)	Sampling ratios
Referred	390	380	272	140	140	35.9	1: 2.76
To Be Continued	2976	906	832	648	140	4.7	1:21.35
Discontinued	6494	988	942	577	140	2.2	1:46.36

Measurement and progress

Seven tests were routinely administered at entry to the programme and at exit (called Discontinuing). Six were from the Diagnostic Survey (Clay, 1985) and one was the nationally standardized Burt Oral Word Reading Test (New Zealand Council for Education Research, 1981).

Interpretations of the research results should acknowledge that while these tests all capture important changes over time in literacy learning they fall into two distinct groups, according to whether the learning occurs in a relatively open-ended variable like text reading or in a finite set of information like all the letters of the alphabet (see Table 22). Finite sets of learning show what is called 'ceiling effects' on the tests as all learners move towards knowledge of the entire set of learning, and this places limitations on quantitative analyses of the data.

Table 22: **Classification of Assessments by Ceiling Effects**

With ceiling effects	Without ceiling effects
Letter Identification Finite set of learning	**Text Reading Level** Discontinuing levels halfway up the scale
Dictation [HRSW] (grapho-phonemic scoring) Limited set of learning	**Writing Vocabulary** Ten-minute limit, open-ended
Concepts About Print Limited set of learning	**Burt Oral Word Reading** (NZCER, 1981) Ceiling at 12- to 13-year level
Clay Word Test Short list of highest frequency words	

Once a week teachers plotted for their own information the current level of book on a gradient of text difficulty, producing a graph of reading progress. While this appears to be linear in shape for most children it is important to note that as the child becomes able to read more difficult texts he is reading more words, in longer stories, written in more complex language. The steps in book level are unequal: those higher on the scale involve bigger increases in the amount to be read and new types of challenges.

Teachers also kept a cumulative record of writing vocabulary used during lessons, including in the count each new word the child demonstrated that he could write correctly without assistance. (Correctness is used to achieve valid scoring by different scorers; it is acknowledged that children move towards correctness through approximations and partially correct transitions.) Not all teachers kept these records, and those who did, did not necessarily keep records at regular intervals. Therefore not all the records were usable, but most were, even when there were missing data points.

Referred children's achievement at follow-up in 1990 was assessed with

- Text Reading of Graded Paragraphs (New Zealand Department of Education, 1984)
- Burt Oral Word Reading (NZCER, 1981)
- Spelling Test (Peters, 1970).

Results

Part One: Progress within the programme

The theory which supports Reading Recovery was derived from studies of children in classrooms learning to read successfully. The intervention conceptualizes literacy learning as complex learning, not controlled by any single variable or type of response, but requiring the orchestration of various responses to derive meaning from text. Each of the assessment tasks measures different clusters of responses, all of which are necessary but none of which is sufficient on its own to 'cause' success in literacy learning.

A large proportion of children in Reading Recovery have entry scores close to zero and it was uncertain how well the Reading Recovery assessment instruments would discriminate between the subgroups at entry, during the programme, and at final testing. It was of interest to know whether at entry those children who would be discontinued could be distinguished from those who would be referred.

Each assessment in the set used to select children for the programme, monitor their progress, and make decisions about referral or discontinuing, worked better than one would expect with such low-scoring children (Clay & Tuck, 1991) but the findings did not suggest that assessment be limited to any single measure or a reduced set of measures. The use of only text reading, or text reading and writing vocabulary is not recommended as each of the seven assessments can be related through theory with the progress.

Relationships were found between levels at entry and the probability of being either discontinued or referred. In general the probability of being discontinued is lowest for the group of children with relatively poor levels of performance at entry. However, it is also the case that individual children unable to score on some of the entry measures were in the Discontinued group, i.e., they reached a level of skill deemed to be average for their class. There are also examples of children who although ultimately in the Referred group scored relatively well on some of the entrance tests. It was concluded that it would be imprudent to exclude individual children on the basis of entry scores. The graphs of progress in reading and writing for one set of research triplets (Figure 5) clearly demonstrate the variability among individual children. These graphs plot the progress of a Discontinued child, a Referred child, and a child who entered the programme late in the year and was to be continued in the following school year (Continued).

Figure 5: Graphs of Progress in Reading and Writing
for One Set of Research Triplets

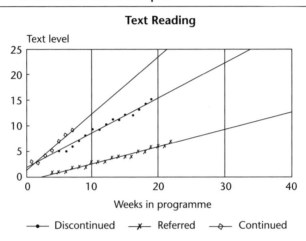

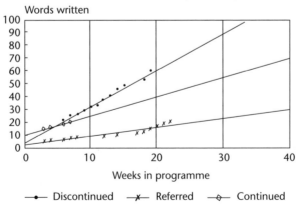

Correlations between entry scores and length of time in the programme (see Table 23) for the successful children (Discontinued) showed that children with the lowest scores tended to take longer to meet the criteria for discontinuing. They had more to learn. For the Referred children the length of time they spent in the programme tended to be unrelated to performance level at entry.

Table 23: **Correlations between Assessments at Entry and Length of Time to Discontinuing or Referral**

Variables	Length of time in weeks to	
	Discontinued	Referred
Text Level	−.53*	−.11
Letter Identification	−.52*	−.12
Concepts About Print	−.34*	−.09
Word Test	−.55*	−.04
Burt Reading (NZCER, 1981)	−.60*	−.10
Writing Vocabulary	−.62*	−.26*
Dictation [HRSW]	−.61*	−.23*

* $p < .01$ (one-tailed)

Note: The N for the correlations ranged from 137 to 140.

Both in New Zealand and overseas the average time in the programme ranges from 12 to 15 weeks, and a recommended upper limit has been set at about 20 weeks, at which time children who cannot be discontinued should be referred for a specialist report. While awaiting a specialist recommendation, and when teacher time was available, schools often kept children in Reading Recovery until a decision on further appropriate programming had been made. This study presents no evidence to suggest a change in this practice. However, a school must be cautious when deciding to retain children in a Reading Recovery programme for longer than 20 weeks because this decision could limit the opportunity for entry of younger children who need it.

Both Discontinued and Referred groups made important gains in test scores over the period of the intervention. The majority of the Discontinued children were performing at or above the New Zealand national average level of Stanine 5 at exit from the programme on each assessment. Many Referred children also reached these levels on some of the measures. There was overlap between the Discontinued and Referred groups on each of the separate measures. Examples of such distributions of individuals in the two groups for Reading Text levels and Writing Vocabulary are shown in Tables 24 a–d.

Table 24a: Instructional Text Level at Entry compared with
Exit Level for Discontinued Group (N = 140)

Text Level at entry	Level when Discontinued							
	9–10	11–12	13–14	15–16	17–18	19–20	21–22	23+
0	1		1	9	6	1		
1 – 2			5	15	8	4	2	
3 – 4			4	15	12	8		
5 – 6			1	4	7	4	3	1
7 – 8			1	3	2	1	4	
9 – 10				3	2	3		
11 – 12					2	3	2	1
13 – 14					2			

Table 24b: Instructional Text Level at Entry compared with
Exit Level for Referred Group (N = 140)

Text Level at entry	Level when Referred									
	0	1–2	3–4	5–6	7–8	9–10	11–12	13–14	15–16	17–18
0		3	14	10	8	5	7	5	3	
1 – 2		3	4	10	11	12	8	3	4	1
3 – 4			3		3	5	8	5	2	
5 – 6							1		1	
7 – 8										
9 – 10							1			

Table 24c: Writing Vocabulary Stanines at Entry compared with
Stanines at Discontinuing for Discontinued Group (N = 139)

Stanine at entry	Stanine when Discontinued								
	1	2	3	4	5	6	7	8	9
1		3	12	23	33	24	12	1	
2			1	1	7	2	1		1
3			1	2	5	3	2		
4					3	2			

Table 24d: Writing Vocabulary Stanines at Entry compared with
Stanines at Referral for Referred Group (N = 117)

Stanine at entry	Stanine when Referred								
	1	2	3	4	5	6	7	8	9
1	33	24	30	16	7	3			
2		1	1	1					
3					1				

As the theory behind the Reading Recovery programme assumes that successful readers and writers learn to bring together information and/or responses from different areas as they problem-solve texts, it is not inconsistent with that theory that Referred children can score relatively well in some areas but still not meet the criteria for discontinuing. Those criteria require that children work relatively independently at problem-solving in all aspects of literacy tasks while reading or writing continuous texts. A series of checks on data patterns found that the tenth week was the earliest that reliable predictions could be made of whether a child would be discontinued (Table 25). At this time predictions were successful for between 70% and 85% of the cases. *However, this means that from 15% to 30% of judgements about outcome would be wrong if made at this time.* An intervention programme affecting children cannot risk such a high level of error.

Table 25: Prediction of Programme Outcomes at 10 Weeks:
Success or Failure of the Prediction

	The prediction was a . . .	Reading	%	Writing	%
All Discontinued	Success	205	78.2[a]	188	75.2[a]
and Referred	Failure	57	21.8	62	24.8
Discontinued	Success	115	85.2	107	79.9
(N = 139)	Failure	20	14.8	27	20.1
Referred	Success	90	70.9	81	69.8
(N = 139)	Failure	37	29.1	35	30.2
No	Discontinued	4		5	
data	Referred	12		23	

a   Predictions made at 10 weeks as to whether a child would be Discontinued or Referred out of the programme would be successful for about three in four cases in either Reading or Writing. Criteria for prediction: Text Level 5 at week 10 and 20 words written at week 10.

Reading. If the criterion was lowered to Text Level 4 and below (instead of Text Level 5) then there would only be six prediction failures for the Discontinued group, and an increase for the Referred group. If the criterion was raised to Text Level 7 or above there would still be 24 failures. This is accounted for by inspection of the graphs and the fact that those Referred children who make a late run at accelerated progress move through many Reading Book levels in the latter part of their programmes.

Writing. If the criterion was lowered to 17 words or below (instead of 20 words and below) then there would be still be 17 prediction failures for the Discontinued group. If the criterion was raised to 23 words or below there would still be 24 failures in the Referred group.

The predictions at 10 weeks were better for Discontinued than for Referred children. Some children with relatively poor levels at 10 weeks make accelerated progress after that time. Because of the high number of incorrect predictions it would be extremely unwise to withdraw children at the tenth week. However, in exceptional individual cases, a decision to refer a child earlier for a specialist report would be appropriate (see Figure 6).

Figure 6: **Progress in Reading and Writing for a Research Triplet in Which an Earlier Referral Could Have Been Made**

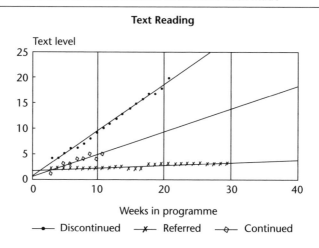

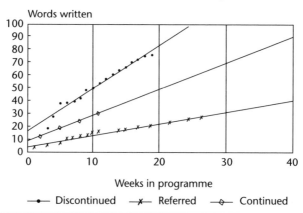

Can children with somewhat higher entry scores be excluded from the programme?

It has been suggested that children who already read texts at Level 7 or above might not need the programme (Glynn et al., 1989). That recommendation assumes that text level is on its own a reliable predictor. Our information shows that individual children can have relatively uneven performance across the various assessments and that it is unwise to rely on only one assessment.

If we accept the risk of predicting only from the text reading assessment, the study leads to the following best prediction.

> 'If the text level is Level 5 or above after 10 weeks in the programme the probability is high that the child will be discontinued.'

However, this rule failed to correctly predict the outcomes for 22% of the combined Discontinued and Referred group. The rule was 'cross-validated' on an independent sample and a similar pattern of 'hits and misses' was observed (Clay & Tuck, 1991). Prediction failure is thus high at 10 weeks of instruction. Applying some Book Level cutting point around the time children enter the programme would probably produce higher risk of being wrong than we obtained at 10 weeks.

To enter the Reading Recovery programme children must be the lowest achievers in their ordinary classroom. Selection is thus relative to the performance of the age cohort in a particular school and children are admitted to the programme up to the limit of resources set aside by that school. The results of the foregoing analyses provide no reason for changing this procedure.

One interesting observation was that the rates of children whose programmes were interrupted by the long summer holiday were similar to those of children whose total programme fell within 1 school year in a) discontinuing rates and b) referral rates. However, a small number of the To Be Continued group were not in Reading Recovery in the following year. The research identified three reasons for not completing their programmes.

- *Change of school.* Children moved schools and were not identified in their new schools.

- *Continued improvement.* Children retested by the Reading Recovery teacher after the summer vacation were then found to be within the average band for their new classes.

- *No teacher resource.* When a Reading Recovery teacher moved to a new school, the new Reading Recovery teacher in training would not be able to work with more than two children who were already halfway through their programmes.

It must be recognized that there is a clear risk of 'slippage' occurring around the long summer vacation.

Part Two: What happens to the 'referrable' children?

A national questionnaire survey was completed and, with the assistance of a network of Reading Recovery Tutors across the country, returns were available for 139 of the 140 Referred children (see Table 26). Of the 45 Referred children in the sample who lived in Auckland, 44 were located. Two educational psychologists interviewed teachers about progress, placements, and instructional assistance in 1989 and 1990, and the children's achievements in reading and spelling were assessed.

Table 26: Action Taken to Refer to a Specialist the Children Who Did Not Reach Criteria for Discontinuing

District	Not applicable or no data	Not Referred	Psychological Service	Direct to RTR (Resource Teacher of Reading)	Other
All districts (N = 139)	7	18	82	28	4
Auckland	3	7	28	15	2
Hamilton	2	2	23	2	0
Gisborne	–	3	2	1	1
Napier	–	–	–	1	–
Taranaki	–	–	3	1	–
Wanganui	–	5	6	1	1
Wellington	1	–	3	1	–
Nelson	–	–	3	3	–
Canterbury	–	–	9	2	–
Otago/ Southland	1	1	5	1	–
	18%			82%	

Eighty-two percent of referrable children were referred by schools for specialist reports (Table 26). Most were being referred by 6-and-a-half years, and this shows that early identification of children who need special help of a continuing kind is possible. Action should be taken to prevent the problem worsening and transfer from Reading Recovery to further specialist teaching on a continuing basis without a break would maximise the carry-over and minimize the loss of what has been already learned. This rate of early referral should be lifted closer to 100%.

From the questionnaire returns for the 139 children, there were 182 individual service entries. Such services fell into the categories discussed below (see Table 27).

Table 27: Following Referral, Action Taken to Provide Services

District	Special class	Main-streamed, with or without IEP[a], or special needs funds	RTR (Resource Teacher of Reading) including waiting list	Reading help of some kind	Other	No data No referrral No action
All districts (N = 182)	22	29	43	67	21	16
Auckland	8	5	22	29	8	7
Hamilton	4	8	3	17	7	2
Gisborne	1	1	5	5	–	1
Napier	–	1	1	1	–	–
Taranaki	2	1	1	1	1	–
Wanganui	2	5	1	2	–	3
Wellington	1	2	1	2	–	1
Nelson	1	1	3	4	–	–
Canterbury	1	3	5	2	4	1
Otago/ Southland	2	2	1	4	1	1
% of entries	28%		23%	36%	11.5%	8%

a   Individual Education Programme.

Note: Table includes multiple entries for some children: 182 entries for 139 children.

Referred children placed in Special Class or mainstreamed with or without an individual educational programme written by a psychologist accounted for 28% of the entries. This provides an estimate of the number of children whose literacy learning may be expected to continue to improve but at slow rates.

Resource Teachers of Reading (RTR) and Reading Assistance teachers (RA) might be expected to see, teach, advise, and guide the progress of the majority of Referred children not in the foregoing group. This is not the case. Only 23% of the entries on the questionnaires showed RTRs and RAs involved in any way. Those entries include placing the child on a waiting list, or offering advice on programming but not teaching the child.

Often the RTR had a pattern of involvement with Referred children which involved three stages. 1) A Referred child was given individual tutoring for several months until a measure of independence in reading and writing was achieved and then 2) the RTR provided guidance to the classroom teacher and monitored the child's further needs until 3) the support service was provided entirely by the school. Shifts of this kind are appropriate to provide the most facilitating environment for the child in a cost-effective way, but this report does not provide data on what criteria were used to guide these shifts and what the implications were for the subsequent progress of the children helped by the RTR.

Reading help delivered by other persons of varied training accounted for 36% of the action taken (including placing the child in a small reading group; using an itinerant reading teacher, a teacher aide, a parent helper, a peer tutor or senior student, an ethnic language teacher, a special needs teacher, or in one entry only, a SPELD (Specific Learning Disabilities) teacher (a non department group). The time available for the service varied greatly from half an hour a week to daily help, as did the duration of the help, for a month or so to 1, 2, or 3 terms of the school year.

The student outcome data for the 45 Auckland Referred children who were followed-up and tested for current achievement levels in literacy two years and some months after their Reading Recovery programme ended has some positive features (seven children were functioning within average-band levels for their class, and most special education students could read and write simple texts) but for the remainder the picture is somewhat negative. Too many of the Referred group were working more than a year below their age group, despite the various services delivered to them in the two years following Reading Recovery (see Clay & Tuck, 1991).

Two general comments on this further programming can be made:

Multiple concurrent services It is appropriate for Referred children to have help from various services, but preferable that they have the skilled attention of highly trained professionals with sound knowledge of literacy learning. What is particularly problematic is that children with literacy learning difficulties need a consistent approach to their slow build-up of competencies. Different approaches delivered over the same period of time are certain to compound their problems.

Multiple services over time There are likely to be some changes over time as specialists, teachers, and parents try to establish the most facilitating programme for an individual child. However, the need for changes should be minimized by seeking specialist guidance early and establishing a programme of long-term help rather than spurts of casual short-term help.

While the quantity of 'reading help' available beyond Reading Recovery appears, on the surface, to be satisfactory, the quality and consistency of that instruction for this hard-to-teach group (who make up less than 1% of the age group) can be questioned. A recommendation was made to the New Zealand Ministry of Education that improvement of this situation be given a high policy priority. Factors requiring attention were identified as follows:

1. Factors relating to more effective delivery of the services, such as

   - access to individual specialist teaching for all Referred children not receiving special services

   - an initial training for Resource Teachers of Reading prior to appointment with continuing in-service updates

   - more Resource Teachers of Reading or Reading Assistance teachers achieving wider coverage throughout the country

   - longer periods of service delivery, and closer supervision during the time when schools are being guided by the RTR to provide a continuing programme

   - research documentation of the RTR service delivery over 3 years, either nationally or in selected areas.

2. Factors related to the knowledge barrier about what are effective ways to work with these children. A research and development programme is needed to uncover new and diverse ways to work with this extremely hard-to-teach group, devising both teaching and

monitoring procedures for a small group of children who are far from homogeneous in their learning characteristics.

Summary of the study of Reading Recovery subgroups

This study refers to the progress of Reading Recovery children in New Zealand who were taught in 1988, and it examines in detail three subgroups: those who were successful in meeting the criteria of average-band performance for their classrooms, those who had incomplete programmes, and those who should have been referred for specialist reports because of unsuccessful progress. *Most children are successful in meeting the programme criteria for discontinuing; only 0.5% to 1% of the age cohort fall into the referable group.* (Italics added for emphasis.)

Study of the three subgroups confirms earlier reports about progress during Reading Recovery but provides illustrations of individual variation in a) test score patterns, b) progress made during the programme, and c) the congruence or otherwise of progress when reading is compared with writing.

Although the study found relationships between the entry characteristics of the children and progress in the programme, it cautioned against using this information in a deterministic fashion. *Predictions of outcome status for individual children from either high or low entry scores, or even after 10 weeks of instruction are likely to be wrong in a significant number of cases. A full programme of instruction (varying according to individual needs from 12 to about 20 weeks) provides at present the best practical estimate of which children will need further individual assistance.* (Italics added for emphasis.)

For several quite different reasons programmes were not always completed for the group To Be Continued in the following school year. Special effort should be made to allow this group to complete a full Reading Recovery programme. Only 82% of referable children were referred for specialist reports. As such referrals allow for a second opinion on children who are very hard to teach, and provide the means of getting expert advice on further instructional programming, it would be desirable for this to occur for all such children.

While schools have seen the need for the referred children to get individual instruction and have in many cases arranged for this, it does not seem reasonable for such children to be faced with multiple approaches to their problems from different tutors concurrently, or over several years of schooling. Consistency in long-term programming is desirable.

Summary of Research Reports

The challenges

Daily, individual instruction might be expected to produce important shifts in children's reading and writing performance. The Reading Recovery programme was associated with such shifts in all the subgroups studied.

Readers are asked to consider again the degree of challenge accepted by the Reading Recovery programme in the Field Trial year.

1. The children with the poorest performance of all the children in their schools at 6:0 were selected for instruction. Teachers used no procedures for excluding any children. They dealt with children in the tail of the achievement distribution for the age-group and included:

   - bicultural Maori children

   - bilingual Pacific Island children

   - children with handicaps

   - children awaiting Special Class placements.

2. It was against normal expectations that any children in the tail end of the achievement distribution could be brought to average levels of attainment:

   - in as little time as 13 to 14 weeks

   - in both reading and writing.

   Above-average levels of attainment would not be expected.

3. Whatever the levels of attainment at the end of individual tutoring, it would be against normal expectations for many children to retain average placements three years later given the ups and downs of school instruction and of child health and family circumstance.

4. It would be almost unreasonable to expect to get any shifts and maintenance of the kinds described with a partially implemented programme which means:

- children who entered school in Term 3 of the field trial year could not receive a full programme as it was only funded for the calendar year (NZ school year), and

- teachers in the field trial year were subsequently found to be not operating the programme as prescribed.

The gains to 1992

The Reading Recovery programme is an effective programme for reducing the number of children with reading difficulties in New Zealand schools (Clay, 1979a; Clay & Watson, 1982). It is a second-chance, early intervention programme. Its aim is to pick up the children who have not begun to read and write after one year at school and provide them with intensive instruction daily and individually. As a result of accelerated progress the children typically leave the programme with average levels of performance in 3 to 6 months. The success gained with the poorest performers of the age group at 6 years runs counter to the assumptions, expectations, and experience in most Western education systems. It is probably related to the specific nature of the instruction delivered by well-trained teachers (Clay, 1982).

Since 1978 the programme has been developed and gradually expanded. Although it was only partially implemented in New Zealand until about 1988, it won support from teachers, principals, school committees, the Department of Education, the media, and the public. Reports of its research and development phase and of two follow-up studies (1 and 3 years later) support its effectiveness across ethnic groups, and the national monitoring figures show how the programme has spread across the education system to reach around 20% of the children.

Quality assurance

The gains were achieved by experienced but non-specialist primary teachers without academic training but who knew how to teach children of this age group, and how, in particular, to teach reading and writing. They were guided by very well-trained Tutors who fully understood why each of the procedures and requirements were in the programme. The Ministry of Education has ensured that the expansion of the programme only proceeds when this necessary support system is already in place. They have also ensured that clear communications to the rest of the education system preceded each expansion of the programme so that all understood the preventive thrust of the programme.

Training for teachers consists of only 50 hours distributed fortnightly throughout the year during the period that teachers are engaged in more than 400 hours of Reading Recovery teaching. Training for Tutors of teachers, who guide the Reading Recovery programme in their district, is a national, year-long University and College of Education-based course which assumes that the Tutor will also work as a Reading Recovery teacher for part of her day.

A national network of Tutors is trained and led by a Director and several National co-ordinators (Trainers) who foster professional development among all Reading Recovery professionals and run training courses for new Tutors.

Some recommendations

The research studies point to some recommendations for Reading Recovery teachers and their schools.

1. When children are to be included in a Reading Recovery programme, contact parents and contract for regular attendance for this second-chance learning opportunity. The school should cooperate with the family to establish appropriate home activities to follow up on lessons.

2. Allow for sufficient time in the programme and apply discontinuing criteria conservatively especially with Maori children.

3. Adopt a watch-dog role for ex-Reading Recovery children in the school and remind staff

   - to monitor their progress sensitively

   - to consider their promotion carefully

   - to provide further individual help if needed and particularly if progress is slow.

Although Reading Recovery children may perform well in their classes they remain at-risk children for 2 or more years after completion of their programme.

Readers with problems

Once this programme is fully implemented its impact within the education system will be felt as each age group moves up through the primary school. There should be a drastic reduction in the numbers of children requiring special teaching for fundamental skills in reading and writing above the second year at school. Many more of the 'slow' children in schools should be able to perform close to average class levels in reading and writing and be able to use these achievements in the service of further learning. This programme will also contribute to the early identification, by 6-and-a-half years or 18 months from school entry, of Referred children requiring the attention of a reading specialist for at least a further year or two.

Gains for the education system

Some of the inefficiencies that have seemed unavoidable in the past should disappear. We should reduce the problems of the teacher in the upper primary or elementary school who tries to teach a non-reader but does not really know how to; the time spent by teachers with the 'low reading groups' should be reduced; the number of children on waiting lists for reading clinics should be reduced. Hopefully children needing continuing help should be able to move straight from Reading Recovery to a reading specialist and not have to wait for a place marking time in a classroom where the programme is beyond them.

Because the effects of the programme run counter to past experience it seems unwise to make undue claims for it. However, the 3-year follow-up research which suggests that for those having daily instruction in Reading Recovery the long-term effects were good for each of three ethnic groups, European, Maori and Pacific Island children, is supported by two other follow-up studies in Victoria, Australia and Ohio, USA.

The cost-effectiveness of the programme depends upon how well it achieves its goal of average performance for most of the children. The programme addresses a problem of Western education systems in that it provides for all children at the lower end of the achievement distribution at 6 years to receive supplementary help with literacy learning. It runs with a minimum of specialist staff. Most importantly, it is a targeted education programme which, if it works, reduces the need for specialist provision in the upper primary (or elementary) school and secondary school.

It has been an exciting exploration of the question 'What is possible when we change the design and delivery of traditional education for the children that teachers find hard to teach?'

References

Clay, M. M. (1966). *Emergent reading behaviour.* Unpublished doctoral thesis. Auckland: The University of Auckland.

Clay, M. M. (1979a). *The early detection of reading difficulties: A diagnostic survey with recovery procedures.* Auckland: Heinemann.

Clay, M. M. (1979b). *Reading: The patterning of complex behavior* (2nd ed.). Auckland: Heinemann.

Clay, M. M. (1982). *Observing young readers: Selected papers.* Portsmouth, NH: Heinemann.

Clay, M. M. (1985). *The early detection of reading difficulties* (3rd ed.). Auckland: Heinemann.

Clay, M. M. (1987). Implementing Reading Recovery: Systemic adaptations to an educational innovation. *New Zealand Journal of Educational Studies, 22*(1), 35–58.

Clay, M. M. (1990). The Reading Recovery programme, 1984–1988: Coverage, outcomes and Education Board figures. *New Zealand Journal of Educational Studies, 25*(1), 61–70.

Clay, M. M. (1991). *Becoming literate: The construction of inner control.* Auckland: Heinemann.

Clay, M. M. (1993a). *Reading Recovery: A guidebook for teachers in training.* Auckland: Heinemann.

Clay, M. M. (1993b). *An observation survey of early literacy achievement* (1st ed.). Auckland: Heinemann.

Clay, M. M. (2002, 2006). *An observation survey of early literacy achievement* (2nd ed.). Auckland: Heinemann.

Clay, M. M. (2005). *Literacy lessons designed for individuals: Part two: Teaching procedures.* Auckland: Heinemann.

Clay, M. M., & Tuck, B. (1991). *A study of Reading Recovery subgroups: Including outcomes for children who did not satisfy discontinuing criteria.* Auckland: University of Auckland.

Clay, M. M., & Watson, B. (1982). *The success of Maori children in the Reading Recovery programme.* Report to the Director of Research. Wellington: Department of Education.

Glynn, I., Crookes, I., Bethune, N., Ballard, K., & Smith, J. (1989). *Reading Recovery in context.* Report to Research Division. Wellington: Ministry of Education.

Neale, M. D. (1958). *Neale analysis of reading ability.* London: Macmillan. (Restandardized by Macmillan, 1988 and NFER, 1989.)

New Zealand Council for Educational Research (1981). *Burt word reading test.* Wellington: NZCER.

New Zealand Department of Education (1984). *LARIC inservice programme.* Wellington: Learning Media.

Nicholson, T. (1989). Research note: A comment on Reading Recovery. *New Zealand Journal of Educational Studies, 24,* 95–97.

Peters, M. L. (1970). *Success in spelling.* Cambridge: Cambridge Institute of Education.

Pinnell, G. S., DeFord, D. E., & Lyons, C. A. (1988). *Reading Recovery: Early intervention for at-risk first graders.* Arlington, VA: Educational Research Service.

Robinson, S. M. (1973). *Predicting early reading progress,* Unpublished master's thesis. Auckland: University of Auckland.

Strickland, D., & Morrow, L. M. (Eds.). (1989). *Emerging literacy: Young children learn to read and write.* Newark, DE: International Reading Association.

Wade, T. (1978). *Promotion patterns in the junior school.* Unpublished thesis. Auckland: University of Auckland.

Wheeler, H. (1986). *Reading Recovery: Central Victorian field trials.* Bendigo: Bendigo College of Advanced Education.

3

Using an Unusual Lens

Billie Askew

Researchers and educators around the world acknowledge Marie Clay's revolutionary contributions to theory, practice, and policy. 'As a researcher, she was a model for us all: fiercely persistent, absolutely ethical, and always open to new evidence and new possibilities' (Johnston, 2007, p. 67). She drew from many disciplines to create an unusual lens to observe and capture emerging literacy behaviours that had not been previously documented. Her choice of that unconventional methodology made possible the early studies reprinted in Chapter 2 that broke the bonds of the ordinary.

Marie Clay was a scientist who pioneered new directions in literacy research. Using a different discipline (developmental psychology) and a different methodology (capturing on-task changes in behaviour across time), she was able to focus on a theory of *learning* that influences teaching. She knew that developmental research could lead to 'ideas of what, when, and how to begin teaching, of the changes that may be expected over time, of the track that most children take, of the variability to be expected, and of different development paths to the same outcomes' (Clay, 1990, p. 43). Her developmental orientation influenced her methodological and theoretical decisions, leading her to describe change over time in children's behaviours, abilities, and processes; to explain what occurs; and to increase opportunities for enhanced development.

In 1963, Marie Clay began her landmark study of 100 New Zealand children. She set herself the research task of exploring exactly what children were learning in their first year at school, knowing that traditional research methodology would be unable to reveal the emerging literacy behaviours of young children, Instead, she chose to use the strategies of biological science to 'describe the variety, complexity, and change observed in reading behaviour during the first year of instruction' (Clay, 1966, p. 4). All scientists use systematic observation of phenomena to gather research data, but they do so under strictly controlled conditions. The unusual lens Marie Clay proceeded to use in her research about young learners was carefully controlled *direct observation*. In the natural setting of their classrooms Clay observed and recorded exactly what happened as children learned to read and write. It was an innovative research methodology, suspect at the time among some reading researchers. Now it is accepted.

I found ways of observing the first steps into reading, became fascinated with early progressions in writing, and began to attend with new interest to changes in oral language acquisition in children of school age. As a developmental psychologist I already had some methodologies for child study and I was particularly concerned with the changes that occurred. How could yesterday's behaviours evolve into tomorrow's? (Clay, 1982, p. 1)

Marie Clay developed and continued to refine research instruments that enabled her to examine acts of literacy processing through an unusual lens, from which she would derive inductively a *grounded theory of literacy processing* (Clay, 1982, 1991a, 1998, 2001). She argued that research in early literacy development cannot begin with a logical experimental question. While theory testing and experimental controls in psychology are needed to answer some questions, observational and participant-observation methodologies are needed to study change in process and knowledge. Therefore, the descriptive mapping of what proficient learners do is a valuable first step in developmental research (Clay, 2004).

Marie Clay combined quantitative and qualitative methodologies. Her quantitative research used appropriate techniques for sampling, data collection, and analysis; appropriate statistical analyses ensured reliability and validity. Her qualitative research met rigorous standards as she 'collected rich data systematically at frequent intervals; used reliable and standardized methods of observing and recording; developed new concepts on the basis of observed patterns in the data (e.g., self-corrections in reading); and then used those concepts to enrich data collection' (Jones & Smith-Burke, 1999, p. 264). Although observation guided her development of theory, she remained open to new discoveries, concepts, and theoretical constructs emerging from her observations.

In this chapter, a tentative attempt is made to define and describe Marie Clay's *unusual lens* and to link her exceptional methodology to her contributions to theory, practice, and policy.

Defining the unusual lens:
A research methodology and ways of observing

Much of Marie Clay's work focused on young children as they were learning to read and write. Capturing their emerging literacy behaviours and how those behaviours changed over time required an *unusual lens.*

Marie Clay called attention to her use of the term 'exceptional lens' to characterize her research methodology.

> When I posed the question 'What is possible for children with reading problems?' people accepted my question but paid little attention to the fact that we began using an exceptional lens to find some answers to it. It was not their error; we underestimated the importance of our methodology and did not articulate its implications. Predictably using a different lens produces a non-conformist view which does not displace existing lenses; rather it is used for limited purposes for which it is particularly suited (like viewing distant things in detail or taking a panoramic photograph). I believe that future developments in early literacy intervention may find some direction by revisiting the history of the evidence we collected when we attended to the detail of beginners trying to read and write texts. (Clay, 2001, p. 41)

To comprehend Marie Clay's *unusual lens* requires an understanding of at least two of her operational definitions:

> 'Literacy' refers to either reading or writing activities considered separately or together. (That arises from my research which began in 1963.) The focus is on behaviours or acts which can be observed and which provide observers with signals. (We began that exploration between 1960 and 1970.) (Clay, 2001, p. 41)

> The phrase 'an unusual lens' refers to any observational or research methodology which gathers detailed data on changes in the literacy behaviours of young children as they learn to read and write continuous texts over a period of time. (Running Records of reading or writing provide one example of an observational lens directed to text processing.) (Clay, 2001, p. 42). It would be an instrument or procedure that could capture how the learner works at learning, and how those ways of working change. It stands in contrast to word tests and comprehension questions which assess what the learner has already learned. (Clay, 2001, p. 82)

Marie Clay's view of measuring progress in literacy processing rejects the historical view that children's progress is to be measured against the teaching curriculum, that is, against what they have been taught. That view leads to the measurement of progress by tests of letters, sounds, words, graded texts, or portfolios. For example, saying a child is 'on text level 18' says nothing about *how* a child reads that text.

Marie Clay's alternative way of assessing progress during literacy acquisition is called a *literacy processing view,* a perspective that leads to the study of *how* children work on texts as they read or write, regardless of how teachers are teaching. This view encourages teachers to help children having literacy difficulty for different reasons. It also encourages teachers to accept reading and writing as complex processes that cannot be reduced to simple explanations. The perspective also suggests that low achievers can move through a somewhat similar succession of changes when supported by appropriate instruction.

Because the literacy processing behaviours of the youngest readers are overt and easily observed, it is possible to describe what occurs before most of their reading becomes silent. Marie Clay's research also used an unusual lens to capture young children's *awareness* of literacy events. She defined *awareness* 'as being able to attend to something, act upon it, or work with it' (Clay, 1998, p. 42). Children may have very different original experiences of literacy awareness. When teachers notice awareness through the *acts* of children, doors are opened for further interactions. Clay uses the term *acts* to refer to both external, observable behaviours and to internal psychological activity.

What makes Marie Clay's unusual lens so exceptional? We get an alternative view of a child's progress on literacy processing behaviors because her observational lens transmits a different kind of information. Rather than an 'additive' model of reading progress which is expressed in scores or counts or enumerated skills, this alternative view gives a *literacy processing* perspective of progress during literacy acquisition — a 'transformation' model of progress that 'describes how different kinds of information in print come to contribute together to a decision and how early primitive decision-making is refined and expanded into more efficient decision making' (Clay, 2001, p. 50).

A theory of literacy processing

Most theoretical models of reading begin at a point where children have already learned to work in primitive ways with print. Marie Clay's research focused uniquely on the formative years of literacy learning. Her research design led to theory development because it was grounded in the careful study of children's behaviours, data gathered from children at the beginning of literacy learning (Jones & Smith-Burke, 1999).

> A grounded theory is one that is inductively derived from the study of the phenomenon it represents . . . It is discovered, developed, and provisionally verified through systematic data collection and analysis of data pertaining to that phenomenon. Therefore, data collection, analysis, and theory stand in reciprocal relationship with each other. One does not begin with a theory, then prove it. Rather one begins with an area of study and what is relevant to that area is allowed to emerge. (Strauss & Corbin, 1990)

Although the term *grounded theory* did not come into use in academic and research literature until 1967, it is clear that Marie Clay was aware of its roots in the biological, social, and cognitive sciences.

Marie Clay's analysis of patterns in literacy behaviours led to what she called 'a literacy processing theory, a theory of assembling perceptual and cognitive working systems needed to complete increasingly complex tasks' (Clay, 2001, pp. 269–70). She described the complex theory in this way:

> In a complex model of interacting competencies in reading and writing the reader can potentially draw from all his or her current understanding, and all his or her language competencies, and visual information, and phonological information, and knowledge of printing conventions, in ways which *extend both the searching and linking processes as well as the item knowledge repertoires*. Learners pull together necessary information from print in simple ways at first . . . but as opportunities to read and write accumulate over time the learner becomes able to quickly and momentarily construct a somewhat complex operating system which might solve the problem. There is no simplified way to engage in the complex activities, but teachers and the public are typically presented with patently untrue simplifications in new commercial instruction kits. (Clay, 2001, p. 224)

Children must learn ways of operating on print. An efficient system uses many kinds of strategic behaviours such as:

- controlling serial order according to the directional rules for the script being read, across lines and within words

- using what you know about in reading to help writing and vice versa

- problem-solving with more than one kind of information

- actively searching for various types of information in print

- using visual information

- using language information

- drawing on stored information

- using phonological information

- working on categories, rules or probabilities about features in print

- using strategies which maintain fluency

- using strategies which problem-solve new features of printed words and meanings

- using strategies which detect and correct error.

(Clay, 2001, p. 199)

A number of theoretical principles emerging from Marie Clay's work have influenced the field of literacy development. While it is not possible to reduce her theory to a list, the following principles underpin her work.

- Reading and writing are complex problem-solving processes.

- Children construct their own understandings.

- Children come to literacy with varying knowledge.

- Reading and writing are reciprocal and interrelated processes.

- Learning to read and write involves a continuous process of change over time.

- Children take different paths to literacy learning.

Within her complex theory of literacy processing, Marie Clay did not ignore writing. In all of her work, relationships among reading, writing, and language are prominent. Her seminal research in oral language development (Clay, 1982, 1991a) supported her work in literacy learning.

> Language can be thought of as a hierarchy of units:
> sentences can be broken down into phrases, phrases into
> words, and words into sounds. The good reader can work
> at any of these levels in the hierarchy. The poor reader
> tends to specialize in words or sounds and may be ignoring
> the details by which letters are distinguished. But this is
> not possible in early writing. All features of the language
> hierarchy must, inevitably, receive attention as the child
> builds letters into words, words into phrases and phrases
> into sentences and stories. (Clay, 1975, p. 2)

In Marie Clay's view of literacy processing, writing plays a significant role in early reading progress. 'It provides for synthetic experience where letters are built into words which make up sentences, reinforcing the left to right principles, and an understanding, however intuitive, of the hierarchical nature of language' (Clay, 1982, p. 208). Writing slows down the complex activity so that all pieces can be interwoven, and contributes to the building of an inner control of literacy learning. To write, a child has to call up his language stores, sound segmentation strategies, phoneme/grapheme associations, and use appropriate motor skills to form a specific letter. He must also use his reading knowledge to check on his written responses (see Clay, 1982, p. 209).

Marie Clay (1982, see pp. 224–225) argued that writing must be included in a recovery programme because it

- facilitates very early reading progress when skills are minimal,

- provides a visible record of progress for the teacher,

- motivates a child because of the sense of power it gives,

- has a reciprocal payoff for letter learning, word recognition, and finding information in new words,

- creates in the child a sense that he can find ways to work on the task, and

- gives the child a sense of personal control over difficulties.

Her theory of literacy processing holds that teachers who are good observers of children have a way of refining their own personal theories of what it is to learn to read (Clay, 1991a). 'An interesting change occurs in teachers who observe closely. They begin to question educational assumptions' (Clay, 1982, p. 3 and Clay, 1998, p. 107). When a teacher observes a child's reading and writing behaviours, she has a way to gather data and a way to keep her teaching in line with what the child can actually do. So teachers can build a kind of *personal theory* of what observed behaviours imply about the underlying cognitive processes and use that theory to make teaching decisions (see Clay, 1991a, p. 232).

Theoretical influences

Marie Clay's unusual research lens revealed the unique constructive nature of learners and how they change over short periods of time. Consider her view of the teaching/learning process: 'Acts of reading are acts of construction rather than instruction. Most instruction . . . serves to fill out children's knowledge sources' (Clay, 2001, p. 137). She viewed the learner as actively constructing new ways of problem-solving with appropriate help from an observing teacher.

The constructive learner

Marie Clay was a champion of the individual. Her research was unique in its attention to the behaviours of the *individual learner*. 'Classes do not learn,' she emphasized. 'Only individuals learn.' Marie Clay's work demonstrated that just as young children construct oral language to gain meaning, the literacy learner with appropriate help from an observant teacher will actively construct new ways to solve problems. Her unusual observational lens verified that children construct their own understandings.

Whether teachers teach learners or learners teach themselves is a longstanding debate in education. Marie Clay viewed the *learner* as the creator of awareness while working on print — paying close attention, trying new responses, noticing and puzzling over new features, and reaching understanding. The actions taken by the *child* pave the route to learning (Clay, 1998). While the teacher works to stimulate, foster, support, and reinforce a learner's reading work, 'only the child can develop strategic control over the experiences and information coded somehow in his brain and governing many of his behaviours' (Clay, 1991a, p. 341).

Active, constructive learners dispel the notion of the empty vessel metaphor that views the teacher pouring learning into children.

Constructive learners also defy the growth-from-within model of learning with the limited view that all that is needed is discovery and self-directed learning. Marie Clay challenged us to recognize the need for the child to actively work on printed messages using all his current abilities and knowledge, while a teacher supports the quickest route to effective processing for that child at that point in time (Clay, 1991a).

By different paths to common outcomes

Marie Clay's unusual lens validated the notion that children take *different* paths to common outcomes. She did not apologize for her view that success is not simply a matter of pedalling harder along the same general path, but 'it is more a matter of initially changing the route several times in order to get to the same destination' (Clay, 2003, p. 298).

What children are able to do when entering school is closely related to their prior opportunities to learn. Because Marie Clay's unusual lens can be used when literacy learning is just beginning, it reflects the 'diversity in children's learning — differences in opportunities, pace, concepts, awareness, understandings, knowledge of items, interests, motivations, and strategies' (Jones & Smith-Burke, 1999, p. 269). Children begin their learning journeys in many different ways; Marie Clay's work enables us to know and help children use their unique footholds to advantage.

An advocate for *accommodating diversity*, she redefined diversity to accommodate any and all variants of individual differences, not limited to cultural, ethnic, and linguistic diversity (Clay, 1998). Being committed to diversity among learners, she refused to accept a stage theory of learning that called for a one-size-fits-all mentality.

> *If I stay with my hypothesis that the outcome of proficient reading and writing can be achieved by taking different paths then it would be an utter waste of time to try to create a table of stages to be achieved at set ages. Nothing so systematic was intended nor is it likely to be found.* (Clay, 2001, p. 77)

Instead, she suggested new questions and discussions, calling for good descriptions to guide contingent teaching. The teacher must find out what the child knows and is able to do — and take the child from there to somewhere else. 'There are many paths to common outcomes of sound literacy processing' (Clay, 2001, p. 303).

Attention to change over time

From the detailed records of active learners, Marie Clay described change over a brief period of historical time. When dealing with short intervals of time, individual differences are large, and theories built on stages of learning become untenable (Clay, 2001). Through close observation, however, teachers gain useful information to improve their teaching day by day. Close observation of emerging readers and writers enables researchers and teachers to assess children's changing literacy behaviours:

> I hope it will also be obvious that I value highly an approach to research which attempts to capture the ways in which children change over time in a reading programme, an approach too rarely taken in reading research. It is not enough to administer achievement tests before and after a programme or to probe deeply into the reading process. An important additional source of research information lies in accounts of what changes occur in what children in what sequences as they learn in their classroom programmes. As a researcher this has interested me; it is, of course, what concerns the teacher. (Clay, 1982, p. xiv)

Documenting how children's literacy acts pass through several different phases in the first year of instruction, Marie Clay concluded, '*What I end up with is not a theory of instruction, but a theory of the construction of an inner control of literacy acts*' (Clay, 2001, p. 46). The focus shifts to observed changes in reading and writing from day to day. And early interventions have to take children by the fastest possible route from where they are to achieving the literacy acts of proficient readers and writers. There is no preferred precise sequence. For example, an 'individual child's progress in mastering the complexity of the writing system seems to involve letters, words, and word groups all at the same time, at first in approximate, specific, and what seem to be primitive ways and later with considerable skill' (Clay, 1975, p. 19).

Practical influences

The theoretical contributions of Marie Clay's work were never isolated from her practical contributions. Because her theoretical work was grounded in observations of children as they were becoming literate, it led to many practical applications. In this section, we consider her contributions to the assessment of young children, to teaching practices based on child learning, and to the prevention of literacy difficulties.

Influence on assessment

The major aim of Marie Clay's (1966) early research was to record in detail the reading behaviour of 100 5-year-old urban New Zealand children at the beginning of instruction. Traditional tools for assessing literacy processing behaviours were not appropriate for emergent readers and writers. Marie Clay met that challenge by creating an array of techniques, instruments, and ways of describing and reporting unfolding early behaviours. Her assessment tools had to (a) be highly sensitive to change over time, (b) provide insights of partial learning, (c) include all areas contributing to literacy learning, and (d) detect individual differences. The tools also had to be easy for classroom teachers to administer and use (Jones & Smith-Burke, 1999).

The observation tasks she developed demonstrate the complexity of her theory of literacy processing. For example, one task required each child to read a selection from his current reading texts while the investigator recorded all aspects of observable literacy behaviour for analysis. Categories and signs of processing behaviour were identified by what became a systematic, valid, and reliable system for recording children's strategic activity while reading text.

Marie Clay argued that educators 'have done a great deal of systematic testing and relatively little systematic observation of learning' (Clay, 2002, 2006, p. 12). Yet educators need to attend 'to the systematic observation of learners who are on the way to those scores on tests' (Clay, 2002, 2006, p. 12). Driven by a theoretical perspective that focused on the individual learner, Marie Clay challenged educators to reconsider current assessment tools for young children. She argued that standardized tests do not discriminate well until considerable progress has been made by the children. Such instruments are dictated by the tyranny of the average! Yet in terms of early learning, 'averages are unable to inform the teacher who is dealing with children who are of similar age *but at different levels of building a literacy processing system*' (Clay, 2001, p. 306).

Her work yielded tasks for educators and researchers to observe young literacy learners with confidence. Years of research and refinement led to the publication of *An Observation Survey of Early Literacy Achievement* (Clay, 1993, 2002, 2006). The Observation Survey comprises multiple tasks that collectively provide a view of a child's awareness and actions related to becoming literate. As noted above, the Running Record of Text Reading is a reliable and valid observational lens to describe how children work on continuous text as they read orally. Survey tasks are briefly described later in this chapter, along with other observational tasks used by Marie Clay to view a child's ways of working with language in reading, writing, and speaking.

Influence on teaching

Marie Clay's development of observation tasks — her unusual lens — led to many questions about teaching.

> How does one manage to support the child's control of literacy activities from the beginning, to interact with an inner control one can only infer, and to progressively withdraw to allow room for the child to control the development of a self-extending network of strategies for literacy learning? (Clay, 1991a, p. 344)

The scope of her contributions to the role of teaching is great. Two representative features of her significant legacy are highlighted here.

1. First, effective teachers need to schedule time to observe exactly what their students are learning. In order to find out what a child knows, thinks, and is able to do, teachers must use observational data supported by a theory of what changes to expect. Rather than test scores and prescriptions of what to teach, teachers need more opportunities to *observe* in order to acknowledge small-step learning (Clay, 2001). Effective teachers will verbalize their observations of behaviours and share tentative hypotheses with colleagues in order to make good decisions about teaching (Clay, 1982).

2. In addition to a theory of what has occurred based on close observation, teachers need theory of how to interact with what can subsequently occur through informed teaching. Marie Clay's view of the teacher's role is not to deliver knowledge, but to arrange for problems to be manageable by the child. In this way the teacher will support the child's problem-solving attempts and maintain flexibility (Johnston, 2007). This reflects Holdaway's (1979) goal for literacy learning — for the learner to operate with motivation and determination within the reach of the teacher's informed help.

Marie Clay's research findings led to several implications for teaching.

- Because children come to school with unique stores of knowledge, literacy instruction should build on their prior knowledge; teachers can work from the learner's strengths.

- Because children come to school with more or less learning in any given area, teachers can help them round out foundational learning as they begin to work with reading and writing.

- Because reading and writing are important in a child's literacy development, instruction should include attention to both processes.

Based on her research on Reading Recovery, Marie Clay identified the following necessary features of teaching that have implications for all teachers of young children (see Clay, 2001, p. 225).

- Make maximum use of a child's existing response repertoire.

- Support the development of literacy processing by
  — astute selection of tasks,
  — judicious sharing of tasks, and
  — varying the time, difficulty, content, interest, method of instruction, and the type and amount of conversation.

- Foster active and constructive problem-solving, self-monitoring, and self-correction from the beginning so that learners take over the expansion of their own competencies.

- Set the level of task difficulty to ensure high rates of correct responding in addition to appropriate challenge so that the child learns from his own attempts to go beyond his current knowledge.

All of these features focus on the teacher's role of facilitating, fostering, and supporting the problem-solving of the learner. An informed teacher who is a careful observer of young children works to ensure the active literacy learning of each child.

Influence on prevention: The legacy of Reading Recovery

Marie Clay's unusual lens allowed researchers and practitioners to determine which children find reading and writing difficult, and demonstrated the need for an early intervention treatment to prevent literacy failure. Reading Recovery was designed to temporarily lift the pace of learning of children experiencing difficulty, to permanently lift their achievement levels, and to build a solid foundation for subsequent literacy learning (see Clay, 2001, p. 217).

Prevention is a central concept in Reading Recovery. The intervention was designed to identify and treat (i.e., *teach individually*) children most at risk of later failure, before serious and pervasive difficulties occur.

> Early identification of children at risk in literacy learning . . .
> should be systematically carried out not later than one year
> after the child has entered a formal programme . . . it is
> sensible to try to predict [failure] only after all children
> have had some equivalent opportunities to respond to
> good teaching. (Clay, 2002, 2006, p. 142)

Five unique principles distinguish Clay's notion of prevention: *early*
detection of literacy difficulties, *early* intervention, individual differences
in learning, intensive one-to-one teaching, and accelerated learning
(Schmitt, Askew, Fountas, Lyons, & Pinnell, 2005).

Again, Marie Clay followed principles of grounded theory. She used
careful, controlled observations of children to develop a theory of literacy
processing; she used that theory to guide procedures for teaching children
with difficulties; she used detailed observations and records to confirm
or revise theory and procedures (Jones & Smith-Burke, 1999). Marie
Clay's Reading Recovery research consisted of a series of eight studies
from 1976 to 1991. These early studies provide the cornerstone of this
book. (See Chapter 2.)

In 1991, Marie Clay reported a number of 'Reading Recovery Surprises'
(Clay, 1991b) based on student outcomes.

- The intervention works with diverse populations.

- The rate of learning accelerates, allowing the lowest achievers to
  'catch up' with their grade level peers.

- Children gain a large measure of independence over how they
  learn.

- Children continue to make progress after the intervention, keeping
  up with their average classmates.

- A high number of children respond to the intervention.

- Children who need more help are identified.

She also expressed some surprising operative concepts (Clay, 1991b).

- Participation is inclusive.

- Selection of children is made by teachers who use observation
  instruments.

- Intervention occurs early.

- The intervention is short-term.

- Every child's intervention is different.
- Children read whole stories, reading a new book each day.
- The volume of reading is increased.
- Children compose and write messages.
- Many sources of information in print are attended to.
- Ordinary classroom teachers are used.
- Teacher training causes teachers to think about their teaching.
- The intervention is designed for expansion.

A significant contribution of Marie Clay's work was the creation of a design to disseminate Reading Recovery to different cultures and government structures while maintaining the integrity and quality of the intervention (Clay, 1997). Her success was based on the interaction of the following components.

Development of professional expertise

Reading Recovery has been touted as an exemplar for effective teacher development. In a review of 10 promising programmes, Herman & Stringfield (1997) praised the professional learning model for Reading Recovery.

> The intensity and methods utilized by Reading Recovery in training and the insistence on high level of Reading Recovery performance provided an almost singularly attractive model for future staff development efforts, regardless of programme type. As schools systematize and create more opportunities for serious staff development, the thoroughness of the Reading Recovery model seems to be well worth emulating. (Herman & Stringfield, 1997, p. 86)

Marie Clay devised three important levels of expertise: the Reading Recovery teacher, the Tutor (Teacher Leader in some countries), and the Trainer of Tutors/Teacher Leaders. Each role requires intensive initial training and ongoing professional development. Professional networks of guidance and collegiality support teacher change. The Reading Recovery professional learning model has been validated in research studies as an important factor in the intervention's success (see Pinnell, Lyons, DeFord, Bryk, & Seltzer, 1994).

Monitoring and evaluating outcomes

As a researcher, Marie Clay knew the importance of monitoring student outcomes. All children involved in Reading Recovery worldwide are accounted for in evaluating the outcomes of the intervention. In addition to monitoring student outcomes, process data are collected to inform implementation decisions. A description of evaluation processes in countries with large implementations of Reading Recovery is provided in Chapter 8 of this volume.

Implementation as a systemic intervention

Unlike most innovations, Reading Recovery developed a plan for implementation, dissemination, expansion, and continuation. Marie Clay understood the importance of attending to implementation issues when placing an innovation into an educational system. Both internal and external structures guide successful implementation; these structures offer a model for implementing other innovations (see Chapter 7).

Nobel Prize-winning physicist and educational reformer Kenneth Wilson and educational journalist Bennett Daviss (1994) call Reading Recovery a model for redesigning education. They suggest that Reading Recovery is one of the most successful educational reforms, thoroughly grounded in the process of redesign:

> It has shaped its methods according to the results of its own and others' research. It has tested and honed its techniques through years of trials and refinements, analogous to industry's processes of product prototyping and test marketing. It equips its specialists with a common body of proven knowledge and skills that allow instructors to tailor each lesson to each child's needs — rather than expecting every child to adapt an identical course of lessons that moves at an inflexible pace. Equally important, the programme maintains rigorous systems of self-evaluation or quality control, and offers ongoing training and support to the teachers in schools . . . that adopt it. (Wilson & Daviss, 1994, pp. 50–51)

The promise of Reading Recovery

Reading Recovery offers promise to the prevention of literacy failure around the world. Marie Clay used the words of Maxine Greene to express her own notion of the important contributions of Reading Recovery.

Through our own attending and the going-out of our own energies, we are able to break the bonds of the ordinary and the taken-for-granted, to move into spaces never known before. And that is what some of us, considering our craft, want for those we teach: the opportunity and capacity to reach beyond, to move towards what is not yet. (Greene, 1986, p. 23)

Describing Marie Clay's observation tasks for capturing early literacy behaviours

The influence of Marie Clay's work on assessment for young learners is unparalleled. *An Observation Survey of Early Literacy Achievement* (Clay, 1993, 2002, 2006) is woven into the fabric of literacy assessment in many primary schools around the world. In this section, tasks of the Observation Survey and other observation tasks used by Marie Clay in her studies of early literacy behaviours are described.

An Observation Survey of Early Literacy Achievement

The first large-scale application of Marie Clay's research was *The Early Detection of Reading Difficulties: A Diagnostic Survey* (Clay, 1972), later revised as *An Observation Survey of Early Literacy Achievement* (Clay, 1993, 2002, 2006). Grounded in a theory of literacy processing, the Observation Survey represents Clay's robust 'conceptualization of early literacy as one that involves the thoughtful application of reading skills and strategies. It also frames reading as an act of constructing meaning. Further, it seeks information about students' procedural knowledge of literacy: the nature of reading, how books work, and the conventions of printed language' (Afflerbach, 2007, p. 118).

An Observation Survey of Early Literacy Achievement has value for assessment, monitoring change over time, teaching, and research. It is a way to observe literacy learning progress at a time when a child's development is difficult to document. Survey tasks capture children's behaviours as they read and write continuous texts and assess knowledge in areas that contribute to reading and writing — items such as letters, print concepts, reading and writing words, and sound–letter relationships. The Survey is 'designed to yield rich information to inform our understanding of students' present needs and challenges and related instruction' (Afflerbach, 2007).

The Observation Survey comprises six tasks: Taking Records of

Reading Continuous Texts (Running Record), Letter Identification, Word Reading, Concepts About Print, Writing Vocabulary, and Hearing and Recording Sounds in Words. Developed over a number of years (1963–1978) and subsequently revised, the tasks are used together to get a comprehensive view of a child's competencies and patterns of literacy behaviour, using real tasks familiar to the child from classroom experiences.

> *All tasks in my observation survey are like screens on which are projected the immaturity or degree of control demonstrated by the young child's tentative responses to print and to books.* . . . A wide-ranging survey of print awareness is necessary to bring out the many things a beginning reader might know, and its array of results will help teachers to *avoid the error of looking at only one aspect of early reading progress and expecting to find in that one aspect an explanation of the beginnings of complex literacy behaviour.* (Clay, 1998, p. 63)

Used by classroom teachers, Reading Recovery teachers, specialist teachers, and researchers, the Observation Survey probes the literacy achievement and progress of individual children. The Survey is a teacher-administered individual assessment, incorporating both open and closed tasks and adhering to characteristics of good measurement instruments: standard tasks, standard administration, real-world tasks to establish validity, and ways of confirming reliability of observations.

Observation Survey tasks have high construct and face validity; they are directly relevant to the reading and writing of continuous text. Validity and reliability data, along with New Zealand and United States norms, are provided in Appendix I (Clay, 2006). Studies have shown a high correlation between the Observation Survey and normed tests (for example, Rodgers, Gómez-Bellengé, Wang, & Schultz, 2005). External documentation supports the validity and reliability of the Survey (for example, Denton, Ciancio, & Fletcher, 2006). The following quote from Jane Hurry (1996) in the United Kingdom illustrates the influence of the Survey in research and evaluation:

> In the United Kingdom evaluation of Reading Recovery this [the Observation Survey] was found to be the most sensitive of the measures used to assess children's reading ability at this age (including the British Ability Scale of Word Reading and the Neale Analysis of Reading) reported in Sylva and Hurry (1995). Elements of this assessment pack

have been used in many Local Education Authorities for some time to identify children at Key Stage 1 with special needs. This is not surprising as it compares favourably with other diagnostic batteries suitable for use with this group of children in a school setting. (Hurry, 1996, p. 97) (quoted in Clay, 2002, 2006, p. 164)

Some researchers have voiced concerns that the Survey does not conform to rules of standardized tests. They argue that behaviours may appear and then disappear and that changes do not occur in equal interval steps. Clay responded to these critics:

This is problematic for literacy researchers whose statistical tools require equal intervals, but it is no reason for discarding a useful tool for observing progress. Using 'an unusual lens' forces us to recognize the utility and the limitations of the analyses we typically make. (Clay, 2001, pp. 46–48)

An Observation Survey of Early Literacy Achievement is available in other languages. A bilingual Spanish-English version (Escamilla, Andrade, Basurto, & Ruiz, 1996) and a Maori-English reconstruction (Rau, 1998) have been published. In French Canada, a full French edition is entitled *Le sondage d'observation en lecture-écriture* (Clay & Bourque, 2003). In addition, the Concepts About Print task has been translated in several languages.

Each task of the Observation Survey is highlighted below, beginning with the one most closely aligned with the reading of continuous text, the Running Record of Text Reading.

Taking records of reading continuous texts (Running Records)

A critically important lens emerging from Marie Clay's research was the Running Record of Text Reading. As she analysed transcripts of what beginners said and did with text, she developed this task for assessing and monitoring change over time in literacy behaviours. Oral responses to the written text were given top priority: true report (accurate reading), error, attack, repetition, and self-correction. The next priority was given to motor responses relating to directional and spatial qualities of the texts (pointing, vocal juncture between words and syllables, and tracking errors).

A Running Record 'transmits a different kind of information from that provided by scores on phoneme, letter, and word tests, or from comprehension questions. So we get an alternative view of progress' (Clay, 2001, p. 46). Clay described a Running Record as

- a systematic procedure for recording reading behaviours observed during text reading,

- a tool for recording and then interpreting how children work on texts, and

- a valid view of change over time in children's reading behaviours.
(Clay, 2001, see pp. 45–46)

Running Records provide a way of analysing imperfect performances, yielding information about the ways in which children monitor and problem-solve as they read. Unexpected responses 'suggest the kind of mental processing taking place and allow us to examine the leading edge of a learner's development' (Johnston, 1997, p. 192). Johnston offered a useful explanation of the importance of error behaviour in literacy learning and in contingent teaching:

> The advantage of mistakes is that you stand to learn something new when you have made one and noticed it. *. . . For teachers, the most useful aspect of errors is that people do not make them randomly.* There is always a reason for them. If you can figure out the reason, then you know where to use your instructional expertise without further confusing the student. (Johnston, 1997, p. 60)

Analysis of errors and self-corrections provides a wealth of information about a child's processing:

- what the child was attending to at the point where error occurred

- whether the child was aware of mismatches between the text and the first selected response

- what the child was attending to in resolving the error

- when the child was relating 'external' information out there in the text to prior 'internal' information that child already had.
(Clay, 2001, p. 200)

An important outcome of Marie Clay's observational research was the noteworthiness of self-correction behaviours to explain the reading process:

Self-correction must contribute to the forward thrust of reading competency. At each substitution the child initiates a search for more information, generates and evaluates hypotheses, and makes decisions. By definition a decision that ends in a self-correction is a correct decision and the reader may have attended to features ignored in the first attempt. We cannot know what information the reader used to reach a correct response which fits perfectly into its textual slot, but when an error is corrected we can ask, 'What information was absent in the error that was subsequently present in the self-correction?' What happens over time to self-correcting needs to be part of an explanation of early reading progress. (Clay, 2001, p. 195)

Self-correction is important to learner and teacher. Self-correction *rates* can show how well readers are monitoring their reading. The self-corrections themselves provide evidence that the reader is 'comparing different sources of information, finding them discrepant, *and* doing something about correcting the discrepancy' (Johnston, 1997, p. 216).

Teachers and researchers use running records to capture change over time in a child's strategic activity while reading continuous text, to assess a text's level of difficulty, and to guide teaching.

Concepts About Print

Concepts About Print was first designed as a means of observing early progress of 5-year-olds in Marie Clay's earliest research. A short story is read to the child; through a book-sharing situation the child shows what he knows about book orientation skills, print and directionality, letter and word concepts, and advanced print concepts. The task attempts to capture children's control over attention to print. The orienting behaviours reveal a motor component (movement), a looking component (visual perception), and a mental, or cognitive, component (Clay, 1998, see pp. 120–121).

As a part of the Observation Survey, the Concepts about Print task reveals children's early reading behaviours during the first year or two in school. Individual differences in literacy awareness are 'highly related to social and cultural factors that limit or extend opportunities to learn' (Clay, 1998, pp. 66–67). Concepts About Print encourages teachers to consider the many ways individual children may start their journey of literacy learning. It can indicate progress and suggest what action the teacher may need to take to provide for children with limited previous literacy learning opportunities.

Letter Identification

The premise of the Letter Identification task is the efficiency of finding out which letters a child already identifies before seeking a fast route to learning the others. This task focuses on the child's identification and visual discrimination of letters one from another and his overt behaviours while responding to the task. It is *not* concerned with learning to write the symbol or linking it to a sound or phoneme (Clay, 2002, 2006).

The Letter Identification task is not a stand-alone predictor of preparation for literacy learning. Used in combination with all other tasks of the Survey, however, it provides information about a child's ability to distinguish letters on any basis — by name, sound, or a word beginning with the letter — and supports teaching to expand the range of known letters and to promote flexibility in ways of labelling them.

Word Reading

Using a list of words appearing frequently in early reading texts, the Word Reading task reveals the extent to which a child is accumulating a reading vocabulary. In addition to information about the child's competence with reading words in isolation and how this changes over time, the observer may use this task to note a child's ways of working with words. For example, attempts and self-corrections may reveal a child's attention to particular understandings or confusions.

Writing Vocabulary

In her early research, Marie Clay noticed that the more competent children made written lists of all the words they knew. From such observations, Susan M. Robinson (1973) developed an observation task now incorporated into the Observation Survey. The task 'is like a screen upon which the child can project what he knows — not only what we have taught him but what he has learned anywhere in his various worlds' (Clay, 2002, 2006, p. 102).

The child is encouraged to write all the words he can in 10 minutes, starting with his name and words he has managed to learn. If he stops writing, the teacher prompts by suggesting words or categories of words he might know how to write.

In addition to change over time in the personal corpus of a child's known writing vocabulary, this task provides a view of the child's approximations or useful behaviours when writing words (e.g., initial and final letters, consonant framework, etc.). The child also has opportunity to write new words by analogy with those he knows.

Hearing and Recording Sounds in Words (phonemic awareness)

This authentic writing task enables the teacher or researcher to observe the child's ability to analyse and sequence the sounds in words he wants to write, and to find appropriate letters to record them. It is a valuable indicator of change over time.

The observer dictates one of five prescribed sentences. The child is asked to say each successive word slowly and to write every sound he hears. Credit is given for every correctly written phoneme even if the word is not correctly spelled. The observer also notes partially correct responses that indicate the cutting edge of the child's knowledge, recording any sequencing errors, omitted sounds, unusual placement of letters within words, and 'good' confusions.

Observation Survey Summary

An Observation Summary Sheet (Clay, 2002, 2006, pp. 124 and 127) brings together the results of the Observation Survey for children whom a teacher wants to look at closely. Class teachers may prepare shorter summaries of children's reading and writing behaviours (Clay, 2002, 2006, pp. 132–137). In addition to a summary of scores for each task, an analysis of the ways in which the child identifies and solves problems or challenges is recorded. Using *all* appropriate tasks in concert, the observer records the child's performance in the following areas (see Clay, 2002, 2006, p. 126):

- Useful strategic activity on text reading

- Problem strategic activity on text reading

- Useful strategic activity with words

- Problem strategic activity with words

- Useful strategic activity with letters

- Problem strategic activity with letters

The teacher who summarizes observed literacy processing behaviours of a child can immediately transfer her observations to teaching that child. The analysis directs the teacher's attention to precisely what she needs to attend to. Teaching becomes contingent upon observed child behaviours rather than scores on unrelated tests.

Assessments of oral language

Marie Clay's contribution to research in oral language is legendary (see

Clay, 1982). In her early research, observation of the oral language of 5-year-olds led to this conclusion:

> From the tapestry of five year old speech we can tease the threads of speech discrimination (which includes discovering the segments), articulation, morphological inflections, syntactic skills, and sentence patterning, transformational rules of sentence structure, and semantic richness. None of these is very meaningful on its own but each contributes to producing a level of language function in the five year old that is either beautiful and intricate, simple and adequate, or scant and barely woven. (Clay, 1966, p. 175)

Marie Clay developed two research tools for observing aspects of language development:

- A sentence repetition task using a set of sentences graded for difficulty (Record of Oral Language) (Clay, Gill, Glynn, McNaughton, & Salmon, 1983, 2007a)
- A task in which the child supplies missing words in short stories (Biks and Gutches) (Clay, 1983, 2007b).

Both tasks have been shown to help teachers observe and understand changes in children's language. Each one can show change over time in a child's control of English (for ages 4 to 7 for English speakers and up to 5 years after beginning to learn English as a second language). Both emphasise teacher observation and child development, not passing or failing.

Record of Oral Language

The Record of Oral Language is intended to help teachers assess a child's ability to handle selected grammatical structures. Levelled Sentences and Diagnostic Sentences are repeated by the child after the teacher.

Sentence repetition techniques are not intended simply to record items a child gets right or wrong. Observing what a child does when trying to repeat a difficult sentence yields valuable information about his oral language control. He may omit or substitute phrases, words, or parts of words. He may expand the sentence or transpose parts of the sentence. When he repeats a difficult sentence in his own words, he often provides evidence of the structures he can control. A careful analysis gives the teacher a detailed description of the child's oral language.

Besides recording changes in a child's control of grammatical structures, the Record of Oral Language guides a *teacher's* own use of grammatical structures with individuals and with the class (Clay et al., 1983, 2007a).

Biks and Gutches

Biks and Gutches (Clay et al., 1983, 2007b) was devised to test a child's control of the inflections of the English language and to observe change over time in his use of inflections. In a natural and conversational tone, the teacher shows the child a picture and reads a story about the picture (using a cloze format), while the child supplies missing words, both real and nonsense.

Assessment of writing

In her longitudinal study of 100 children in their first year in school, Marie Clay observed them as they progressed along different paths and at different rates in writing as well as reading.

> The shifts were individually paced as children moved from idiosyncratic starting points, ranging from scribble and discovery to tracing or copying a model, through a period of dependent appeals for help when they knew they did not know, to self-initiated, self-organized sequences of behaviour carried out with a minimum of outside support (Clay, 1967, 1975). (from Clay, 1998, p. 133)

Believing that the writing samples collected from those children might help teachers sharpen their observation of children's writing, Marie Clay began work on the book *What Did I Write?* (1975). Initially, she had no organizational scheme in mind but found when she analysed the samples that they revealed children's assumptions about language and the task. She considered these *implied assumptions and principles* important because a child's work took a leap forward in complexity when he began to operate according to one of these principles for the first time (Clay, 1982).

Principles emerging from her analysis of writing samples guided Clay's thinking about observable behaviours over time. She observed a *flexibility principle* as children experiment with letter forms, exploring the limits of variation while still maintaining identity. Flexibility could be critically important to early stages of complex learning. The *recurring principle*, or the ability to repeat an action, is especially important when the child realizes that the same elements can recur in variable patterns.

And the *generating principle* allows the child to use what he knows to produce or generate new learning. These principles, among others, provided a new and unusual lens for observing children's change over time in written literacy.

What Did I Write? is considered innovative in its impact on the role of writing in early literacy processing. Marie Clay illustrated 'some of the insights that a child gains during his first contacts with written language and some of the points at which he can become confused' (Clay, 1975, p. 2). Not intended to specify teaching procedures, the book's theme was the child's gradual development of a perceptual awareness of the arbitrary customs used in written English. Ann Haas Dyson said the book 'gripped my attention. It promised intellectual interest in and respect for children's actions — not didactic prescriptions for teachers. My own research path began there, that day, in the bookstore aisle' (Gaffney & Askew, 1999, p. 286).

Marie Clay's observational data led her to create yet another instrument for observing early progress in writing (see Clay, 2002, 2006, pp. 99–100). She suggested the collection of three writing samples on consecutive days at intervals throughout the first year of instruction. Samples are analysed to observe improvement in three areas: Language Level, Message Quality, and Directional Principles. She created a scale to serve as a rough guide to a child's instruction needs (see page 66 in Clay, 1975 or pages 99–100 in Clay, 2002, 2006*)*.

A child's written work provides 'objective evidence of what the child has learned. We have an opportunity to see how the child organises his behaviour as he writes' (Clay, 1982, p. 220).

The legacy of Marie Clay's unusual lens

It is not possible to convey adequately the magnitude of the legacy left by Marie Clay's unusual lens for observing acts of early literacy processing. Her understanding of multiple scientific methodologies freed her to use an exceptional methodology to study literacy behaviours of young readers and writers. Her observational research led to

- a grounded theory of literacy processing that accounts for *early* literacy development,

- an emphasis on observation as a basic phase of teaching,

- assessment tasks for observing progress of young literacy learners over time, and

- a powerful and replicable intervention for preventing reading failure (Reading Recovery).

The legacy of Marie Clay's unusual lens extends to practitioners and researchers. Practitioners are challenged to observe and record children's reading and writing behaviours in order to explore teacher-child interactions. She cautioned that test scores do not lead directly to teaching, but coded observations that are supported by a theory of expected changes can be used to guide teaching.

Marie Clay challenged researchers to observe and to do it well, with imagination, with boldness, with dedication, and in valid and reliable ways (Bakeman & Gottman, 1986). Through controlled and sequential observations, we can become aware of patterns and the discovery of patterns can give rise to theories.

> So systematic observations which are analysed for sequential patterns usually yield new insights in areas previously restricted to quantitative analysis of test scores or probes at several isolated points of time. A sequential analysis of patterns in reading behaviours could lead to what I call a literacy processing theory, a theory of assembling perceptual and cognitive working systems needed to complete increasingly complex tasks. (Clay, 2001, pp. 269–270).

Legacies endure only if they continue to thrive and build. Marie Clay's work will continue as teachers and researchers use an observational lens that gives rise to new questions with theoretical and practical consequences.

References

Afflerbach, P. (2007). *Understanding and using reading assessment K-12.* Newark, DE: International Reading Association.

Bakeman, R., & Gottman, J. M. (1986). *Observing interaction: An introduction to sequential analysis.* Cambridge: Cambridge University Press.

Clay, M. M. (1966). *Emergent reading behaviour.* Unpublished doctoral thesis. Auckland: University of Auckland.

Clay, M. M. (1967). The reading behaviour of five-year-old children: A research report. *New Zealand Journal of Educational Studies, 2*(1), 11–31.

Clay, M. M. (1972). *The early detection of reading difficulties: A diagnostic survey.* Auckland: Heinemann.

Clay, M. M. (1975). *What did I write?* Auckland: Heinemann.

Clay, M. M. (1982). *Observing young readers.* Portsmouth, NH: Heinemann.

Clay, M. M. (1990). Child development. In J. Flood, J. Jensen, D. Lapp, & J. R. Squire (Eds.), *Handbook of research on teaching the English language arts* (pp. 40–45). Newark, DE: International Reading Association and National Council of Teachers of English. (Reprinted in *Journal of Reading Recovery*, Fall 2007.)

Clay, M. M. (1991a). *Becoming literate: The construction of inner control.* Auckland: Heinemann.

Clay, M. M. (1991b). Reading Recovery surprises. In D. E. Deford, C. A. Lyons, & G. S. Pinnell (Eds.), *Bridges to literacy* (pp. 55–74). Portsmouth, NH: Heinemann.

Clay, M. M. (1993). *An observation survey of early literacy achievement* (1st ed.). Auckland: Heinemann.

Clay, M. M. (1997). International perspectives on the Reading Recovery programme. In J. Flood, S. B. Heath, & D. Lapp (Eds.), *Handbook of research on teaching literacy through the communicative and visual arts* (pp. 655–667). New York: Macmillan Library Reference USA (a project of the International Reading Association). (reprinted in *Journal of Reading Recovery*, Fall 2007)

Clay, M. M. (1998). *By different paths to common outcomes.* Portland, ME: Stenhouse.

Clay, M. M. (2001). *Change over time in children's literacy development.* Auckland: Heinemann.

Clay, M. M. (2002, 2006). *An observation survey of early literacy achievement* (2nd ed.). Auckland: Heinemann.

Clay, M. M. (2003). Afterword. In S. Forbes & C. Briggs (Eds.), *Research in Reading Recovery, Volume Two* (pp. 297–303). Portsmouth, NH: Heinemann.

Clay, M. M. (2004). Simply by sailing in a new direction you could enlarge the world. In C. M. Fairbanks, J. Worthy, B. Maloch, J. V. Hoffman, & D. L Schallert (Eds.), *Fifty-third yearbook of the National Conference* (pp. 60–66). Oak Creek, WI: National Reading Conference. (Reprinted in *Journal of Reading Recovery*, Fall 2007.)

Clay, M. M. (2007). *Biks and gutches: Learning to inflect English.* Auckland: Heinemann.

Clay, M. M., & Bourque, G. (2003). *Le sondage d'observation en lecture-écriture.* Montréal (Québec), Canada: Chenelière/McGraw-Hill.

Clay, M. M., Gill, M., Glynn, T., McNaughton, T., & Salmon, K. (1983). *Record of oral language and biks and gutches.* Auckland, NZ: Heinemann.

Clay, M. M., Gill, M., Glynn, T., McNaughton, T., & Salmon, K. (2007). *Record of oral language: Observing changes in the acquisition of language structures.* Auckland: Heinemann.

Denton, C. A., Ciancio, D., & Fletcher, J. (2006). Validity, reliability, and utility of the Observation Survey of Early Literacy Achievement. *Reading Research Quarterly, 41,* 8–34.

Escamilla, K., Andrade, A. M., Basurto, A. G. M., & Ruiz, O. A (1996). *Instrumento de observación de los logros de la lecto-escritura inicial.* Portsmouth, NH: Heinemann.

Gaffney, J. S., & Askew, B. J. (1999). *Stirring the waters: The influence of Marie Clay.* Portsmouth, NH: Heinemann.

Greene, M. (1986). How do we think about our craft? In A. Lieberman (Ed.), *Rethinking school improvement: Research, craft, and concept.* New York: Teachers College Press.

Herman, R., & Stringfield, S. (1997). *Ten promising programmes for educating all children: Evidence of impact.* Arlington, VA: Educational Research Service.

Holdaway, D. (1979). *Foundations of literacy.* Sydney: Ashton Scholastic.

Hurry, J. (1996). What is so special about Reading Recovery? *The Curriculum Journal, 7*(8), 93–108.

Johnston, P. H. (1997). *Knowing literacy: Constructive literacy assessment.* York, ME: Stenhouse.

Johnston, P. H. (2007). Revolutionary contributions. *Journal of Reading Recovery, 7*(1), 67–68.

Jones, N. K., & Smith-Burke, M. T. (1999). Forging an international relationship among research, theory, and practice: Clay's research design and methodology. In J. S. Gaffney & B. J. Askew (Eds.), *Stirring the waters: The influence of Marie Clay* (pp. 261–283). Portsmouth, NH: Heinemann.

Pinnell, G. S., Lyons, C. A., DeFord, D. E., Bryk, A. S., & Seltzer, M. (1994). Comparing instructional models for the literacy education of high-risk first graders. *Reading Research Quarterly, 29,* 8–39.

Rau, C. (1998). *He Mātai Āta Titiro Ki Te Tūtukitanga Mātātupu Pānui Tuhi*. The Maori reconstruction of *An observation survey of early literacy achievement*. Ngaruawahia: Kia Ata Mai Educational Trust.

Robinson, S. M. (1973). *Predicting early reading progress*. Unpublished master's thesis. Auckland: University of Auckland.

Rodgers, E. M., Gómez-Bellengé, F. X., Wang, C., & Schulz, M. M. (2005, April). *Examination of the validity of the observation survey with a comparison to ITBS*. Paper presented at the annual meeting of the American Educational Research Association, Montreal, Quebec. (www.ndec.us)

Schmitt, M. C., Askew, B. J., Fountas, I. C., Lyons, C. A., & Pinnell, G. S. (2005). *Changing futures: The influence of Reading Recovery in the United States*. Worthington, OH: Reading Recovery Council of North America.

Strauss, A., & Corbin, J. (1990). *Basics of qualitative research: Grounded theory procedures and techniques*. Newbury Park, CA: Sage Publications.

Wilson, K., & Daviss, B. (1994). *Redesigning education*. New York: Henry Holt.

Part Two
Continuing the Search for Possibilities

4

Reading Recovery Research in New Zealand and Australia

Sue McDowall

A major theme integral to the development of Reading Recovery is the enduring commitment to the child becoming an independent reader and writer. The impact of Reading Recovery on individual children's achievement was central to Marie Clay's early research reported in Chapter 2. Subsequently, many different aspects of Reading Recovery as an early literacy intervention have been investigated. However, the research reported in this review from New Zealand and Australia, and in the two following reviews, focuses on the principal tenet of Reading Recovery, literacy outcomes for children.

This chapter begins with an overview of published research findings on student outcomes during Reading Recovery and in the months and years following the intervention. Evidence of the relative impact of Reading Recovery for different groups of children within the intervention follows, taking into account factors such as type of school attended and such student characteristics as ethnicity, first language, and initial achievement. Finally, the influence of implementation factors and the school context of Reading Recovery are examined, focusing on factors that may affect children's progress such as classroom instruction before, during, and after Reading Recovery.

The New Zealand and Australian research is presented together in this chapter for several reasons. One is that geographical proximity has resulted in close social and cultural ties between these two countries and similarities in approaches to literacy instruction. Another is because of the connections between the studies in these two countries. One study, for instance, involves both New Zealand and Australian children in the sample, while another compares the Reading Recovery entry levels of New Zealand and Australian children.

Differences in the New Zealand and Australian contexts, however, should not be overlooked. New Zealand has a longer history of Reading Recovery than Australia and, unlike Australia, since 1983 it has been implemented nationally. There are also differences in school entry practices. In New Zealand children start school on, or close to, their fifth birthday which means continuous entry into beginning classrooms. Correspondingly, there is continuous entry into Reading Recovery. In Australia children start school at the beginning of the school year. This means children are at varying ages when they enter Reading Recovery. Regardless of school entry differences, however, in both countries every child who enters Reading Recovery towards the end of the school year and does not reach the point at which lessons can be discontinued is carried over into the following year. Lessons then resume, continuing until the child's competency indicates the series of lessons can be discontinued.

Impact of Reading Recovery on student outcomes

The studies presented in this chapter define and measure the effectiveness of Reading Recovery in different ways. The research questions asked, the definitions of 'effectiveness' used, and the ways in which effectiveness is measured all have a bearing on the conclusions that can be drawn. As observed by Marie Clay (2001), some are more appropriate for an intervention such as Reading Recovery than others. Definitions of effectiveness include whether or not children

- reach the point at which they no longer need supplementary support, that is lessons are discontinued,

- make greater progress than could be expected without the intervention,

- reach the average band of achievement for their class,

- reach the average level or band of achievement for their region, state, or national cohort, and

- maintain satisfactory progress in the short, medium, or longer term following the cessation of the intervention.

The next section focuses on student achievement by the end of Reading Recovery, keeping in mind the points discussed above. The section that follows focuses on the months and years after Reading Recovery has ceased. Some of the longitudinal studies have produced findings pertinent to more than one of these sections and are included in each.

Student achievement by the end of Reading Recovery

When interpreting findings of studies of student achievement by the end of Reading Recovery lessons, the methods used need to be considered. In this section, three groups of studies are presented:

- studies without comparison groups,
- studies with comparison groups or with the use of comparative cohort data, and
- studies with randomized control groups.

Studies without comparison groups

One method used to evaluate the impact of Reading Recovery is to measure shifts in children's achievement between entry and exit points. As described in Chapter 8, the New Zealand Ministry of Education provides annual reports on national Reading Recovery data [that is, results from the Observation Survey (Clay, 2002, 2006) and the Burt Word Reading Test — New Zealand Revision (Gilmore, Croft, & Reid, 1981)] which show that the majority of Reading Recovery children make the shifts needed to have their series of lessons discontinued.

A recent evaluation of Reading Recovery (McDowall, Boyd, Hodgen, with van Vliet, 2005) carried out by the New Zealand Council for Educational Research (NZCER) for the New Zealand Ministry of Education included an analysis of the national data collected in 2003.[1] The effect sizes (Cohen's *d*) for students whose lessons were discontinued suggest considerable growth (Instructional Text Level scores, 7.7; Burt Word Reading Test scores, 3.8; and Clay Writing Vocabulary scores, 2.6). The effect sizes for students who were referred also indicate growth although, as would be expected, to a lesser degree (Instructional Text Level scores, 2.2; Burt Word Reading Test scores, 1.7; and Clay Writing Vocabulary scores, 1.6). Both sets of effect sizes are likely to be conservative.[2] They do not discount for growth as a result of maturation or expected classroom progress, or for regression to the mean.

In an earlier and much smaller New Zealand study, Fletcher-Flinn, White, and Nicholson (1998) also produced effect sizes for the Text Level

---

1 In addition to analysis of the national data, this evaluation involved a national survey of Reading Recovery teachers; a national survey of principals from Reading Recovery and non-Reading Recovery schools; interviews with staff from eight case study schools selected for their effective implementation of Reading Recovery; interviews with a sample of Reading Recovery Tutors/Teacher Leaders and teachers; and focus groups with regional Reading Recovery Tutors/Teacher Leaders and teachers.

2 The effect sizes are likely to be conservative for two reasons. One is that correlation coefficients were not used (the correlations between initial and final scores were low), and the other is because, for consistency, the standard deviations associated with the final, as opposed to initial, scores were used (typically there is a greater spread in the post-intervention scores).

and Burt Word Reading Test scores for the 13 Reading Recovery students in their study (0.63 and 0.76 respectively). If the same calculations used to determine effect sizes in the study of McDowall et al. (2005) are used with the means and standard deviations provided by Fletcher-Flinn et al., the effect sizes increase (1.98 and 2.02 respectively). These are closer to the figures McDowall et al. cite for referred students than for those whose lessons were discontinued. This might be expected given that Fletcher-Flinn et al. tested after an average of only 50 lessons, and consequently only two of the children had made the progress necessary to have their lessons discontinued.

There has been some criticism of data showing the effectiveness of Reading Recovery using student results on tests from the Observation Survey (e.g., Center, Wheldall, & Freeman, 1992; Chapman & Tunmer, 1991). Such critics argue that

- the text reading level measures are not standardized and are therefore subject to tester interpretation,

- the text reading level scale is not an interval scale, and children with lower starting points progress more quickly through the levels,

- none of the tests from the Observation Survey adequately assess metalinguistic skills shown to be necessary for reading success, for example phonological recoding,

- the tests focus on what is taught, and so make it more likely for Reading Recovery children to attain higher scores; and that

- the same Reading Recovery teachers who teach the children also do the testing (an inaccurate claim).

Such critics argue that in addition to the Observation Survey, studies of Reading Recovery should include standardized and criterion-referenced assessments, including those focusing on metalinguistic skills. A number of studies have done this. Fogarty and Greaves (2004) measured changes in the phonological awareness and recoding skills of 29 Year 1 Reading Recovery children from six schools in Melbourne, Australia. A comparison of the pre- and post-test data showed significant differences on 11 of the 15 phonological processing measures, and the authors acknowledge that ceiling effects may have accounted for a lack of significance in the remaining four. These results, particularly the positive results on the tests requiring phonological recoding, led the authors to conclude that the children had acquired the alphabetical principle. They expressed surprise at this finding given their understanding that

Reading Recovery does not offer systematic training in phonological recoding skills. They acknowledge that their results lend support to Clay's (1991) claim that the alphabetic principle can be acquired incidentally in Reading Recovery lessons.

The Fletcher-Flinn, White, and Nicholson (1998) study discussed earlier also focused on the acquisition of phonemic awareness and phonological processing skills. They found that on average the 13 Reading Recovery children made 'significant and substantial gains' on all the literacy and language measures used at pre- and post-test (p. 13). The largest effect sizes were from a test of children's phonemic awareness (2.66) and from a test of their verbal understanding and general language skills (2.13). If the method of calculation used on the McDowall et al. (2005) figures are used here, these effect sizes are lower (1.42 and 0.75 respectively). Unlike the findings of Fogarty and Greaves (2004), few children at post-test could pronounce the pseudowords in the test of phonological recoding. The authors concluded from these results that Reading Recovery should be adapted to include systematic instruction in phonological processing skills and tests to assess progress in these skills. Caution should be taken when drawing conclusions such as this, however, due to the small sample size, because tests were conducted after an average of only 50 lessons [the equivalent of 10 weeks compared with the 15-week time period used by Fogarty and Greaves (2004)], and because only two of the children had made the progress needed to have their lessons discontinued.

Findings discussed in this section indicate that Reading Recovery children make considerable progress during Reading Recovery as measured by the Observation Survey assessments and by other standardized and criterion-referenced tests focusing on a wide range of different skills. These include reading words in context and isolation, comprehension, verbal and general language skills, and metalinguistic skills. However, without comparison or control groups it is difficult to gauge whether, or by how much, the progress made is greater than could be expected without the intervention. With this in mind, attention shifts to studies with comparison data.

Studies with comparison groups

Studies with comparison groups help show whether shifts in children's achievement during Reading Recovery are greater than those which would occur without the intervention as a result of maturation and general classroom progress. It is important to be aware of the composition of comparison groups in different studies. Of the studies presented in this section, two compare the achievement shifts of Reading Recovery children with their cohorts in over 160 schools (Ainley & Fleming, 2000;

Ainley, Fleming & McGregor, 2002), one with a comparative normative group (Auditor General of Victoria, 2003), and three with low progress comparative groups (Chapman, Tunmer, & Prochnow, 2001; Glynn et al., 1989; Trethowan, Harvey, & Fraser, 1996). In all cases the comparison groups comprise children with higher initial scores than the Reading Recovery groups, even the studies with low-progress comparison groups. This is because the low-progress comparison groups comprise children whose initial achievement is not low enough to make them candidates for Reading Recovery. For all these studies, some of the 'increase' displayed by Reading Recovery children could be attributable to regression to the mean. This is a statistical phenomenon whereby those with the lowest pre-test scores are more likely to show a greater rate of improvement regardless of the amount of learning that occurs.

A measure common to four of these studies is text reading level. The Auditor General of Victoria (2003) found that the gap between text reading levels of Year 1 children who participated in Reading Recovery in 1999 to 2001 and that of the comparative, normative group was considerably reduced. Data on 4529 Year 1 Australian children from Catholic primary schools in Victoria in 1998 (Ainley & Fleming, 2000) and 5393 in 2000 (Ainley, Fleming & McGregor, 2002) showed that Reading Recovery children gained on average four text reading levels more than the rest of their cohort. The smaller Melbourne study of Trethowan et al. (1996) and New Zealand study of Glynn et al. (1989) also showed that on average the Reading Recovery group made greater shifts in text reading levels than the low progress comparison groups. However, comparisons made between shifts in text reading level need to be treated with caution when the initial text levels of the Reading Recovery group are lower than the comparison group, as is the case with these studies. This is because the text reading level scale is not an interval scale, and so a gain of equal magnitude cannot be assumed to represent an equal gain in achievement when the starting book levels are different (Clay, 1993). It is therefore difficult to tell in real terms how much greater the gains made by Reading Recovery children really were.

In addition to shifts in text reading level, Trethowan et al. (1996), Ainley and Fleming (2000), and Ainley et al. (2002) used the Burt Word Reading Test (Gilmore, Croft, & Reid, 1981). Trethowan et al. found that on average the 12 Reading Recovery children achieved significantly higher results on the Burt Word Reading Test than the low-progress children. Ainley and Fleming found for the 1998 cohort, and Ainley et al. for the 2000 cohort, that by the end of Year 1, the Reading Recovery students made greater gains on the Burt Word Reading Test than all other children, although this difference was not statistically significant for the 2000 cohort.

In addition to text reading level and the Burt Word Reading Test, Ainley and Fleming (2000) used the five other tests from the Observation Survey to gain a composite measure of reading achievement at the beginning and end of Year 1. They then used hierarchical linear modelling — a method which enables analysis of influences at different levels (in this case school/class and student) to identify factors which influence reading development. They found a significant effect on achievement growth over Year 1 for students participating in Reading Recovery and that students in Reading Recovery made greater progress during Year 1 than other students, other things being equal.

In a smaller New Zealand study, Chapman, Tunmer, and Prochnow (2001) produced quite different findings. By the end of Year 2, the 26 discontinued Reading Recovery children did not perform significantly better on text reading level or on measures assessing phonological processing skills, contextual facilitation, word identification, reading comprehension, and spelling than the 20 children in the poor reader comparison group. Nor were there significant differences in the reading and academic self-concept of the two groups.

Chapman et al. (2001) acknowledge their results might appear surprising given those reported in the international research. They explain the differences by hypothesizing that New Zealand children are more likely to be encouraged to use context cues to identify unfamiliar words. They base this on their finding that the Reading Recovery and poor reader comparison groups had deficiencies in phonological processing skills prior to and during Reading Recovery, and that Reading Recovery did not reduce these deficiencies.

As previously observed by Schwartz (2005) and McGee (2006), an alternative explanation is that the poor reader comparison group may in fact have been an average or low average group. This may have come about because the retrospective matching procedures excluded any low-performing children who entered Reading Recovery after the start of the second year from the poor reader comparison group. If the poor reader comparison group were actually an average/low average group, the similarity in performance of this group and the Reading Recovery group following the intervention would be expected. That there were no significant differences at the end of Year 1 on all of the tests used might be seen to disconfirm Schwartz's argument. However, while there were no significant differences for each of the tests individually, the pattern across all the tests is the same, that is, the poor reader comparison group outperformed the Reading Recovery group. If the poor reader comparison group truly were comprised of low-progress children comparable to those of the Reading Recovery group, you would expect a more variable pattern. Chapman et al.'s use of a series of analyses of variance only shows one part of the story in this study because of the extreme variability within groups on some tests. It is possible that a wider analysis looking at not only changes in mean but variability in the groups would give a richer picture of what is happening in the tests. As McGee (2006) notes, given that up to 14 tests were used at any one data collection point, it is surprising that the authors used a series of analyses of variance rather than multivariate analysis of co-variance, which would control for initial differences. McGee also argues that the initial difference between the Reading Recovery and comparison group may have been significant if a less conservative statistic than Scheffes was used. Finally, caution should also be taken with the results of Chapman et al. (2001) due to the small and not necessarily representative sample.

Schwartz's argument can also be applied to the small New Zealand study conducted by Glynn et al. (1989), summarized in Chapter 2, which found no significant differences in the post-test scores of their New Zealand Reading Recovery and low-progress comparison groups on a cloze test used to measure syntactic awareness. In this study, the initial performance of the low-progress comparison group was much higher than the Reading Recovery group — a difference Clay (1991, p. 88) describes as a 'major threat' to the internal validity of the study. If the low-progress comparison group were really an average/low average group, the similarity in performance of this group and the Reading Recovery group following the intervention would be expected.

As illustrated in this section, it can be difficult to draw conclusions about the relative shifts of Reading Recovery and comparison groups due to the lack of equivalence in their initial performance. Consequently, there has been an ongoing call for studies with randomized controlled trials (Center et al., 1992; Nicholson, 1989; Reynolds & Wheldall, 2007).

Randomized controlled trials

In randomized controlled trials (RCTs), low-progress readers are randomly allocated to experiment and control groups. This method is the most effective in demonstrating causality and controlling threats to internal validity. However, there are ethical issues associated with RCTs because they require that some children identified as needing intervention either miss out or have their entry delayed. Consequently, very few studies of this nature have been conducted in New Zealand and Australia.

One study using RCTs was conducted in New South Wales, Australia (Center, Wheldall, Freeman, Outhred, & McNaught, 1995). The sample consisted of low-progress children from 10 schools randomly assigned to a Reading Recovery group (31 students), or to a control group (39 students). Children were tested at four time points: just before the intervention (pre-test); 15 weeks later (post-test), approximately 15 weeks after the post-test (short-term maintenance); and 12 months after the post-test (long-term maintenance).

The authors used eight measures, categorized into two groups: one group of five tests focusing on words read in context and isolation and one group of three tests focusing on metalinguistic skills. At post-test the Reading Recovery children average score was significantly higher than control children on all five tests measuring words read in context or isolation and on the Word Attack Skills Test measuring phonological recoding. There were no significant differences on the Syntactic Awareness (Cloze) Test and the phonemic awareness measure. These differences were achieved in only 15 weeks. Reading Recovery is designed to vary according to individual need, and the final weeks are shown to be those in which the hardest-to-teach Reading Recovery children make the greatest shifts (Clay, 2001).

Discussion of Reading Recovery outcomes for children

Studies reviewed in this section show the complexities in drawing conclusions about the relative impact of Reading Recovery given the associated sampling and ethical issues discussed — and in particular the very small sample sizes of some studies. However, taking into account these complexities, the studies from New Zealand and Australia, with the exception of Chapman et al. (2001), suggest that children receiving Reading Recovery make greater progress than could be expected without the intervention on measures from the Observation Survey and on external standardized measures assessing reading words in context and isolation, and reading comprehension. These findings are consistent with the conclusions drawn in overviews and meta-analyses of the international research literature (Askew, Kaye, Frasier, Mobasher, Anderson, & Rodriguez, 2003; D'Agostino & Murphy, 2004; Rhodes-Kline, 1997; Shanahan & Barr, 1995; Wasik & Slavin, 1993).

It is more difficult to draw conclusions on tests assessing metalinguistic skills because different measures are used in different studies, making comparisons difficult. Chapman et al. (2001) found no significant differences between the Reading Recovery and low-progress comparison group outcomes on their tests of metalinguistic skills. As discussed, however, their findings may in part be attributable to the nature of their sample. This is not in question for the study of Center et al. (1995) who found in their RCT study that the Reading Recovery children had a significantly higher averaged score on the test of phonological recoding. There were no significant differences in the experimental and control groups on tests of phonemic and syntactic awareness.

Some argue that Reading Recovery could be more effective if it included systematic instruction in phonological processing skills (Chapman et al., 2001; Fletcher-Flinn et al., 1998). This argument has, from time to time, been picked up by policy advisers. For example, the New Zealand Literacy Experts Group (Ministry of Education, 1999b, p. 6) recommended to the New Zealand Government that 'further New Zealand research be carried out to determine whether Reading Recovery is effective as it could be' and that Reading Recovery place 'greater emphasis on explicit instruction in phonological awareness and the use of spelling-to-sound patterns in orgnizing unfamiliar words in text.'

To date, no research on the inclusion of the systematic instruction of phonological processing skills in Reading Recovery lessons (and the associated changes to the intervention that would be necessary to accommodate this) has been conducted in New Zealand or Australia. It is therefore not possible to comment on the relative impact this would have on the effectiveness of the intervention. It would be unwise to proceed with the second recommendation unless research indicates that such an approach increases the effectiveness of Reading Recovery.

Progress of students after Reading Recovery

There has been much interest in the achievement of children once they leave Reading Recovery. In this section, research findings are reported on children's achievement three to four months following Reading Recovery, one year after, and in the longer term.

Progress in the three to four months following Reading Recovery

As outlined earlier, Center et al. (1995) assessed the Reading Recovery and control groups in their RCT 15 weeks after the post-test. They found the Reading Recovery group still scored significantly higher than the control group on all five tests measuring words read in context or isolation. This time the Reading Recovery group scored significantly higher than the control group on the Phonemic Awareness Test but not on the Word Attack Skills Test — a reversal of the post-test finding discussed earlier. As in the post-test, there were no significant differences in the Syntactic Awareness (Cloze) Test. Center et al. found that although the Reading Recovery group still had a significantly higher average score than the control group in six of the eight tests used, there was a decrease in the large effect sizes shown in the post-test.

This finding of slower rates of progress immediately following Reading Recovery is consistent with Glynn et al. (1989) who claimed that the Reading Recovery children in their study gained no text reading levels during the 3 months following the intervention. Meta-analyses and overviews of the international research literature also show slower rates of progress after Reading Recovery lessons end (D'Agostino & Murphy, 2004; Shanahan & Barr, 1995). This finding could be expected given that children are no longer receiving daily, one-to-one tutoring with a specialist. Interestingly, the meta-analyses and overviews of the literature show that an initial slower rate of progress on completion of Reading Recovery tends to be followed by a later increased rate of growth in the subsequent 1 to 2 years (D'Agostino & Murphy 2004; Shanahan & Barr, 1995).

Progress one year after Reading Recovery

There is relatively little evidence from New Zealand and Australia about Reading Recovery student outcomes one year after completing the intervention. This makes it difficult to comment on whether or not the longer-term trend described above is evident in these contexts.

Smith (1994) used the entry and exit Reading Recovery and post-intervention achievement data of children from a region in New Zealand to conduct a two-phase study of children who received Reading Recovery in 1986–1988. The second phase involved comparing the text reading, word identification, and writing vocabulary scores of 37 matched pairs of ESOL (English for Speakers of Other Languages) and non-ESOL students in each of the 3 years after Reading Recovery lessons were discontinued. Smith found that the majority (95%) of the Reading Recovery children in her study were able to read at or above their chronological age 1 year after participating in Reading Recovery but that their ability to read words in isolation had slowed. However, without a comparison group comprising low-progress children who did not receive Reading Recovery, it is difficult to determine the relative meaning of the gains.

Center et al. (1995) compared the Reading Recovery and control groups in their Randomized Controlled Trials 12 months after the post-test. They found the Reading Recovery group had a significantly higher text reading level average than the control group, but they did not attain significantly higher averaged scores on the other seven tests. However, the authors recommend caution when considering these results because, by the time of testing, the control group included only 16 of the original 39 children. Fifteen of the lowest achieving original control group had been removed from the study as they had been selected to participate in Reading Recovery. The authors acknowledge that the remaining members of the control group would therefore be those with the highest initial scores and so no longer comparable with the Reading Recovery group.

Chapman et al. (2001) found that one year after Reading Recovery lessons ended there were no significant differences between the Reading

Recovery and poor reader comparison groups in text reading level or on any of the other measures of reading achievement or reading self-concept. This is not surprising given that in this study no significant differences in the performance of the Reading Recovery and the poor reader comparison groups were found at the first checkpoint.

Given the small amount of evidence and the mixed findings relating to children's performance 1 year after Reading Recovery lessons are discontinued, it is difficult to draw conclusions. However, the studies presented in the following section provide evidence to suggest that many New Zealand and Australian Reading Recovery children maintain their gains in the longer term.

Progress in the longer term

Because of the sampling challenges and ethical issues of longitudinal experimental or quasi-experimental designs, few studies focusing on Reading Recovery outcomes in the longer term involve comparison or control groups. Instead, some make use of statewide or national standards. For example, the Annual Report of the New South Wales Department of Education and Training (2004) concludes that many ex-Reading Recovery children continued to perform at a level considered acceptable for their class cohort by showing that most reached the minimum literacy standard set for the Year 3 (77.4%) and Year 5 (84.7%) Basic Skills Test.

Smith (1994) refers to assessment norms to measure continuing progress. She found the majority of the students in her study were able to read at or above their chronological age in their second and third years following Reading Recovery. Her finding that by the third year only about a quarter were reading isolated words with achievement ages at or above their chronological age led her to conjecture that some children might have benefited from further in-class instruction on word level analysis at the multisyllabic word level after finishing Reading Recovery with average levels of achievement.

In the absence of comparison or control groups, other studies use statewide cohort assessment results for comparative purposes. When considering the findings of these studies, it is important to remember that one aim of Reading Recovery is to lift a child's achievement to within the average band of achievement for his or her *class*. You therefore could not reasonably expect all low-performing children to reach the average achievement of their cohort statewide, but if Reading Recovery was meeting its aim there would be a decreased variation in the statewide distribution.

Rowe's (1997) study of factors affecting students' literacy development from 1988 to 1991 involved a sample of 5000 school entry to Grade

6 children and their teachers from 100 schools in Victoria, Australia. Rowe concluded that Reading Recovery is meeting its intended purpose on finding the variation in reading comprehension and Reading Profile Band test scores of the 147 ex-Reading Recovery children in his longitudinal study to be smaller than those of their non-Reading Recovery counterparts. By Grades 5 and 6, the Reading Recovery children in the study, whose scores were clustered at the low range when entering Reading Recovery, had the same range of scores and fewer low scores than the general school population, suggesting the effectiveness of Reading Recovery in the longer term.

Ainley et al. (2002) followed the progress of the 1998 cohort of Year 1 children (4529 children from 164 schools) in the study of Ainley and Fleming (2000) through to the end of Year 3. As could be expected, they found the Reading Recovery students scored lower than their peers on the statewide assessment programme, the Achievement Improvement Monitor (AIM) administered at the end of Year 3. They had, however, made greater gains on average than the average cohort gains. The *Improving Literacy Standards in Government Schools* (Auditor General of Victoria, 2003) report shows the 2000 cohort of Year 3 children were close to reaching the levels of their non-Reading Recovery peers on the statewide AIM test at the end of Year 3. There was less variation in the distribution of scores for the Reading Recovery children compared with the remainder of the Year 3 cohort. These findings suggest that the Reading Recovery students improved and moved closer to the achievement levels of their peers.

The authors of *Improving Literacy Standards in Government Schools* (Auditor General of Victoria, 2003) concluded that their capacity to comment on the effectiveness of Reading Recovery was hindered by their research design. The results of Reading Recovery children would need to have been compared, not with the whole cohort of Year 3 students, but with a group of children with similarly low initial scores. Such an argument might also apply to the study of Ainley et al. (2002) described earlier. The Auditor General of Victoria recommended that the Department develop a rigorous evaluation methodology involving the establishment of comparative groups of children not involved in Reading Recovery.

The only study which does compare longer-term Reading Recovery children's outcomes with other initially low-performing children is Wade and Moore (1998). They compared the performance of 121 former Reading Recovery children then in Years 5 and 6 from 13 schools in New Zealand and two states of Australia with 121 non-Reading Recovery children of a similar age and with similar primary school experiences drawn from the same schools. The comparison group was made up of children who were mainly average or below average readers for their class, but more able than the Reading Recovery children in Year 1. Results showed that the ex-Reading Recovery children had significantly higher reading accuracy and comprehension scores on the Neale Analysis of Reading Ability, reported significantly more positive attitudes to reading as measured by a Likert scale, and reported reading significantly more books. In response to an open-ended interview question 'What do you do if you are stuck on a word?' Reading Recovery children mentioned specific strategies 136 times compared with 64 mentions from the comparison group. The authors concluded that Reading Recovery children were continuing to use the strategies they were taught to become independent readers and that improvement in reading achievement and attitudes to reading can be retained in the long-term.

Discussion about progress after Reading Recovery

There are some limitations in studies using statewide cohort data for comparative purposes. This information is not fine grained enough to tell us what proportion of the Reading Recovery children were working within the average band of their particular classes in their particular schools. The lack of comparison groups with similarly low initial reading performance limits the possibility of determining how the Reading Recovery children might have performed without the intervention. The one study involving a low-progress comparison group to examine the relative outcomes of Reading Recovery children in the longer term (Wade & Moore, 1998) suggests that Reading Recovery children can continue to outperform their low-progress peers.

The question of whether or not Reading Recovery can be considered an 'inoculation' that accounts for all, most, or some children remaining at average class achievement levels in the longer term is worthy of some consideration. The focus of reading instruction changes over time with increasing emphasis placed on the capacity to comprehend more complex text, requiring the development of strategic activities not necessarily needed by 6-year-olds in Reading Recovery. Inadequate classroom literacy instruction in the years following Reading Recovery will therefore impact on children's later achievement — something beyond Reading Recovery's sphere of influence.

Out-of-school factors may also contribute to children's continuing progress after Reading Recovery. Illness, absenteeism, and home circumstances may continue to have an ongoing impact on children's reading performance in the years following Reading Recovery.

Given these caveats, there exists noteworthy evidence of children who appear to have retained the benefits of a series of Reading Recovery lessons, as many as 4 to 5 years afterwards.

Progress of particular groups within Reading Recovery

What does the research tells us about the comparable gains made by different groups of children *within* Reading Recovery? Of particular importance in New Zealand is the effectiveness of Reading Recovery for Maori[3] children and Pacific[4] children relative to their New Zealand European Reading Recovery peers. This arises from concern about the findings of international (Telford & Caygill, 2007; Chamberlain, 2008) and national (Crooks & Flockton, 2005) assessments, showing Maori and Pacific children to be over-represented in the tail of literacy performance. In this context, the New Zealand Literacy Taskforce (Ministry of Education, 1999a) emphasized the importance of cultural affirmation of children by Reading Recovery teachers, and the New Zealand Literacy Experts Group (Ministry of Education, 1999b) recommended further research into the effectiveness of Reading Recovery for Maori and Pacific children, and for other children whose home language differs from the language of instruction. Similarly, the Australian research literature as summarized by Exley and Bliss (2004) identifies groups of indigenous children as those most at risk of being disaffected by schooling, and least able to enhance their future opportunities in Australian education systems.

The following sections examine the relative impact of Reading Recovery for different groups of children whose lessons were discontinued and for children who were referred[5] to other forms of intervention.

Children whose lessons are discontinued

This section focuses on Reading Recovery children who made the progress needed to have their lessons discontinued. It considers the relative gains of these students (according to personal characteristics such as ethnicity and first language; school characteristics, such as decile; and scores on entry to Reading Recovery) in relation to their peers.

School and personal characteristics

In response to the need for further research into the effectiveness of Reading Recovery for Maori and Pacific children, McDowall et al. (2005) analysed the 2003 national Reading Recovery data collected by

---

3 Indigenous people of New Zealand.

4 Pacific is a general term used to describe a wide range of Pacific nations such as Samoa, Tonga, Niue, and so forth. The term represents a diverse range of cultures and languages, not a homogeneous group.

5 Children are usually 'referred' to other specialist help if, after approximately 20 weeks, it is judged that they will not be able to continue learning in the classroom programme without additional support.

the New Zealand Ministry of Education according to school and student characteristics. They found that differences in averaged initial scores varied in relation to ethnicity, school decile, school authority, school size, the size of the population centre, and the proportion of Maori enrolment. Many of these characteristics are associated. For example, many low-decile schools have high Maori or Pacific enrolment, and the majority of Pacific children attend schools in mainly urban areas. Children's averaged initial scores decreased with decreasing decile schools and decreased with an increase in proportion of Maori enrolment.

McDowall et al. (2005) found that the inequalities which were a feature of averaged initial scores were diminished in the final scores for children whose lessons were discontinued. Those with the lowest initial scores tended to make the greatest gains. Overall, the outcomes for Maori and Pacific children who had their Reading Recovery lessons discontinued were equitable with those of other children given their different entry points and the ceiling effect of some tests. In general, Maori and Pacific students whose series of lessons were discontinued received a greater number of lessons than other students. This finding supports the practice of providing more lessons to those students with greatest need in order to ensure equitable outcomes. This equalizing effect was particularly evident for the discontinued Pacific children. Outcomes for Maori and Pacific children were related more to the socio-economic status of the school they attended than ethnicity. These findings are consistent with Clay and Watson's (1982) early study on the outcomes of Maori children relative to their New Zealand European peers (summarized in Chapter 2).

New Zealand research (Smith, 1994) also demonstrates that children with first languages other than English can make similar gains to other Reading Recovery children and can, like their peers with English as a first language, continue to succeed after Reading Recovery without further assistance — a finding consistent with the international literature (Ashdown & Simic, 2000; Hobsbaum, 1995; Yukish & Fraas, 2003). Smith analysed the achievement data of 1503 children from a region in New Zealand whose Reading Recovery lessons had been discontinued due to successful results. She found no significant differences between the ESOL and other children in the average text reading level attained by the end of their Reading Recovery lessons. The 37 pairs of ESOL and non-ESOL children who were matched according to their text reading level, word identification, and writing vocabulary scores at the point their lessons were discontinued, continued to progress in each of the 3 succeeding years. At each of the three checkpoints there were no significant differences between the two groups' average text reading levels, the average Burt Word Reading Test scores, or the average raw score or range in scores on the Daniels and Diack spelling test.

Scores on entry to Reading Recovery

In New Zealand it is recommended practice to offer Reading Recovery to children considered to be making the slowest progress on completion of their first year of instruction and as near as possible to their sixth birthday. In Australia (as mentioned earlier) intake policy means there is variation in the amount of time children have been in school prior to entry to Reading Recovery, with resultant age differences.

Some argue that not all children are best placed to make sustained progress at this particular age or stage and that either they should be excluded or their entry delayed. For example, Glynn et al. (1989) and the subsequent *Report of the Literacy Taskforce* (Ministry of Education, 1999a) recommended greater flexibility in the stage at which Reading Recovery is delivered to reflect the range in children's language acquisition. Underlying such recommendations is the belief that there may be an optimal achievement level at which children will most benefit from the intervention — an issue of particular importance to those concerned about the cost effectiveness of Reading Recovery. However, the findings of McDowall et al. (2005) and Anand and Bennie (2005) show very clearly that entry data on the Observation Survey are not predictive of outcomes. These findings are consistent with those of Clay and Tuck's (1991) much earlier study (summarized in Chapter 2) and support their conclusion that it would be ill advised to establish entry criterion according to initial performance.

Referred children

This section focuses on the relative outcomes of different groups of Reading Recovery children referred to other interventions.

McDowall et al. (2005) found that children's initial scores and school and personal characteristics alone did not give enough information to reliably predict whether the outcome for a child would be discontinued or referred — a finding consistent with analysis of the national Reading Recovery data collected by the New Zealand Ministry of Education (Anand & Bennie, 2005). However, initial scores and personal and school characteristics were found to be *suggestive* of outcomes.

Another finding in the McDowall et al. (2005) study was that fewer children from low-decile schools made the accelerated progress needed to have their lessons discontinued, and they spent less time in Reading Recovery before referral decisions were made. The most common reasons for this were transience and referral. There is not enough data to be sure of the reasons for this increased likelihood of referral, but McDowall et al. surmise from their survey and interview data that likely contributing factors were (a) pressure for Reading Recovery places due to low levels of implementation relative to need, (b) less experienced Reading Recovery teachers, and (c) less effective home-school partnerships.

McDowall et al. (2005) also found that Maori students and Pacific students were less likely than those of other ethnicities to make the progress needed to have their lessons discontinued — a finding consistent with concurrent and subsequent Ministry of Education findings (e.g., Ng, 2006). McDowall et al. acknowledge that this may in part be because a high proportion of Maori and Pacific students attend low-decile schools. However, they found that even *within* low-decile schools, Maori and Pacific students received fewer lessons before referral than children of other ethnicities who had similar initial achievement. McDowall et al. also found that while Reading Recovery was effective in reducing initial differences by ethnicity and school type in performance of children whose lessons were discontinued, this was not the case for the small group of children who were referred. They recommend a closer look at the Reading Recovery and classroom experiences of children who are referred, an examination of school decisions about their referral, and fine-tuning of practices where needed. McDowall et al. also suggest that some teachers may need more support developing a wider range of strategies for identifying the cognitive, linguistic, and cultural resources of Maori and Pacific students.

The Queensland study of Exley and Bliss (2004) provides a good example of research into possible approaches for developing such strategies. In their study involving 17 Reading Recovery teachers and 38 children across 13 schools, Exley and Bliss found that children whose Reading Recovery teachers had access to texts developed in collaboration with indigenous writers and artists, and who had access to professional development in a culturally responsive interactive framework were able to make the progress needed to have their lessons discontinued 3½ weeks sooner than those who did not. The authors acknowledge some limitations to this study — in particular the small sample size. However, the study is important in highlighting the need for those working with culturally diverse children to 'cast a critical lens on the appropriateness of resources and teaching interactions to ensure they are providing the most effective teaching experiences' (Exley & Bliss, 2004, p.15).

Discussion of diversity of outcomes

In general, evidence suggests that Reading Recovery meets its aim of producing 'a common outcome despite initial differences' (Clay, 2001, p. 250). The research findings show children's school characteristics (such as socio-economic status) and personal characteristics (such as ethnicity, first language, and initial achievement) do not alone give enough information to reliably predict outcomes, and that the differences in average initial scores are diminished by the point at which lessons are discontinued. This is not surprising given that the intervention is tailored to suit the strengths, needs, pace of learning, and prior knowledge and experiences of individuals in order 'to iron out differences and avoid the negative effects of any prior variables' (Clay, 2001, p. 249).

Many features of Reading Recovery are consistent with those of a recent New Zealand Best Evidence Synthesis of the research (Alton-Lee, 2003[6]), and work in the area of multiliteracies (The New London Group, 2000) show to be important for ensuring successful outcomes for diverse student populations. These features include (a) immersion activities in a secure environment where learners can take risks; (b) broad and flexible guidance that takes into account the sociocultural needs of learners, and draws on their out of school experiences, communities, and discourses; and (c) explicit instruction which includes scaffolding learning, assisting the learner to take control over their learning, using meta-languages to describe discourses of practice, and formative assessment. These criteria appear to align with the characteristics of Reading Recovery.

However, the New Zealand research shows that for a very small group of children — those who do not make the progress needed to have their series of lessons discontinued — initial differences by ethnicity and school decile are not diminished by the point of referral. It is important that further research be carried out to investigate the school and Reading Recovery experiences of these children and the decisions made about their referral. The findings of McDowall et al. (2005) suggest that a useful starting point may be research into teachers' expectations of and instructional approaches with children from diverse cultural backgrounds.

School context of Reading Recovery

According to Clay (2001), the success of Reading Recovery is dependent on organizational change in schools as well as behavioural change in teachers and children. Consistent with this claim is research that shows a strong association between the performance of Reading Recovery children and the *particular* school they attend (Auditor General of Victoria, 2003; McDowall et al., 2005). Differences between schools are likely to reflect differences in contributing populations and to a lesser extent in the implementation of Reading Recovery. Differences in implementation

---

6 In particular, the work of McNaughton (2002).

may include factors such as the degree of resource given to Reading Recovery; classroom instruction in the years before, during, and after Reading Recovery; and the interactions between Reading Recovery and classroom teachers.

Reading Recovery was designed to be 'something extra' for the lowest performing children following 1 year of quality classroom instruction, as opposed to an intervention for all children making slow progress in reading. Robinson (1989) asks whether the introduction of Reading Recovery into schools often precludes analysis of Year 1 instruction and the ways in which Year 1 instruction itself may contribute to the problem of early reading difficulties. She warns that as a result, schools where staff consider the majority of 6-year-olds to need Reading Recovery may reject the intervention because it reaches too few children for the cost of its provision.

The findings of McDowall et al. (2005) suggest that this may be the case in New Zealand, especially in low decile schools where Reading Recovery is less likely to be offered. From their national survey, they found that principals and Reading Recovery teachers from low-decile schools reported large numbers of their children needed Reading Recovery and were more likely to report that five or more children had missed out on a place that year, even when they offered Reading Recovery to 20% or more of the 6-year-old cohort. The main reason schools chose not to offer Reading Recovery was the belief that other interventions better met school and children's needs or could be offered to more children at the same or less cost.

Respondents to the McDowall et al. (2005) national survey reported that the most commonly offered alternative interventions were provided by (a) teacher aides; (b) specialist teachers such as Resource Teachers: Learning and Behaviour, and Resource Teachers: Literacy; and (c) a variety of phonics programmes. McDowall et al. cite survey data suggesting that many schools were not monitoring the effectiveness of these other interventions. They concluded that some schools rated the effectiveness of these other interventions by the number of children they targeted, without taking into account their relative impact on children's performance.

An alternative approach — and one which aligns more closely with Marie Clay's initial intention for Reading Recovery — is to lift the quality of literacy instruction in Year 1. This was a possible alternative to delaying entry into Reading Recovery considered by Wheldall, Center, and Freeman (1993), on finding that a control group of later entrants into Reading Recovery needed significantly fewer lessons to reach the same text reading level as a group who entered after the requisite 12 months.

Evidence from New Zealand and Australia shows that by lifting the quality of literacy instruction in Year 1 it is possible to reduce the number of children who need Reading Recovery and improve their rates of progress (Center, Freeman, & Robertson, 2001; McDowall et al., 2005; Phillips, McNaughton, & MacDonald, 2002; Robinson, 1989). For example, Center et al. found that after literacy professional development for teachers of junior children in six New South Wales schools, children entered Reading Recovery with higher scores, spent significantly less time in Reading Recovery, were less likely to be referred, performed better on four standardized reading measures, and were more likely to be viewed as having had successful experiences of transition from Reading Recovery.

Reading Recovery teachers from eight New Zealand case study schools (McDowall et al., 2005) reported that when policies and practices for ensuring quality literacy instruction in Year 1 were adopted, fewer children needed Reading Recovery, and those who did entered and completed at higher levels than previously. These practices included (a) placing experienced teachers in Year 1 classes; (b) keeping teacher-child ratios low; (c) providing teacher professional development; (d) providing supplementary literacy instruction to Year 1 students considered at risk of falling behind; and (e) providing literacy activities, such as shared story-reading sessions, for the parents and preschool children in the local community.

The staff in one of Robinson's (1989) case study schools also reported that by improving literacy instruction in junior classes, through close collaboration with the Reading Recovery teacher, they had reduced the numbers of children needing Reading Recovery, and decreased the likelihood of them slipping behind once they had finished their series of lessons.

Research findings also suggest a relationship between the quality of classroom instruction during and after Reading Recovery, and progress of ex-Reading Recovery children in the immediate and longer term. Smith (1987 and 1988 cited in Smith, 1994) found that issues relating to post-Reading Recovery classroom instruction were the strongest influence on children's subsequent progress. The factors found to have a negative impact included frequent changes of teacher, no classroom instructional reading, no opportunity to read books independently at an appropriate level, and instruction based on texts that were either too easy or too difficult (Office for Standards in Education, 1993). Wheldall et al. (1993) and Glynn et al. (1989) also hypothesized that the placement of children at incorrect reading levels after leaving Reading Recovery may account for the initial lack of progress by some children.

Both Robinson (1989) and McDowall et al. (2005) found that staff from New Zealand case study schools which focused on lifting the quality of classroom instruction in Years 2 to 3 reported more positive outcomes for children. Close collaboration with Reading Recovery teachers enabled classroom teachers to provide current and ex-Reading Recovery children with reading material at the appropriate level and to provide the opportunities to practice the skills learnt in Reading Recovery considered necessary for their ongoing progress. It also ensured closer monitoring of their achievement which meant ex-Reading Recovery children were less likely to slip behind. Collaborative practices included Reading Recovery teachers engaging in ongoing professional conversations with classroom teachers, demonstrating evidence-based enquiry through their use of achievement data, observing and providing feedback on teachers' literacy instruction, modelling literacy instruction for teachers, and having teachers observe Reading Recovery lessons. They also participated in school literacy initiatives and decision making beyond Reading Recovery.

It is not the primary purpose of Reading Recovery to influence classroom instruction in order to lift the achievement of non-Reading Recovery children. However, some research, while not conclusive, suggests that this may occur in schools with the collaborative practices described above, and in which there are high numbers of teachers trained in Reading Recovery (Elley, 2003).

In March 2003, a representative sample of 61 New Zealand primary schools participated in an NZCER national trial to produce norms for the Supplementary Test of Achievement in Reading (Elley, 2003) for Year 3. At 13 schools, the Year 3 students had much better scores than others at the same decile levels. Subsequent research (Elley, 2004) found 92% of these schools offered Reading Recovery (compared with 67% nationwide). Of the Years 1 and 2 teachers surveyed from these schools, 46% had trained in Reading Recovery. Many of these teachers and all of the principals considered that this training led to improved literacy instruction because it helped teachers understand how their children were learning to read and to identify next teaching steps.

The corollary to these findings is research showing that when these conditions do not exist, Reading Recovery does not have an impact on achievement of non-Reading Recovery children. Wheldall et al. (1993) concluded from their Sydney-based study that Reading Recovery had little impact on classroom programmes. They found no difference on the Macquarie Battery of Tests between children in Reading Recovery schools and matched, low-progress comparison children in non-Reading Recovery schools. They concluded that Reading Recovery was operating independently of school-wide organizational structures. At the time of this study Sydney schools were only in their second year of implementing Reading Recovery, a time period not long enough for the potential systemic benefits of hosting Reading Recovery to be developed. Marie Clay (2001, p. 260) argued that unless research into the effectiveness of Reading Recovery occurs in an education system with a minimum of 3 years' experience of making the intervention work it 'may merely document the growing pains of starting something new, rather than provide a valid test of the programme's effectiveness' and observes that it may take 'three to five years to bed down a programme in a new school setting.'

Findings in the international research literature show the importance for children's achievement of consistency between one-to-one interventions and class settings (Wasik & Slavin, 1993) and of school-wide coherence in approaches to instruction (Newmann, Smith, Allensworth, & Bryk, 2001). The original design of Reading Recovery in which Reading Recovery teachers had concurrent classroom teaching responsibilities, and in which there were frequent changes of teachers in Reading Recovery positions, is one that is likely to support the establishment of school-wide coherence.

When the Reading Recovery teacher is part-time and employed only to deliver Reading Recovery, there is an increased risk of Reading Recovery being seen as a separate remedial programme rather than supplementary to the classroom literacy instruction. When the Reading Recovery teacher is not at staff, syndicate, and literacy meetings and school-wide professional development, schools miss out on the input of a literacy specialist. There are also fewer opportunities for informal conversations between Reading Recovery and classroom teachers during interval and lunchtime breaks. In turn, Reading Recovery teachers may miss out on school-wide professional development and risk losing touch with the context and culture of the school.

In their 2004 national survey, McDowall et al. (2005) found that less than one-third of the Reading Recovery teachers surveyed reported having a class of their own. This was because nearly one-half of these teachers worked part-time to deliver Reading Recovery in one school, or provided Reading Recovery to a range of different schools, and nearly one-quarter of the teachers were employed full-time within one school just to deliver interventions in addition to Reading Recovery.

The decreasing number of Reading Recovery teachers with classroom responsibilities may have contributed to changing perceptions of the purpose and nature of Reading Recovery, as something that exists in isolation from classroom practice and from the wider life of the school. These findings may help explain why over 40% of the principals and Reading Recovery teachers surveyed by McDowall et al. (2005) did not rate their schools' processes for ensuring ongoing communication between Reading Recovery and classroom teachers as 'very effective.'

One solution would be for schools to implement Reading Recovery as it was initially designed. This would involve full-time classroom teachers spending part of each day out of their classroom taking Reading Recovery for a 3- to 4-year period, and then having new teachers taking over this role so that expertise could grow across the school. However, not all schools are in the position to do this.

Another solution can be found in the establishment of a school culture in which the expertise of all staff, including the Reading Recovery teacher, is shared. This raises the question of roles and responsibilities. Who is responsible for ensuring that two-way sharing of literacy expertise between Reading Recovery teachers and other school staff members occurs? Some, such as Robinson (1989), suggest that this is the responsibility of Reading Recovery Tutors/Teacher Leaders and teachers. In contrast, McDowall et al. (2005) concluded that while Reading Recovery teachers saw themselves as having an important role to play in sharing their expertise, they did not have the scope over and above their Reading Recovery work to take on the full responsibility for ensuring this occurred, nor the capacity to lead school change. They found that in the effective case study schools, staff in management positions had established processes and modelled attitudes which supported the development of professional learning communities in which Reading Recovery teachers were valued members. The findings of Timperley, Phillips, and Wiseman (2003) indicate that the responsibility of managing and monitoring systems to support the establishment of strong professional learning communities and to address any barriers to them lies with school leaders.

Discussion of school contexts

Reading Recovery is dependent on organizational change in schools and behavioural change in teachers, and is predicated on quality classroom instruction before, during, and after participation in the intervention (Clay, 2001).

The research findings presented in this section suggest that the type of instruction occurring in junior classes influences the number of children who need Reading Recovery, their achievement on entry, time spent in the intervention, their achievement on leaving, and their progress in the subsequent year. It is important that schools do not lose sight of the fact that Reading Recovery is a supplementary intervention designed for the lowest performing readers after 1 year of quality classroom teaching and learning at school, rather than a remedial programme for all children considered to be making slow progress.

To harness maximum benefit for students in Reading Recovery and for teachers and children across the school as a whole, research suggests that schools can build consistency across Reading Recovery and classroom settings, and incorporate Reading Recovery expertise into school-wide approaches to literacy instruction.

Conclusions

The weight of the New Zealand- and Australian-based research evidence suggests that children who successfully complete Reading Recovery make greater progress than could be expected without the intervention. This is shown to be so when measures associated with Reading Recovery and external measures are used. There is also some evidence to suggest that gains may be retained in the longer term.

Reading Recovery has existed for many years. As Marie Clay (2001) observed, given the changing nature of the societies and school systems in which Reading Recovery operates, further research into its effectiveness is necessary. According to Marie Clay (2001, p. 272), such research is needed 'when a legitimate question is "Do the same results and explanations still hold true?" given that times and settings have changed. Sometimes the answer will be yes, they still hold true; at other times a search for explanations for the directions of change will be indicated.'

One of the most notable changes since the inception of Reading Recovery is the increased cultural and linguistic diversity of local communities resulting from globalization. Research and assessment results suggest that certain groups of children achieve consistently lower scores on international and national literacy assessments. It is important to be assured that interventions such as Reading Recovery address this situation. This necessitates investigation into the relative effectiveness of Reading Recovery for different groups of children receiving the intervention. To date, little research of this nature has been conducted in New Zealand and Australia. The study of McDowall et al. (2005) shows that the outcomes of referred children tended to reflect the same differences by ethnicity shown in initial scores, indicating the importance of further research into the experiences of these children. However, for discontinued children, differences in initial achievement are diminished by the end of Reading Recovery lessons. Such a finding is perhaps not surprising given that one of the aims of Reading Recovery is to produce 'a common outcome despite initial differences' (Clay 2001, p. 250) by tailoring instruction to the strengths and prior experiences of individuals.

References

Ainley, J., & Fleming, M. (2000). *Literacy advance research project: Learning to read in the early primary years.* Melbourne: Catholic Education Commission of Victoria.

Ainley, J., Fleming, M., & McGregor, M. (2002). *Three years on: Literacy advance in the early years and middle primary years.* Melbourne: Catholic Education Commission of Victoria.

Alton-Lee, A. (2003). *Quality teaching for diverse students in schooling: Best evidence synthesis.* Wellington: Ministry of Education.

Anand, V., & Bennie, N. (2005). *Annual monitoring of Reading Recovery: The data for 2003.* Wellington: Ministry of Education.

Ashdown, J., & Simic, O. (2000). Is early literacy intervention effective for English language learners? Evidence from Reading Recovery. *Literacy Teaching and Learning, 5*(1), 27–42.

Askew, B., Kaye, E., Frasier, D., Mobasher, M., Anderson, N., & Rodriguez, Y. (2003). Making a case for prevention in education. In S. Forbes & C. Briggs (Eds.), *Research in Reading Recovery, Volume Two* (pp. 133–158). Portsmouth, NH: Heinemann.

Auditor General of Victoria. (2003). *Improving literacy standards in government schools.* Melborne: Government Printer for the State of Victoria.

Center, Y., Wheldall, K., Freeman, L., Outhred, L., & McNaught, M. (1995). An experimental evaluation of Reading Recovery. *Reading Research Quarterly, 30*(2), 240–263.

Center, Y., Freeman, L., & Robertson, G. (2001). The relative effect of a code-oriented and a meaning-oriented early literacy program on regular and low progress Australian students in Year 1 classrooms which implement Reading Recovery. *International Journal of Disability, Development and Education, 48*(2), 207–232.

Center, Y., Wheldall, K., & Freeman, L. (1992). Evaluating the effectiveness of Reading Recovery: A critique. *Educational Psychology, 12*(3–4), 263–274.

Chamberlain, M. (2008). *PIRLS 2005/2006 in New Zealand: An overview of the national findings from the second cycle of the Progress in International Reading Literacy Study (PIRLS).* Wellington: Ministry of Education.

Chapman, J., & Tunmer, W. (1991). Recovering Reading Recovery. *Australian and New Zealand Journal of Developmental Disabilities, 17*(1), 59–71.

Chapman, J., Tunmer, W., & Prochnow, J. (2001). Does success in the Reading Recovery program depend on developing proficiency in phonological-processing skills? A longitudinal study in a whole language instructional context. *Scientific Studies of Reading, 5*(2), 141–176.

Clay, M. M. (1991). Syntactic awareness and Reading Recovery: A response to Tunmer. *New Zealand Journal of Educational Studies, 26*(1), 87–91.

Clay, M. M. (1993). *Reading Recovery: A guidebook for teachers in training.* Auckland: Heinemann.

Clay, M. M. (2001). *Change over time in children's literacy development.* Auckland: Heinemann.

Clay, M. M. (2002, 2006). *An observation survey of early literacy achievement* (2nd ed.). Auckland: Heinemann.

Clay, M. M., & Tuck, B. (1991). *A study of Reading Recovery sub-groups: Including outcomes for children who did not satisfy discontinuing criteria.* Auckland: University of Auckland.

Clay, M. M., & Watson, B. (1982). *The success of Maori children in the Reading Recovery programme: An overview.* Auckland: Department of Education, University of Auckland.

Crooks, T., & Flockton, L. (2005). *National Education Monitoring Project reading and speaking assessment results 2004.* Otago: Educational Assessment Research Unit.

D'Agostino, J., & Murphy, J. (2004). A meta-analysis of Reading Recovery in United States schools. *Educational Evaluation and Policy Analysis, 26*(1), 23–38.

Elley, W. (2003). *STAR Supplementary test of achievement in reading: Year 3.* Wellington: New Zealand Council for Educational Research.

Elley, W. (2004). Effective reading programmes in the junior school: How some schools produce high literacy levels at Year 3. *Set: Research Information for Teachers, 1,* 2–6.

Exley, B., & Bliss, J. (2004). Using culturally relevant texts and Grant's Holistic Framework to connect indigenous early readers to SAE print-based texts. *Practically Primary, 9*(3), 11–15.

Fletcher-Flinn, C., White, C., & Nicholson, T. (1998). Does Reading Recovery improve phonological skills? *Queensland Journal of Educational Research, 14*(2), 4–28.

Fogarty, J., & Greaves, D. (2004). The overlooked role of phonological processing abilities for successful Reading Recovery program outcomes. In B. Knight & W. Scott (Eds.), *Learning difficulties: Multiple perspectives* (pp. 51–65). Frenchs Forest, NSW: Pearson Education.

Gilmore, A., Croft, C., & Reid, N. (1981). *Burt Word Reading Test — New Zealand revision.* Wellington: New Zealand Council for Educational Research.

Glynn, T., Crooks, T., Bethune, N., Ballard, K., Smith, J., Sherrel, J., Crooks, M., & Mohi, L. (1989). *Reading Recovery in context.* Wellington: Department of Education.

Hobsbaum, A. (1995). Reading Recovery in England. *Literacy, Teaching and Learning: An International Journal of Early Literacy, 1*(2), 22–39.

McDowall, S., Boyd, S., & Hodgen, E., with van Vliet, T. (2005). *Reading Recovery in New Zealand: Uptake, implementation, and outcomes, especially in relation to Maori and Pacifika students.* Wellington: Ministry of Education. Available at: http://www.tki.org.nz/r/literacy_numeracy/pdf/reading_rec_uptake.pdf

McGee, L. (2006). Research on Reading Recovery: What is the impact on early literacy research? *Literacy Teaching and Learning, 10*(2), 1–50.

McNaughton, S. (2002). *Meeting of minds.* Wellington: Learning Media Ltd.

Ministry of Education. (1999a). *Report of the Literacy Taskforce; Advice to the Government that 'By 2005, every child turning nine will be able to read, write, and do maths for success.'* Wellington: Ministry of Education.

Ministry of Education. (1999b). *Literacy Experts Group: Report to the Secretary for Education.* Wellington: Ministry of Education.

New South Wales Department of Education and Training (2004). 2004 Annual Report, Statistical Compendium. At: https://www.det.nsw.edu.au/reports_stats/annual_reports/report2004.htm

Newmann, F., Smith, B., Allensworth, E., & Bryk, A. (2001). Instructional program coherence: What is it and why it should guide school improvement policy. *Educational Evaluation and Policy Analysis, 23*(4), 297–321.

Ng, L. (2006). *Annual monitoring of Reading Recovery: The data for 2005.* Wellington: Ministry of Education.

Nicholson, T. (1989). A comment on Reading Recovery. *New Zealand Journal of Educational Studies, 24*, 95–97.

Office for Standards in Education. (1993). *Reading Recovery in New Zealand: A report from the office of Her Majesty's Chief Inspector of Schools.* London: Office for Standards in Education.

Phillips, G., McNaughton, S., & MacDonald, S. (2002). Picking up the pace: Effective literacy interventions for accelerated progress over the transition into decile 1 schools. Wellington: Ministry of Education.

Reynolds, M., & Wheldall, K. (2007). Reading Recovery 20 years down the track: Looking forward, looking back. *International Journal of Disability, Development and Education, 54*(2), 199–223.

Rhodes-Kline, A. (1997). *Sustained effects of Reading Recovery: A review of the literature.* Orono, ME: University of Maine Center for Early Literacy.

Robinson, V. (1989). Some limitations of systematic adaptation: The implementation of Reading Recovery. *New Zealand Journal of Educational Studies, 24*(1), 35–45.

Rowe, K. (1997). Factors affecting students' progress in reading: Key findings from a longitudinal study. In S. Swartz & A. Klein (Eds.), *Research in Reading Recovery* (pp. 53–101). Portsmouth, NH: Heinemann.

Schwartz, R. (2005). Literacy learning of at-risk first-grade students in the Reading Recovery early intervention. *Journal of Educational Psychology*, *97*(2), 257–267.

Shanahan, T., & Barr, R. (1995). Reading Recovery: An independent evaluation of the effects of an early instructional intervention for at risk learners. *Reading Research Quarterly*, *30*(4), 958–995.

Smith, P. (1994). Reading Recovery and children with English as a second language. *New Zealand Journal of Educational Studies*, *29*(2), 141–159.

Telford, M., & Caygill, R. (2007). *PISA 2006: How ready are our 15-year-olds for tomorrow's world?* Wellington: Ministry of Education.

The New London Group. (2000). A pedagogy of multiliteracies designing social futures. In B. Cope & M. Kalantzis (Eds.), *Multiliteracies: Literacy learning and the design of social futures* (pp. 9–37). London: Routledge.

Timperley, H., Phillips, G., & Wiseman, J. (2003). *The sustainability of professional development in literacy: Parts one and two.* Wellington: Ministry of Education.

Trethowan, V., Harvey, D., & Fraser, C. (1996). Reading Recovery: Comparison between its efficacy and normal classroom instruction. *The Australian Journal of Language and Literacy*, *19*(1), 29–37.

Wade, B., & Moore, M. (1998). Attitudes to reading: A longitudinal study of the effectiveness of Reading Recovery. *New Zealand Journal of Educational Studies*, *3*(1), 3–17.

Wasik, B., & Slavin, R. (1993). Preventing early reading failure with one-to-one tutoring: A review of five programmes. *Reading Research Quarterly*, *28*(2), 179–200.

Wheldall, K., Center, Y., & Freeman, L. (1993). Reading Recovery in Sydney primary schools. *Australasian Journal of Special Education*, *17*(2), 51–63.

Yukish, J., & Fraas, J. (2003). Success of old order Amish children in a strategy-oriented program for children at risk of failure in reading. In S. Forbes & C. Briggs (Eds.), *Research in Reading Recovery, Volume Two* (pp. 39–52). Portsmouth, NH: Heinemann.

5

Reading Recovery Research in North America

Robert M. Schwartz

The initial development of Reading Recovery in New Zealand established the foundation for early literacy intervention. This foundation included teaching procedures grounded in theory and expert practice, continuously modified through ongoing observation, objective recording of behaviour, and analysis of children's literacy learning examined in the light of theory. It also included initial research evidence on intervention effects, implementation variables, replication, sustained effects, and subgroup performance. Research in North America over the last 25 years has built on this foundation. This research, together with the international research reviewed in the contiguous chapters, epitomizes research in support of evidence-based practice.

Since Marie Clay's initial development studies, a strong and varied international research base has developed around the practices and outcomes of Reading Recovery. For instance, there have been carefully controlled experimental studies that show the efficacy of Reading Recovery in lifting students' literacy achievement in schools. Numerous evaluation studies continue to be undertaken every year that show the replication of results across thousands of education settings. More recently there have been meta-analyses and large-scale independent assessments of the body of research arising from Reading Recovery. And data from research at every level have been used to continuously develop and refine Reading Recovery professional practice, optimising the outcomes of local implementations everywhere.

This chapter is organized in three parts. The first section highlights experimental research on Reading Recovery outcomes for children published in North America, with specific attention to five selected studies. The second section validates experimental research evidence by focusing on Reading Recovery evaluation research that documents the intervention's effectiveness, sustained effects, and reduction of achievement gaps among subgroups. Finally, the research efforts are set in the context of the political and educational climate in North America, particularly the United States.

Experimental studies extending Marie Clay's Reading Recovery research

When Reading Recovery was introduced in the United States during the 1984–1985 school year, it was not possible to predict the future impact the intervention would have throughout North America. Yet the faculty at The Ohio State University realized that the endeavour required a long-term commitment to evaluation and research in the new context. They immediately put in motion a research agenda that built on the foundational research of Marie Clay in New Zealand. Subsequently researchers at other Reading Recovery university training centres and independent researchers explored the effectiveness of the intervention.

Across the years, a number of rigorous experimental trials have been conducted and published in peer-reviewed journals. Five of those studies are presented in this section in the order in which they were published. The Pinnell (1989) and the Schwartz (2005a) studies compared the progress of Reading Recovery children with similar low-performing students without the intervention from the same schools. Studies by Pinnell, Lyons, DeFord, Bryk, & Seltzer (1994), Schwartz (2005a), and Quay, Steele, Johnson, and Hortman (2001) all used random assignment procedures to compare the progress of initially equivalent groups with and without intervention support. The Pinnell et al. (1994) and the Iversen and Tunmer (1993) studies provided component analyses of various aspects of Reading Recovery and early intervention.

Pinnell (1989)

This first large-scale experimental study of Reading Recovery in the United States is described fully in Pinnell, DeFord, & Lyons (1988). The study included 32 Reading Recovery teachers, 12 with 1 year of Reading Recovery experience and 20 who were receiving training during the 1985–1986 data collection. Like Marie Clay's initial studies, this research was based on a relatively new implementation of Reading Recovery. The research groups included first grade students from the lowest 20% of students in classrooms taught by the Reading Recovery teachers, and similar low-performing students from other first grade classrooms in the same schools. A shared-classroom staffing model was used where Reading Recovery teachers taught first grade for half of their assignment and Reading Recovery for the other half of their day.

The Reading Recovery teachers taught all children in the bottom 20% of their classrooms. Children who qualified in the other first grade classrooms were randomly assigned to Reading Recovery tutoring or to an alternative compensatory programme (control group). This alternative programme was provided by aides to groups of two to four students, a pre-existing and valued component of the district's student support programme. The aides were given considerable support by means of professional development during the year. Both groups were compared with a random sample of average and high progress first graders (N = 102) as an indication of average.

Reading Recovery children scored significantly higher than the children in the small-group compensatory programme on a variety of reading and writing performance measures including a standardized test. Children whose Reading Recovery lessons were discontinued when they met the criteria had scores within an average band of the random sample group. In follow-up studies in second and third grades, Reading Recovery children continued to make progress while the control group fell behind. Again, those Reading Recovery students whose lessons were discontinued performed within the average range for their class peers in the random sample.

Because of the higher quality of literacy teaching in classrooms taught by Reading Recovery teachers, random assignment to treatments only occurred for the other classrooms. This is the aspect of the study that was analysed and reported in the What Works Clearinghouse report. This resulted in a sample of 38 Reading Recovery students and 53 students in the alternative compensatory programme. Table 1 summarizes the results for the randomized control group trial reported in the What Works Clearinghouse report (2007b, Appendix A3.2).

Table 1: **Means (Standard Deviations) and Effect Sizes for the Comparison Between the Reading Recovery and Control Group**

Outcome Measures	Reading Recovery		Control Group		Effect Size
	Mean	(SD)	Mean	(SD)	
DS[a]: Letter Identification	48.05	(1.41)	49.61	(8.33)	−0.24
DS[a]: Word Test	13.29	(1.63)	11.98	(3.92)	0.41
DS[a]: Concepts About Print	19.24	(2.91)	13.98	(3.31)	0.89*
DS[a]: Dictation [HRSW]	30.52	(6.13)	23.80	(7.99)	0.92*
DS[a]: Writing Vocabulary	33.21	(13.49)	25.37	(14.33)	0.56*
CTBS[b]: Reading Comprehension	36.67	(19.27)	27.33	(13.95)	0.56*
CTBS[b]: Reading Vocabulary	36.64	(11.93)	28.07	(17.00)	0.57*

a Diagnostic Survey (Clay, 1985); renamed Observation Survey (Clay, 1993a, 2002, 2006); Dictation task later renamed Hearing and Recording Sounds in Words.

b Comprehensive Test of Basic Skills.

* Indicates significant difference (p < .05).

The negative effect size for the Letter Identification task in Table 1 is due to a ceiling effect on this measure: by mid-year the children in both groups recognized most of the letters. Results on the Text Reading Level measure from the Clay assessment were not reported by the What Works Clearinghouse because they did not have individual scores on this measure for every child in the experimental and control group. This requirement was based on their concern that this task did not have an equal interval measurement scale (What Works Clearinghouse, 2007d, personal communication). However, since Reading Recovery students scored higher than the control group students, calculations based on an equal interval assumption would provide a conservative estimate of the effect size on this measure. The effect size for text reading level in this study was .96, or an improvement index of 33 percentile points.

Iversen and Tunmer (1993)

Iversen and Tunmer (1993) compared two versions of individual instruction, one labelled 'Standard Reading Recovery' and the other 'Modified Reading Recovery.' The modified version used the same lesson framework as the standard Reading Recovery approach but incorporated systematic instruction designed to make children aware of the relationship of visual patterns and the sounds shared by words with those patterns. The modification was introduced in the fourth week of instruction and replaced a segment of the lesson devoted to letter identification. The teachers in the modified Reading Recovery group used this time to provide instruction on visual and phonological elements of words based on phonograms. This involved children in manipulating magnetic letters (e.g., to change *and* to *band* or *sand* or *big* to *bag* or *bug*). The description of this modified programme is very similar to procedures that Clay (1993b) describes in Section 10 of *Reading Recovery: A Guidebook for Teachers in Training*. It seems likely that the modification assessed in this study and the revised guidebook sections are both responses to the same body of research on the role of phonological awareness in early literacy. This element of Reading Recovery instruction and training has continued to evolve in the latest version of Reading Recovery procedures, *Literacy Lessons Designed for Individuals, Part Two* (Clay, 2005b, see Sections 5 and 11–13).

Iversen and Tunmer worked with teachers who were receiving initial training in the use of Reading Recovery procedures. Iversen herself provided this training and implemented the treatment conditions by varying the training received by each group. (Iversen had previously trained in New Zealand as a Reading Recovery Tutor/Teacher Leader, but was not involved in ongoing Reading Recovery professional development at the time of this research.) A total of 23 schools and 26 Reading Recovery teachers engaged in their initial year of training worked with 64 children from 34 classrooms for the two Reading Recovery groups. Seven reading specialists in seven schools taught a comparison group that included 32 children who were matched with the Reading Recovery participants on entry scores and demographic characteristics. The comparison students were taught in small groups of six to seven students in the schools' Chapter 1 (now Title 1) programmes.

The three groups (Standard Reading Recovery, Modified Reading Recovery, Small Group Comparison) scored equally low on all pre-test measures. When the Reading Recovery lessons were discontinued, both the standard and modified Reading Recovery groups scored significantly higher on all outcome measures than the students receiving small group instruction. For measures like Text Reading Level, with no ceiling effects, the differences were extremely large (more than eight standard deviations on this measure and more than two standard deviations for the Dolch Word Recognition Test). Both Reading Recovery groups closed the achievement gap with their average classmates who had very similar profiles on the post-intervention measures.

The two Reading Recovery groups performed similarly on most measures, including phonemic measures used to assess the effectiveness of the modified Reading Recovery approach. The authors did find a difference in the number of lessons prior to the decision to discontinue the intervention for students in the standard Reading Recovery group (57.31) versus the modified Reading Recovery group (41.75). The authors claim that this analysis indicates increased efficiency of the modified lesson component. Since the authors did not discuss the number of lessons received before discontinuing as a variable in the methods section, this appears to be an exploratory analysis.

There are several possible difficulties with this analysis. First, the decision to discontinue a student's series of lessons is somewhat subjective and was completely under the control of the lead author. Second, the reported difference may be due to the lesson component, but it may also be due to any other variation that occurred in the training of the two groups. Finally, the difference may be due to differences among the teachers in the two Reading Recovery groups. There is no indication that teachers were randomly assigned to treatment conditions or matched on the basis of previous knowledge or experience. In any event, the efficiency claim is debatable since a lesson component very close to the modified method is part of the standard intervention in Clay's (1993b, 2005b) guidebooks.

Pinnell, Lyons, DeFord, Bryk, and Seltzer (1994)

This study, often referred to as the MacArthur Study because it was funded externally by the MacArthur Foundation, examined several factors that may contribute to the effectiveness of early intervention — factors related to individual instruction, instructional approaches, and professional development. To explore the contribution of these components to the effectiveness of early intervention, researchers compared four treatment groups: (a) standard Reading Recovery, (b) a Reading Recovery-like intervention delivered by teachers who received a considerably shortened period of professional development (Reading Success), (c) a Reading Recovery-like intervention taught by experienced Reading Recovery teachers working with small groups (Reading/Writing Group), and (d) a basic skills, small group intervention focusing primarily on teaching the alphabetic principles (Direct Instruction Skill Plan).

A complex hierarchical design and analysis were used to compare these four treatments. Within each participating school district, one school had already implemented Reading Recovery. That school was designated as the Reading Recovery treatment site and three additional schools in the district were randomly assigned to one of the three alternative treatments. Within each school the 10 lowest performing first grade students were identified; 4 of these students were randomly assigned to the treatment condition at their school and the others constituted a randomized comparison group. A total of 403 students representing two rural, two suburban, and six urban school districts participated in the study.

Data were collected at the beginning, middle, and end of first grade and at the beginning of second grade. Measures included the Dictation [later renamed Hearing and Recording Sounds in Words (Clay, 1993a)] and Text Reading Level tasks from Clay (1985), the Woodcock Reading Mastery Test, and the Gates-MacGinitie Reading Test. Researchers at the University of Chicago independently analysed the data. In addition, the MacArthur Foundation appointed a national panel of renowned researchers who were not involved in Reading Recovery to provide oversight for analysing results.

Analyses indicated that Reading Recovery was the only treatment with significant effects on all four measures at the end of the intervention period. The Reading Recovery group also showed sustained gains on the Text Reading measure and Dictation (Hearing and Recording Sounds in Words) at the beginning of second grade. The study indicates that differences in professional development, group size, and instructional approach influence early intervention outcomes.

Quay, Steele, Johnson, and Hortman (2001)

Quay et al. (2001) studied initial Reading Recovery implementations, looking for evidence of Reading Recovery intervention effects on standardized measures of reading achievement, systematic observational measures, teacher ratings of academic and social characteristics, and promotion rates. A quasi-experimental procedure was used to establish equivalent experimental and comparison groups. Within 34 schools, one first grade classroom was randomly assigned to receive Reading Recovery and another classroom assigned as a control classroom. Based on teacher rankings and six tasks from Clay (1993a), the lowest performing children were identified for Reading Recovery or the comparison group, with 107 children in each group. The two groups were equivalent by gender (60% boys), ethnicity (70% African-American), free or reduced lunch (a majority of each group), and performance on the Observation Survey (Clay, 1993a) and the scales of the Iowa Test of Basic Skills.

The Reading Recovery group received a full series of one-to-one lessons in addition to regular classroom instruction. The comparison group participated in classroom instruction and other supplemental literacy activities. For 66% of the comparison group, this included daily, small group literacy support conducted by the Reading Recovery teacher.

As shown in Table 2, the effect sizes are large and significant on the Observation Survey measures (Clay, 1993a) and the Gates-MacGinitie Reading Test. On the Iowa tasks, results are more moderate but still significant on four of the six measures. This study also included teacher ratings of student progress on nine scales related to achievement, work habits, and self-confidence. Teachers rated the Reading Recovery students significantly higher on each of these scales.

The What Works Clearinghouse did not include this study in their analysis. In the intervention report they cited the reason for this omission as 'disruption problems that made it difficult to attribute study outcomes to the intervention, as delivered' (WWC, 2007a, p. 11). Yet nothing in the design or analysis of this study indicated that 'disruption' was any more of a factor in this research than in any of the other studies included in their analysis. Perhaps this quote from the discussion section in Quay et al. (2001) confounded the analysis:

> However, in addition to the Reading Recovery treatment, forces such as maturation, reading instruction in the first-grade classroom, and a variety of other school-related experiences occur during the interval between the pre- and post-tests. Thus, whether Reading Recovery is responsible for the achievement gains cannot be determined conclusively with these methodologies (p. 17).

Possibly the What Works Clearinghouse reviewer assumed the authors were describing serious faults in their study when in reality what they provided is a good definition of disruption factors. When read in context, Quay et al. (2001) explain that they conducted an experimental versus comparison group study to avoid confounds that might interfere with the interpretation of pre- and post-test only design. Fortunately, the What Works Clearinghouse had sufficient experimental evidence to produce a highly positive report even without the strong evidence from this experiment.

Table 2: Means, Standard Deviations, and Effect Sizes on Outcome Measures

	Reading Recovery Group		Comparison Group		Effect Size
	Mean	(SD)	Mean	(SD)	
Iowa Test of Basic Skills					
Listening	39.57	(18.04)	38.67	(17.11)	.05
Reading Comprehension	48.60	(13.41)	39.08	(14.40)	.68*
Vocabulary	39.64	(16.57)	38.67	(17.11)	.06
Word Analysis	36.55	(16.85)	29.52	(18.66)	.40*
Reading Total	43.88	(14.60)	39.13	(15.96)	.31*
Language Total	39.34	(14.33)	33.85	(16.50)	.36*
Gates-MacGinitie Reading Test					
Initial Consonant	13.30	(1.80)	11.59	(2.90)	.70**
Final Consonant	12.36	(2.34)	9.80	(2.85)	.98**
Vowels	12.23	(2.55)	9.16	(3.61)	.98**
Context in Sentence	13.07	(2.54)	9.44	(3.38)	1.21**
Observation Survey (Clay, 1993a)					
Letter Identification	52.89	(4.85)	51.10	(6.57)	.31*
Word Test	18.20	(3.03)	13.41	(5.71)	1.05**
Concepts About Print	20.65	(3.04)	16.03	(3.64)	1.38**
Writing Vocabulary	46.37	(12.20)	29.98	(13.40)	1.23**
Dictation [HRSW]	33.92	(4.30)	26.96	(8.84)	1.00**
Text Reading Level	16.38	(6.15)	6.72	(5.55)	1.65**

* $p < .05$
** $p < .001$

Schwartz (2005a)

Schwartz (2005a) also provided a randomized clinical trial of Reading Recovery's effectiveness. Thirty-seven Reading Recovery teachers from across the United States agreed to participate in this study and submitted complete data sets on at-risk first grade students randomly assigned to receive the Reading Recovery intervention during the first or second half of the school year. Data were also reported on high-average and low-average students receiving the same classroom instruction as the at-risk students. The study compared the progress of these students at the beginning of first grade, at the transition from first to second round intervention service around mid-year, and at the end of the school year. The primary measures of intervention effectiveness came from the comparison of the randomly assigned at-risk students at the mid-year transition. These comparisons showed the effect of the intervention compared to the achievement of similar low-performing students in the same classrooms (the control group).

While the Pinnell (1989) study showed the effectiveness of the initial implementation in Ohio, the Schwartz (2005a) study looked at effectiveness of a more mature national implementation. The teachers were volunteers, some with many years of experience with the Reading Recovery intervention.

Students who participated in the Reading Recovery intervention (Intervention Group) during the first half of the year performed significantly better at mid-year than similar at-risk students (Control Group) from the same classrooms (see Table 3). The differences were large and significant on measures of Clay's (2002) Text Reading Level, Word Reading, Concepts About Print, Writing Vocabulary, and Hearing and Recording Sounds in Words, as well as the Slosson Oral Reading Test. The two groups did not differ on Letter Identification, two measures of phonemic segmentation, or the Degrees of Reading Power test.

The effect size reported in Table 3 for Text Reading Level is based on the standard calculation for an interval measure. The What Works Clearinghouse was provided with the individual scores for each student, so they were able to use a non-parametric procedure to calculate the effect size (What Works Clearinghouse, 2007b). They reported the effect size for Text Reading Level of 2.49 compared to the 2.02 value reported by Schwartz (2005a).

Table 3: Means, Standard Deviations, and Effect Sizes for the Intervention and Control Groups at Mid-Year

Measure	Maximum Score	Intervention[a]		Control Group[b]		
		M	SD	M	SD	ES
Text Level	30	12.35	4.80	4.70	2.40	2.02
Letter Identification	54	52.68	1.27	51.68	2.78	.23
Word Test	20	14.94	3.99	8.87	4.75	1.38
Concepts About Print	24	19.35	2.55	16.68	2.30	1.10
Writing Vocabulary	–	42.03	11.42	31.00	12.94	.90
Hearing & Recording Sounds	37	34.97	2.70	29.08	7.37	1.06
Slosson Oral Reading	200	30.58	14.41	18.12	11.87	.94
Degrees of Reading Power	28	4.82	3.88	4.27	3.88	.14
Phonemic Segmentation	22	17.70	4.93	15.27	5.43	.47
Phonemic Deletion	10	6.64	2.56	5.58	2.50	.42

a $n = 37$ b $n = 37$

Comparison of the Reading Recovery intervention group with the high-average and low-average classroom groups showed that the at-risk students had closed the literacy achievement gap with their average peers. A further efficiency analysis similar to that conducted by Center, Wheldall, Freeman, Outhred, & McNaught (1995) showed that selection procedures identified students in most need of intervention, and that the Reading Recovery intervention reduced the number of children who appeared to need long-term literacy support from 17% to 5% of the first grade cohort.

Evaluation research validation

The experimental studies discussed above make a strong case for the effectiveness of Reading Recovery. At-risk first grade students do make large and significant gains during this 12- to approximately 20-week intervention. However, experimental demonstrations of effects are a necessary but not sufficient foundation for evidence-based practice as controlled experimental studies may produce results that cannot be disseminated and replicated on a large scale. Marie Clay recognized the need for replication studies, conducting the first such study in 1979 (see Chapter 2). She also established a system for collecting data on every child who received a series of Reading Recovery lessons.

In a meta-analysis of Reading Recovery in the United States, researchers compared rigorous Reading Recovery studies with other studies incorporating broader design parameters (D'Agostino & Murphy, 2004). They did not find large discrepancies in results between the less and more selective analyses: results on more rigorously designed studies seemed to converge with the bulk of available evidence. They found no evidence that methodological flaws or weaknesses in individual studies were responsible for previously identified effects.

Studies and research reviews in peer-reviewed journals have documented a variety of outcomes of Reading Recovery and Descubriendo la Lectura (Reading Recovery in Spanish) and have explored factors related to the intervention. These have included phonological awareness, self-efficacy, self-regulated behaviours, achievement gaps, one-to-one teaching, writing strategies, and reduction of long-term services (see Schmitt, Askew, Fountas, Lyons, & Pinnell, 2005 for summaries of Reading Recovery research). Some of the evaluation outcomes are summarized below.

Effectiveness data

The evaluation data collected and reported by the National Data Evaluation Center (NDEC) at The Ohio State University and the Canadian Institute of Reading Recovery (2007) provide annual evidence that the results obtained in small scale experimental studies are replicated in hundreds of districts and schools across the US and Canada. Table 4 provides one example of the data reported by the National Data Evaluation Center (2007) for the 91,089 Reading Recovery children with year-end data in the 2006–2007 school year, showing changes in text reading level for children with different end-of-intervention outcome categories. (Outcome categories are described in Chapter 8.)

Table 4: Progress on Text Reading Level: Reading Recovery, 2006–2007

Intervention Status/ Study Group	Fall			Year-end			Gain	
	n	mean	SD	n	mean	SD	n	mean
Discontinued	39,909	1.2	1.2	54,241	19.2	3.8	38,801	18.2
Recommended	19,598	0.6	0.8	19,434	9.9	4.7	18,767	9.3
Incomplete	7410	1.1	1.1	15,236	10.3	3.8	7348	9.5
Moved	3331	0.7	0.9	273	10.7	6.4	234	10.1
None of Above	2246	0.6	0.9	1902	7.7	5.5	1666	6.9
All Served	72,494	1.0	1.1	91,086	15.5	6.1	66,816	14.4
Complete Intervention	59,507	1.0	1.1	73,675	16.8	5.8	57,568	15.3
Random Sample	13,062	4.7	5.8	12,116	20.4	7.1	12,011	15.6

Note: Mean gain is based only on children with both fall and year-end Text Reading Level scores.

In Table 5, changes in text reading level for children in Descubriendo la Lectura are provided.

Table 5: **Progress on Text Reading Level:**
Descubriendo la Lectura, 2006–2007

Intervention Status/ Study Group	Fall			Year-end			Gain	
	n	mean	SD	n	mean	SD	n	mean
Discontinued	496	0.8	1.0	694	19.5	4.3	484	18.9
Recommended	283	0.5	0.6	282	9.6	5.8	266	9.2
Incomplete	84	0.5	0.8	211	7.9	4.0	82	8.3
Moved	54	0.5	0.8	6	7.5	5.2	3	6.7
None of Above	32	0.3	0.5	33	6.8	6.3	28	6.7
All Served	949	0.6	0.9	1226	14.8	7.1	863	14.5
Complete Intervention	779	0.7	0.9	976	16.6	6.6	750	15.5
Random Sample	260	3.9	4.8	235	20.2	7.1	234	16.2

Note: Mean gain is based only on children with both fall and year-end Text Reading Level scores.

The end-of-year text reading level for the students who met Reading Recovery and Descubriendo la Lectura criteria to discontinue their series of intervention lessons shows these students reading texts at a second grade level. Although there is no comparison to an initially equivalent control group in these evaluation data, the previously reviewed experimental studies clearly establish that the intervention made a significant contribution to student progress across the year. Data from the classroom Random Sample show average performance levels for first grade children at the beginning and end of the year. Reading Recovery students who meet exit criteria (*discontinued*) are achieving at grade level on text reading level and other year-end measures. The Recommended group includes children that have completed around 20 weeks of individual literacy lessons, but need some form of additional support for a time. Identification of this group of children is also a positive intervention outcome of Reading Recovery (Jones, Johnson, Schwartz, & Zalud, 2005).

As a developmental psychologist by training, Marie Clay (1987) always regarded early intervention as a necessary component in identifying children who required long-term literacy support. In the United States the current emphasis on Response to Intervention (RTI) mirrors her vision. By using intensive pre-referral interventions as part of the identification process, the aim is to reduce the percentage of children referred for special education. Reading Recovery serves this function well as demonstrated in both evaluation and experimental studies (Gómez-Bellengé & Rodgers,

2007; O'Connor & Simic, 2002; Schwartz, 2005a; Vellutino, Scanlon, Sipay, Small, Pratt, & Chen, 1996).

Evaluation research in North America has also addressed two critical issues that are difficult to explore with experimental studies — *sustained effects* and *closing the gap* studies. Clay and Watson (Clay, 1993b and Chapter 2 in this volume) investigated both issues in a 3-year follow-up study with Maori, Pacific, and NZ/European students from the 1978 cohort of children who received Reading Recovery in New Zealand. North American researchers have continued to address these issues, finding that children continue to progress with their peers after Reading Recovery and that the intervention closes or reduces the achievement gap among subgroups.

Closing the gap research

Early research in New Zealand by Marie Clay and Barbara Watson (Clay, 1993b and Chapter 2 in this volume) asked, 'Was Reading Recovery suitable for Maori children?' In the United States, educators wanted to determine whether the gains made by minority group participants are sufficient to reduce or eliminate the disparities in achievement observed between racial or socio-economic groups in the broader population. US national evaluation data were examined to indicate the relationship of economic status, race/ethnicity, and early intervention to predictions of end-of-first grade reading achievement (Rodgers, Gómez-Bellengé, & Wang, 2004; Rodgers, Gómez-Bellengé, Wang, & Schulz, 2005). These studies demonstrated that the Reading Recovery intervention is effective across race/ethnic and socio-economic groups and that access to the Reading Recovery intervention reduces but does not eliminate the achievement gap among these groups. Regression procedures indicated that the strongest predictor of literacy success in first grade was *access* to the Reading Recovery intervention. The regression model included economic status as a predictor variable, but race did not contribute to the prediction of success beyond these two main factors. These results suggest that effective early intervention is a critical component towards providing educational opportunity for all students.

Closing the achievement gap for English language learners is also a major concern of North American educators. Kelly, Gómez-Bellengé, Chen, and Shultz (2008) examined the performance of 17,792 English language learners from the national evaluation data. They found only a slight difference in the outcome status, success rate, and performance levels between English language learners and native speakers. The length of interventions did not differ between these groups, nor was it related to the rating of oral English proficiency prior to the intervention.

Sustained effects research

The 1981 3-year follow-up study in New Zealand (Clay, 1993b and Chapter 2 in this book) was a response to educators' enquiries about the long-term outcomes of Reading Recovery. Marie Clay and Barbara Watson asked, 'Were the children who had been given Reading Recovery lessons in 1978 continuing to progress with the average groups in their classes in December 1981?' Similarly, North American educators wanted to determine if the gains due to intervention dissipate after the intensive intervention is discontinued or whether these students continue to benefit from classroom instruction like their average peers.

Sustained effects are a complex issue for any early intervention. What is a reasonable expectation? The view of Reading Recovery as an inoculation against all future literacy difficulties is certainly unrealistic (Shanahan & Barr, 1995). The *recovery* envisioned in the intervention name was never of the medical type. Developed in New Zealand, a country familiar with small boats and planes, a *recovery* was an adjustment in course, a return to the flight path, one that brought the learner back on track for further development. With good instruction, children whose series of lessons is discontinued at grade level criteria (70% to 90% of those receiving a full intervention) should continue to show average progress in classroom instruction. They should be no more at risk than other average readers at the end of first grade. Still, over time any group of average readers will begin to display a normal distribution of scores, with some children making more rapid progress and others showing slower learning rates. By definition, an average group will be half above average and half below average. Marie Clay's (2005a) expectation was

> that children who successfully complete the early literacy intervention, Reading Recovery, should operate in reading and writing in ways that put them on track for being silent readers with self-extending processing systems during the next two years at school. With good classroom instruction and moderate personal motivation that should be achievable. (Clay, 2005a, p. 52)

Experimental studies of sustained gains are difficult to conduct. A strong design would require random assignment or matching of students to treatment and control conditions. If the treatment is a 12 to about 20 weeks early intervention like Reading Recovery, what would constitute the control comparison? Effectiveness studies have shown that Reading Recovery students perform significantly better than comparison groups at the end of the intervention period. If the groups performed at equal levels at the end of third or fifth grade, what would that indicate? Would it suggest that several years of small group support was equivalent to a half term intervention in first grade? What would this suggest about the cost effectiveness of these different approaches? Would there be other benefits of reducing the number of struggling readers and writers in a classroom with early intervention beyond the gains to these particular students?

Since maintaining a control group for several years is difficult and possibly unethical, most of the evidence on sustained effects comes from evaluation research. In evaluation studies, comparisons are usually made with a random sample of average peers rather than an equivalent group of initially at-risk students who are not given the intervention. D'Agostino and Murphy (2004) used a combination of meta-analysis and regression procedures to examine 36 US studies conducted between 1984 and 1995. Most of these studies were unpublished evaluation reports by districts implementing Reading Recovery. From this set of data they examined the evidence of whether gains from Reading Recovery were sustained through second grade. They report that

> Compared to similar needy students, discontinued students actually widened the gap from post-test to second-grade follow-up on standardized achievement tests, and they closed the gap at follow-up with regular students. At follow-up, the not-discontinued students surpassed the low achievers on standardized tests. In sum, the results seem to indicate a lasting programme effect, at least by the end of second grade, on broad reading skills. (D'Agostino & Murphy, 2004, p. 35)

Other evaluation studies have tracked the progress of Reading Recovery students through third, fourth, and fifth grades on standardized measures and high stakes state assessments (Askew, Kaye, Frasier, Mobasher, Anderson, & Rodriguez, 2002; Briggs & Young, 2003; Brown, Denton, Kelly, & Neal, 1999; Escamilla, Loera, Ruiz, & Rodriguez, 1998; Schmitt & Gregory, 2005). While the details of these studies differ, the overall pattern is quite similar. Schmitt et al. (2005) provide a summary description of these studies. Sample findings are summarised below:

- On the Texas Assessment of Academic Skills at the end of fourth grade, 85% of the Reading Recovery sample passed the reading test compared to 90% of the random sample of the general population (Askew et al., 2002).

- On the Gates-MacGinitie vocabulary, comprehension, and overall reading scores in fourth grade, the Reading Recovery sample was equivalent to a grade level stratified random sample of their peers (Briggs & Young, 2003).

- On the Iowa Test of Basic Skills and the Stanford Achievement Test, 9th edition, 65% to 85% of Reading Recovery students performed at average levels from second through fifth grades (Brown et al., 1999).

- On Spanish Text Level Reading and the Spanish Reading Achievement Test, students who received the Spanish reconstruction of Reading Recovery (Descubriendo la Lectura) were equivalent to or above their peers in bilingual classrooms (Escamilla et al., 1998).

- On the Indiana State Test of Educational Progress in fourth grade, the Reading Recovery sample was approximately normally distributed with a mean at the 45th percentile and a standard deviation of 21.7 (Schmitt & Gregory, 2005).

When examining evaluation studies of sustained effects, it is important to carefully examine the sample included in the analysis. For most of these evaluation studies, researchers have tracked the progress of students who made accelerated gains during the intervention and discontinued their lessons by meeting grade level criteria. Following the progress of these students makes sense in studies of sustained gains.

Shanahan and Barr (1995), on the other hand, suggest this practice might be 'the most serious flaw in Reading Recovery research' (p. 991). The exclusion of students who struggle during the intervention may be a serious flaw in effectiveness studies like those reviewed by the What Works Clearinghouse, but this is not the case in studies of *sustained* effects. National data evaluation in the United States and Canada includes every student that enters Reading Recovery, even if they only participate in a very few lessons. In studies of sustained gains, however, it makes perfect sense to focus on the subsequent progress of a subset of the entering students — those who reached grade-level performance at the end of the Reading Recovery intervention. Despite continuing efforts to correct this misconception related to Reading Recovery research (Reading Recovery Council of North America, 2002), this misunderstanding continues to be cited by critics (Elbaum, Vaughn, Hughes, & Moody, 2000; Reynolds & Wheldall, 2007).

Separate analyses by outcome categories make even more sense given the recent emphasis on Response to Intervention approaches for identification of students needing long-term literacy support.

> The Reading Recovery early intervention was designed
> to accelerate literacy acquisition for most of the children
> falling into the lowest 20% of literacy learners after a year
> at school. It also acts as a pre-referral intervention and
> provides a diagnostic period of teaching to identify a small
> residual group of children who still need extra help and
> probably further specialist guidance. Reading Recovery
> enables an education system to deliver those two outcomes.
> (Clay, 2005a, p. 18).

A few studies in North America have tracked the progress of students who
are recommended or referred for additional assessment and possibly for
additional support (Dorn & Allen, 1995; James, 2005; Matczuk, 2007).
This type of research is becoming more important as teachers attempt
to foster every student's learning by matching instructional contexts
to the student's strengths and needs (Clay, 1987; McEneaney, Lose, &
Schwartz, 2006).

Influence of the US political and educational climate

For several decades, education authorities and policy makers in the
United States have extolled the importance of research-based practices
in schools. Reading Recovery's strong research base was a major factor
contributing to the growth of the intervention in the United States during
the 1980s and 1990s. For the first time, an evidence-based intervention
was available to serve the lowest literacy achievers in Grade 1 before a
cycle of failure prevailed.

In recent years, the political context in the United States has increased
the demand for research evidence while narrowing the definition of
research and acceptable evidence. Some of these political influences are
described in this section.

Scientifically based reading research

Federal legislation has tied funding decisions to literacy programmes
supported by scientifically based reading research. The US Department
of Education's definition of scientifically based reading research includes
both observational and experimental methods that employ 'rigorous,
systematic and objective procedures to obtain valid knowledge relevant
to reading development, reading instruction and reading difficulties'

(Office of Elementary and Secondary Education, 2002, pp. 3–4). Criteria for scientific research included

- systematic, empirical methods that draw on observation or experiment,
- rigorous data analyses that are adequate to test stated hypotheses,
- measurements or observational methods that provide valid data across evaluators and observers and across multiple measurements and observations, and
- acceptance by a peer-reviewed journal or approved by a panel of independent experts through a comparably rigorous, objective, and scientific review.

Reading Recovery met all of these criteria for evidence-based research (see descriptions of experimental studies earlier in this chapter) and was poised for access to funding sources that called for interventions based on scientific research.

Report of the National Reading Panel

The National Reading Panel report (National Reading Panel, 2000) also strongly influenced federal guidance for selecting materials, programmes, strategies, and professional development. They used meta-analysis procedures to examine the available experimental or quasi-experimental research to determine the components of instruction with a causal link to gains in measures of reading achievement. These components were phonemic awareness, phonics, fluency, vocabulary, and comprehension. Reading Recovery incorporates all components of reading instruction identified by the National Reading Panel. An analysis is provided in Chapter 13 of *Changing Futures: The Influence of Reading Recovery in the United States* (Schmitt, Askew, Fountas, Lyons, & Pinnell, 2005).

The importance ascribed to the five components identified by the National Reading Panel has been widely used to make decisions about practice. Findings from the full report, however, have sometimes been ignored when recommendations for practice are cited. For example, findings have been used to endorse a phonics-first curriculum. Yet the National Reading Panel (National Institute of Child Health and Human Development, 2000) acknowledged the complexity of the literacy learning process and issued some important cautions about placing a total, early emphasis on phonics.

Because phonics is not a total reading program, phonics instruction should not become the dominant component in a reading program, neither in the amount of time devoted to it nor in the significance attached. (See the Report of the National Reading Panel: Reports of the Subgroups, National Institute of Child Health and Human Development, 2000, pp. 2/97.)

Programs should acknowledge that systematic phonics instruction is a means to an end. .... although children need to be taught the major consonant and vowel letter-sound relationships, they also need ample reading and writing activities that allow them to practice using this knowledge. (See Put Reading First, National Institute of Child Health and Human Development, 2001, p. 17.)

Reading Recovery teachers give strong support to children as they develop letter-sound knowledge and learn to apply that knowledge to their reading and writing (Schwartz & Gallant, in press).

Impact on federal and state funding streams

Under policy guidelines provided by the US Department of Education Policies (Office of Elementary and Secondary Education, 2002), state and local educational agencies are responsible for ensuring that instructional materials, programmes, strategies, and professional development funded under the federal Reading First legislation were (a) based on scientifically based reading research and (b) included the five components of instruction identified by the National Reading Panel. In order to qualify for state grants, education agencies were required to meet those two criteria, but *how* to meet them was not clear. At the time, there was no readily available summary or comparison of research evidence on the effectiveness of classroom programmes, supplemental programmes, or instructional materials. As a result, funding was allocated for one of five widely adopted basal reading series and a limited set of supplemental materials; none of these programme adoption decisions was based on research evidence of the effectiveness of the particular programme (Reading Recovery Council of North America, 2007).

In several instances, state grants that included Reading Recovery as part of their comprehensive literacy plan were questioned, rejected, or returned for revision (Reading Recovery Council of North America, 2007). It seemed a contradiction that an intervention that met both the standards of scientific research and included all components of reading instruction was denied Reading First funding in several instances while programmes with little or no documented evidence were supported. The Reading Recovery Council of North America (2007) challenged this practice and a federal investigation concluded that the Reading First initiative had indeed been mismanaged. It became essential for Reading Recovery leadership to publicize the existing research-based evidence of Reading Recovery's effectiveness, and to monitor decisions about future funding streams and their impact on the availability of Reading Recovery to schools that choose to adopt it.

Validation from the What Works Clearinghouse (WWC)

The task of determining whether particular programmes were supported by scientifically based reading research was left to the What Works Clearinghouse (WWC) that was established in 2002 by the US Department of Education's Institute of Education Sciences 'to provide educators, policymakers, researchers, and the public with a central and trusted source of scientific evidence of what works in education' (WWC, 2008). It established rigorous criteria for inclusion of research studies in its evidence review (WWC, 2006). These 'best evidence' standards were designed to ensure that any reported gains in student performance could be attributed to the programme or intervention and not to other uncontrolled factors or contaminants in the research. Well-designed experimental studies are the primary means of establishing this type of causal validity.

Initially, it appeared that the What Works Clearinghouse would give priority to the review of beginning reading programmes. This priority would coincide with the emphasis given to early literacy in the 2002 No Child Left Behind legislation with its Reading First component that limited funding to programmes supported by research. In May 2003, the Reading Recovery Council of North America and the North American Trainers Group Research Committee submitted information about Reading Recovery's research base to the WWC. This submission included four experimental studies conducted in the US and one study from Australia: Pinnell (1989); Iversen & Tunmer (1993); Pinnell, Lyons, DeFord, Bryk, & Seltzer (1994); Center, Wheldall, Freeman, Outhred, & McNaught (1995); and Quay, Steele, Johnson, & Hortman, (2001).

Almost 4 years later, in March 2007, the What Works Clearinghouse posted its intervention report on Reading Recovery (WWC, 2007a, 2007b) and in August 2007, its summary topic report on beginning reading programmes (WWC, 2007c). Investigators examined 78 Reading Recovery studies identified in their search of the research literature. Of these studies, four met their standards for determining causal validity (Pinnell, 1989; Iversen & Tunmer, 1993; Pinnell et al., 1994; Schwartz, 2005a), and one study met their standards with reservations (Baenen, Bernhole, Dulaney, & Banks, 1997).[1]

The What Works Clearinghouse looked for evidence of programme effects on four domains of measures related to beginning reading — alphabetics (phonemic awareness, phonological awareness, letter identification, print awareness, and phonics); fluency; comprehension; and general reading achievement. Reading Recovery was the only intervention reviewed that received positive or potentially positive ratings in each of the four outcome domains.

They also reported effect size measures as a way to compare different programmes. Effect size is often reported in terms of standard deviation units (Cohen, 1988). An effect size of 1.0 indicates that the intervention group has an average score one standard deviation above the mean of the control group. This corresponds to 34 percentile points above the mean of the control group. The WWC reports effect size as an improvement index that ranges from 0 to 50 percentile points. An improvement index of 0 indicates that the experimental and control groups have the same mean score. An improvement index of 50 indicates that (within rounding error) the mean of the experimental group is higher than that achieved by any student in the control group. Negative improvement index scores in this range are also possible, indicating that the control group scored higher than the intervention group. Because in education and social science research the range of individual scores is usually much larger than the difference between treatment means, Cohen (1988) suggests that effect sizes of more than 0.8 standard deviations are considered large. This is equivalent to an improvement index of 29 percentile points.

The Reading Recovery research (WWC, 2007a) indicated relatively large effect sizes in each domain:

---

1 Although included in the What Works Clearinghouse analysis of Reading Recovery as a randomized clinical trial, the Baenen et al. study is more a local evaluation study. The What Works Clearinghouse was only able to extract one finding of equivalent retention rates for the experimental and control groups in second grade. Since the retention rates were relatively low for both groups, this finding is likely to relate more to district policy than to intervention effectiveness. As a clinical trial Baenen et al. provide little information about the teachers involved, the number of teachers and schools participating, details of the randomization procedure within schools, demographic information on the participating children, the pre-test and post-test scores or standard measures used in Reading Recovery, the number of lessons in complete and partial programmes, or any supplemental small group support provided by the Reading Recovery teacher or other teachers to students in the control group. It is therefore suggested that the study is not as comprehensive as needed to make definitive statements about program effectiveness.

- alphabetics, 34 percentile points

- fluency, 46 percentile points

- comprehension, 14 percentile points

- general reading achievement, 32 percentile points.

Compared to other programmes, these Reading Recovery effect sizes ranked first for fluency and general reading achievement, second on alphabetics and tied for third on comprehension. Comprehension is a difficult construct to assess at the middle or even the end of first grade (WWC, 2007c).

When publishing the report on beginning reading interventions, the What Works Clearinghouse identified a total of 887 studies which included 153 beginning reading programmes. Twenty-seven of these studies met their evidence standards and another 24 met their standards with reservations. Based on this body of research, they produced reports on 24 beginning reading programmes that had one or more studies meeting their evidence standards (with or without reservation). This left 129 programmes with no studies that met these standards. The five Reading Recovery studies included in the report provide documentation of a substantial research base and strong support for a causal link to student achievement gains.

The What Works Clearinghouse (2007a) intervention report on Reading Recovery replicates and extends the early research that Marie Clay conducted from 1976 to 1978 to establish the effectiveness of her newly designed Reading Recovery intervention procedures (see Chapter 2). This research continues to demonstrate that specially trained, knowledgeable teachers can adapt a set of early intervention procedures to the learning needs of individual children, and produce literacy gains that far exceed those of similar, low-performing students receiving classroom or classroom plus small group instruction.

A final word

Marie Clay (2001) devoted her final chapter in *Change Over Time in Children's Literacy Development* to a discussion of issues and cautions related to early intervention research. She gave particular attention to the limitations of control group studies like those included in the What Works Clearinghouse (2007a) report. She valued research based on systematic observation for the insights it can provide to develop and refine our theories of literacy learning and instruction (for a few examples, see Lyons, Pinnell, & DeFord, 1993; Rodgers, 2004; Schwartz, 1997, 2005b).

Marie Clay (2001, p. 247) quoted Eliot Eisner of Stanford University, citing the relevance of his comments for all who work internationally in the field of early literacy interventions. His words speak to the importance and the challenges we will face in order to continue to make a difference around the world:

> ... the major aim of the common enterprise in which we are engaged ... has to do with the improvement of educational practice so that the lives of those who teach and learn are themselves enhanced ... we do research to understand. We try to understand in order to make our schools better places for both the children and the adults who shared their lives ... In the end, our work lives its ultimate life in the lives that it enables others to lead. Although we are making headway toward that end, there will continue to be difficulties and uncertainties, frustrations and obstacles. (Eisner, 1993, p. 10)

The research reviewed here is more than just a set of group means and effect sizes. It represents the extraordinary accomplishment of Marie Clay in fostering the professional learning of thousands of literacy professionals across North America and their ability to transform the literate lives of millions of struggling first grade children.

Research, in all its varied forms, has always been at the heart of the Reading Recovery intervention. Peter Johnston (2007) reminded the literacy community that research was a critical part of Marie Clay's legacy: 'As a researcher she was a model for us all; fiercely persistent, absolutely ethical, and always open to new evidence and new possibilities' (p. 67). To continue the legacy of Marie Clay's research is a daunting but essential challenge.

Reading Recovery sets a standard for educational research. It combines a strong theoretical base with evidence of its effects and ability to be replicated in thousands of schools across North America. Administrators, educators, and policymakers have scientific, research-based evidence to enhance educational opportunity for many of our most promising, but at-risk children. Are we willing to act on the evidence?

References

Askew, B. J., Kaye, E., Frasier, D. F., Mobasher, M., Anderson, N., & Rodriguez, Y. (2002). Making a case for prevention in education. *Literacy Teaching and Learning: An International Journal of Early Reading and Writing, 6*(2), 43–73.

Baenen, N., Bernhole, A., Dulaney, C., & Banks, K. (1997). Reading Recovery: Long-term progress after three cohorts. *Journal of Education for Students Placed at Risk (JESPAR), 2*(2), 161–181.

Briggs, C., & Young, B. K. (2003). Does Reading Recovery work in Kansas? A retrospective longitudinal study of sustained effects. *The Journal of Reading Recovery, 3*(1), 59–64.

Brown, W., Denton, E., Kelly, P., & Neal, J. (1999). Reading Recovery effectiveness: A five-year success story in San Luis Costal Unified School District. *ERS Spectrum: Journal of School Research and Information, 17*(1), 3–12.

Canadian Institute of Reading Recovery (2007). *National implementation data 2006–2007.* Toronto, CA: Canadian Institute of Reading Recovery.

Center, Y., Wheldall, K., Freeman, L., Outhred, L., & McNaught, M. (1995). An evaluation of Reading Recovery. *Reading Research Quarterly, 30*(2), 240–263.

Clay, M. M. (1985). *The early detection of reading difficulties.* Auckland: Heinemann.

Clay, M. M. (1987). Learning to be learning disabled. *New Zealand Journal of Educational Studies, 22,* 155–173.

Clay, M. M. (1993a). *An observation survey of early literacy achievement.* (1st ed.). Auckland: Heinemann.

Clay, M. M. (1993b). *Reading Recovery: A guidebook for teachers in training.* Auckland: Heinemann.

Clay, M. M. (2001). *Change over time in children's literacy development.* Auckland: Heinemann.

Clay, M. M. (2002, 2006). *An observation survey of early literacy achievement.* (2nd ed.). Auckland: Heinemann.

Clay, M. M. (2005a). *Literacy lessons designed for individuals: Part one.* Auckland: Heinemann.

Clay, M. M. (2005b). *Literacy lessons designed for individuals: Part two.* Auckland: Heinemann.

Cohen, J. (1988). *Statistical power analysis for the behavior sciences* (2nd ed.). Hillsdale, NJ: Lawrence Erlbaum Associates.

D'Agostino, J. V., & Murphy, J. A. (2004). A meta-analysis of Reading Recovery in United States schools. *Educational Evaluation and Policy Analysis, 26*(1), 23–38.

Dorn, L., & Allen, A. (1995). Helping low-achieving first-grade readers: A programme combining Reading Recovery tutoring and small-group instruction. *ERS Spectrum, 13*(3), 16–24.

Eisner, E. (1993). Forms of understanding and the future of educational research. *Educational Researcher, 22*(7), 5–11.

Elbaum, B., Vaughn, S., Hughes, M. T., & Moody, S. W. (2000). How effective are one-to-one tutoring programmes in reading for elementary students at risk for reading failure? A meta-analysis of the intervention research. *Journal of Educational Psychology, 92*(4), 605–619.

Escamilla, K., Loera, M., Ruiz, O., & Rodriguez, Y. (1998). An examination of sustaining effects in Descubriendo la Lectura programmes. *Literacy Teaching and Learning: An International Journal of Early Reading and Writing, 3*(2), 59–81.

Gómez-Bellengé, F. X., & Rodgers, E. M. (2007). *Reading Recovery and Descubriendo la Lectura national report 2005–2006.* Columbus: OH: The Ohio State University.

Iversen, S., & Tunmer, W. E. (1993). Phonological processing skills and the Reading Recovery programme. *Journal of Educational Psychology, 85*(1), 112–126.

James, K. V. (2005). *Reading Recovery and small group literacy intervention: A layered approach for comprehensive intervention.* Unpublished educational specialist's thesis, University of Arkansas at Little Rock, Little Rock, Arkansas.

Johnston, P. (2007). Revolutionary contributions. *Journal of Reading Recovery, 7*(1), 67–68.

Jones, N., Johnson, C., Schwartz, R., & Zalud, G. (2005). Two positive outcomes of Reading Recovery: Exploring the interface between Reading Recovery and special education. *Journal of Reading Recovery, 4*(3), 19–34.

Kelly, P., Gómez-Bellengé, F. X., Chen, J., & Schulz, M. (2008). Learner outcomes for English language learner low readers in an early intervention. *TESOL Quarterly, 42*(2), 135–160.

Lyons, C. A., Pinnell, G. S., & DeFord, D. E. (1993). *Partners in learning: Teachers and children in Reading Recovery.* New York, NY: Teachers College Press.

McEneaney, J. E., Lose, M. K., & Schwartz, R. M. (2006). A transactional perspective on reading difficulties and response to intervention. *Reading Research Quarterly, 41*(1), 117–128.

Matczuk, A. (2007). *Study of Canadian students recommended for long term support after Reading Recovery.* Toronto, CA: Canadian Institute of Reading Recovery.

National Data Evaluation Center (2007). *2006–2007 Reading Recovery statistical abstract for the U.S.* Columbus: OH: The Ohio State University. (www.ndec.us)

National Institute of Child Health and Human Development (2000). *Report of the National Reading Panel. Teaching children to read: An evidence-based assessment of the scientific research literature on reading and its implications for reading instruction: Reports of the sub-groups* (NIH Publication No. 00-4754). Washington, DC: US Government Printing Office.

National Institute of Child Health and Human Development, NIH, DHHS (2001). *Put reading first: Helping your child learn to read.* Washington, DC: US Government Printing Office.

National Reading Panel (2000). *Teaching children to read: An evidence-based assessment of the scientific research literature on reading and its implications for reading instruction* (NIH Publication No. 00-4769). Washington, DC: National Institute of Child Health and Human Development.

O'Connor, E. A., & Simic, O. (2002). The effect of Reading Recovery on special education referrals and placements. *Psychology in the Schools, 39*(6), 635–646.

Office of Elementary and Secondary Education. (2002). *Guidance for the reading first programme.* Washington DC: US Department of Education. Retrieved on 6 March, 2008 from http://www.ed.gov/programmes/readingfirst/guidance.pdf

Pinnell, G. S. (1989). Reading Recovery: Helping at-risk children learn to read. *The Elementary School Journal, 90*, 161–181.

Pinnell, G. S., DeFord, D. E., & Lyons, C. A. (1988). *Reading Recovery: Early intervention for at-risk first graders.* Arlington, VA: Educational Research Service.

Pinnell, G. S., Lyons, C. A., DeFord, D. E., Bryk, A. S., & Seltzer, M. (1994). Comparing instructional models for the literacy education of high risk first graders. *Reading Research Quarterly, 29*, 8–39.

Quay, L. C., Steele, D. C., Johnson, C. I., & Hortman, W. (2001). Children's achievement and personal and social development in a first-year Reading Recovery programme with teachers-in-training. *Literacy Teaching and Learning, 5*(2), 7–25.

Reading Recovery Council of North America (2002). *What evidence says about Reading Recovery.* Columbus, OH: Reading Recovery Council of North America.

Reading Recovery Council of North America (2007). *Reading Recovery and Reading First: Facts, findings, and recommendations for change.* Columbus, OH: Reading Recovery Council of North America.

Reynolds, M., & Wheldall, K. (2007). Reading Recovery 20 years down the track: Looking forward, looking back. *International Journal of Disability, Development and Education, 54*(2), 199–223.

Rodgers, E. M. (2004). Interactions that scaffold reading performance. *Journal of Literacy Research, 36*(4), 501–532.

Rodgers, E., Gómez-Bellengé, F. X., & Wang, C. (2004). *Closing the literacy achievement gap with early intervention.* Paper presented at the annual meeting of the American Educational Research Association. San Diego, CA.

Rodgers, E., Gómez-Bellengé, F. X., Wang, C., & Schulz, M. (2005). *Predicting the literacy achievement of struggling readers: Does intervening early make a difference.* Paper presented at the annual meeting of the American Educational Research Association. Montreal, Quebec.

Schmitt, M. C., Askew, B. J., Fountas, I. C., Lyons, C. A., & Pinnell, G. S. (2005). *Changing futures: The influence of Reading Recovery in the United States.* Columbus, OH: Reading Recovery Council of North America.

Schmitt, M. C., & Gregory, A. E. (2005). The impact of early literacy intervention: Where are the children now? *Literacy Teaching and Learning: An International Journal of Early Reading and Writing, 10*(1), 1–20.

Schwartz, R. M. (1997). Self-monitoring in beginning reading. *The Reading Teacher, 51*(1), 40–48.

Schwartz, R. M. (2005a). Literacy learning of at-risk first grade students in the Reading Recovery early intervention. *Journal of Educational Psychology, 97,* 257–267.

Schwartz, R. M. (2005b). Decisions, decisions: Responding to primary students during guided reading. *The Reading Teacher, 58*(5), 436–443.

Schwartz, R. M., & Gallant, P. (in press). The role of self-monitoring in initial word recognition learning. In C. Wyatt-Smith, J. Elkins, & S. Gunn (Eds.), Multiple perspectives on literacy learning and numeracy. Springer.

Shanahan, T., & Barr, R. (1995). Reading Recovery: An independent evaluation of the effects of an early instructional intervention for at-risk learners. *Reading Research Quarterly, 30*(4), 958–996.

Vellutino, F. R., Scanlon, D. M., Sipay, E. R., Small, S. G., Pratt, A., & Chen, R. (1996). Cognitive profiles of difficult-to-remediate and readily remediated poor readers: Early intervention as a vehicle for distinguishing between cognitive and experiential deficits as basic causes of specific reading disability. *Journal of Educational Psychology, 88*(4), 601–638.

What Works Clearinghouse (2006). *What works clearinghouse study design classification.* Retrieved from Institute of Education Science, US Department of Education: http://ies.ed.gov/ncee/wwc/twp.asp

What Works Clearinghouse (2007a). *Reading Recovery intervention report.* Retrieved from Institute of Education Science, US Department of Education: http://ies.ed.gov/ncee/wwc/reports/beginning_reading/ reading_recovery/

What Works Clearinghouse (2007b). *Reading Recovery intervention report technical appendices.* Retrieved from Institute of Education Science, US Department of Education: http://ies.ed.gov/ncee/wwc/reports/beginning_ reading/reading_recovery/

What Works Clearinghouse (2007c). *Beginning reading: WWC topic report.* Retrieved from Institute of Education Science, US Department of Education: http://ies.ed.gov/ncee/wwc/reports/beginning_reading/topic/

What Works Clearinghouse (2007d). Personal communication.

What Works Clearinghouse (2008). *Who we are.* Retrieved from Institute of Education Science, US Department of Education: http://ies.ed.gov/ncee/wwc/overview/

6

Reading Recovery Research in the United Kingdom and Ireland

Sue Burroughs-Lange

Literacy has mattered to the United Kingdom for centuries and continues to be of popular and political interest today. Debate has centred on absolute versus relative standards of achievement (e.g., recently, PIRLS, 2006; Hilton, 2006; Whetton, Twist, & Sainsbury, 2007), while popularly literacy is often characterized as an indicator of education standards generally and is therefore regarded as everyone's concern. An important shift has been gaining more acceptance within the English education system: the view that the measure of success lies not only in achievement norms but also in how many struggling learners are left behind. In the 1980s, that concern provided impetus for Marie Clay to begin working with educators on the introduction of Reading Recovery. Her influence has been felt even beyond the field of early intervention. In a review interweaving research, policy, and practice, this chapter reveals why and how a New Zealander's ideas came to influence education in the United Kingdom and Ireland.

The return journey: ideas from New Zealand colonising education in England

In response to the impact of Marie Clay's visit to Cambridge University in the late 1980s, the Surrey Local Education Authority sent experienced educator Jean Prance from Runnymede to New Zealand to train as the United Kingdom's first Reading Recovery Tutor/Teacher Leader. Douëtil (2007a) found historical symmetry in this action: '. . . the name Runnymede has a special significance as the site, in 1215, of the signing of the Magna Carta and the birthplace of British democracy. How appropriate, then, that the nearby Runnymede Education Centre should be the birthplace of Reading Recovery in Britain.'

By 1991–1992, with Jean Prance about to train her third group of Surrey teachers, Marie Clay and three New Zealand Reading Recovery professionals were established as visiting academics at the University of

London Institute of Education (ULIE) and began training nine Tutors/ Teacher Leaders and four groups of teachers for London. In this first year, the work was funded by the ULIE and a charitable foundation. In the second year (1992–1993) the New Zealanders, still active in London, helped to establish Reading Recovery training sites in other cities. Two Reading Recovery Trainers of Tutors/Teacher Leaders were trained concurrently. As daily teaching of individual children is required at every level of Reading Recovery training, 900 children received individual literacy lessons that year (Hobsbaum & Clay, 1993). By 1993–1994, the UK enterprise became autonomous in training and coordination. Government special funding (GEST — Grants for Education Support and Training) which had supported the expansion of the previous year continued over a 3-year development period until July 1995.

It had been a well-planned, effective introduction of a literacy innovation into a different national education system by a process replicating Reading Recovery's successful implementation in several states of Australia and the United States of America. In the light of English educational history where few 'imports' have lasted, Reading Recovery's success was remarkable.

Introducing Reading Recovery in England: the context

By 1995, there were 50 Tutors/Teacher Leaders training hundreds of teachers across England. What new research or political press had prompted the overtures made to Marie Clay in the 1980s? Why was the English education system so receptive to Reading Recovery at that time?

An explosion of reading research activity between 1960 and 1990 (see, for example, Raban, 1990) had stirred academic debate about theory and practice, but there was a lack of consensus that might have driven curriculum guidance for the teaching of reading. The wider publicity given to international evaluations of literacy probably played a part. There was general consternation when the Organization for Economic Cooperation and Development (OECD) comparisons of national reading standards showed New Zealand at the top of the list and England much lower down (Elley, 1992). The report from a group of Her Majesty's Inspectors (HMI) who visited New Zealand to investigate Reading Recovery in operation noted that in general 'literacy is accorded the supremely important place in the New Zealand system' (Office of Standards in Education, 1992, p. 22). Amongst many observations of Junior Class teaching, they noted a high quality of literacy activities that resulted in children 'receiving appropriate help and instruction, and developing independent reading interests and abilities' (Office of Standards in Education, 1992, p. 20). They stated that 'there is no reason to suppose [Reading Recovery] is not transferable to other education systems' (Office of Standards in Education, 1992, p. 23).

Special Educational Needs (SEN) and labelling children

A report on Special Educational Needs (Warnock, 1978) had shown that around a fifth of the school population could be expected to exhibit Special Educational Needs (SEN) in at least some period of their schooling. Warnock intended to save resources by refining the labelling of SEN children whose individual learning needs were now to be written in a straightforward *Statement* to be acted upon. But a decade later the SEN budget had exploded. Hope then transferred to the development of a National Curriculum to improve classroom practice in order to better meet the needs of most children. At the same time, the Kingman Committee reported that the centrality of literature in the English curriculum had led to a neglect of the teaching of early reading and writing (Department of Education and Science, 1988). Several years later these two concerns converged on an urgency to address the poor literacy achievement of the lowest group of children.

The National Curriculum and shifting the locus of control in educational decision-making

In 1989, the British Government became the locus of control of educational decision-making at all levels including curriculum content and process. It did so in a context of damaged national pride, public mistrust of schools' programmes, and seriously inadequate funding of Local Education Authorities (LEAs). Schools and teachers lost their autonomy and LEAs their authority, their funding, and any means of improving standards (Stannard & Huxford, 2007).

In this environment of reaction against child-centred, topic-organized curriculum, Reading Recovery was introduced — philosophically different, and (worse) foreign. Only very skilled strategists would be able to demonstrate that this exceptionally effective educational innovation could succeed in England, too. Marie Clay and Reading Recovery were equal to that challenge.

Going national — a dichotomy

The publication of international comparisons of literacy standards coincided with the period when Reading Recovery was set to expand across England. On the OECD ranked list, England's outcomes differed from many other countries performing in the same 'middle' group, in that there existed 'a long 'tail' of underachievement which is relatively greater than that of other countries' (Brooks, Pugh, & Schagen, 1996, p.10). However, the educational response did not adopt a logic of directing attention and resources to the lowest groups. Instead, the National Literacy Strategy was introduced in 1997, going well beyond the guidance of the National Curriculum of 1989. The National Literacy Strategy set national achievement targets, such as, 'By 2002, 80% of 11-year-olds should reach the standard expected for their age in English' in national standardized assessments. Yet at the time it was set, merely 57% of students were reaching the standard. About the remaining 20% not expected to reach the standard, little was said or planned until much later.

The development of the National Literacy Strategy (NLS)

Despite very positive evaluations of the efficacy of Reading Recovery in the English context (Hobsbaum, 1997; Hobsbaum & Clay, 1993; Moore & Wade, 1998; Wright, 1992), working with individual children in Reading Recovery was not part of the new National Literacy Strategy (NLS). The NLS drew support from the Literacy Task Force report (1997) *How Can We Teach Every Child to Read Well?* but ignored the Task Force's favourable report on the impact of Reading Recovery on children's literacy achievement. The National Literacy Strategy adapted the 'searchlight' model of the reading process (Bickler, Baker, & Hobsbaum, 1998). By acknowledging the reader's four main sources of information and the role of redundancy in text in its 'Framework for Teaching' (Department of Education & Employment, 1998), it resembled Marie Clay's complex theory of reading. However, the role of the individual reader in a complex task of 'orchestrating' the many perceptual, cognitive, and physical activities was lost in the NLS representation. The urge to simplify and reduce the model (ostensibly to assist classroom teachers) foreshadowed the 'simple view of reading' and an emphasis on phonics which has replaced it (Department for Education & Skills, The Rose Review, 2006).

Evaluations of the National Literacy Strategy (Earl, Watson, Levin, Leithwood, Fullan, & Torrence, 2003; Office of Standards in Education, 1998) reported some evidence of literacy progress in classrooms. Clay's theory of reading acquisition had been applied to classroom practice to some extent (Stainthorp, 2000), but without the concomitant depth of professional development that can in Fullan's words 'empower people' to effect change in practice. Yet Clay 'built her work around a sound understanding of, and sympathy for, 'teachers' . . . recognized them as partners and accorded them respect' (Mortimore & Mortimore, 1999, pp. 221–222).

The near demise of Reading Recovery in England: its ascendancy in Northern Ireland

Throughout the National Literacy Strategy years, much-reduced funding limited the ability of local education authorities to employ a Reading Recovery Tutor/Teacher Leader and of schools to employ Reading Recovery teachers. In 1992, the future of Reading Recovery had looked promising, rather as it does now in 2009. The favourable HMI report from New Zealand and early data on children's progress in Reading Recovery were both impressive. Labour Education Minister Jack Straw had announced a 3-year funding scheme: 'Reading Recovery is an expensive method. We want to set up pilot schemes to see whether it is cost effective' (Straw, 1992).

But in 1995, despite Reading Recovery's continuing impressive results, the Conservative Government withdrew all funding. Local councils and schools became pressured to prioritize the National Literacy Strategy demands and few could find the funding to continue Reading Recovery. Funding previously assigned to Special Educational Needs and early literacy was now diverted to employing teaching assistants, three of whom could be employed for the same cost as an experienced Reading Recovery teacher. Stainthorp (2000) warned that '. . . children who show atypical development need the most qualified and highly skilled teachers' (p. 299). But all the evidence that Reading Recovery works was unable to save it from near extinction.

Meanwhile, in the province of Northern Ireland interest in Reading Recovery was growing. Years of violent civil disorder had produced a focus on working for peace rather than investing in such social infrastructure as schooling. Children's education had been disrupted and the curriculum fossilized in its pre-'Troubles' form. Reading Recovery was now embraced as a means of tackling underachievement in literacy and giving children with a tough start in life a second chance at stability and success. Although unstated at the time, and only emerging in the later evaluations conducted on Reading Recovery in Northern Ireland, there was a hope that Reading Recovery's methods and theoretical base would also come to influence classroom practice (Gardner, Sutherland, & Meenan-Stain, 1998; Munn & Ellis, 2005).

Expansion of Reading Recovery in Northern Ireland was funded largely from grants from the European Economic Commission (EEC) in its support for the restoration of the social and physical fabric of war-torn countries. So pot-holed roads were mended and new ones built, schools were repaired, murals lauding hooded gunmen were gradually replaced by new terrace housing, and a plan for Reading Recovery to reach every school in Northern Ireland was put in place. By 1994, in the first 2 years of implementation, 50 schools had taken on Reading Recovery (Gardner et al., 1998).

In 2004, about one-quarter of Northern Ireland schools had Reading Recovery teachers in training. Munn and Ellis (2005) reported, 'Reading Recovery has achieved resounding success as an individual programme' (p. 341), observing that 'approximately two-thirds of schools had adopted practices from Reading Recovery that had widened their literacy curriculum' (p. 356). In England, the National Literacy Strategy had introduced classroom literacy programmes loosely based on Marie Clay's theory and New Zealand classroom teaching practices while ignoring the needs of children experiencing most difficulty. Northern Ireland's goal, by contrast, was to expand Reading Recovery coverage in response to the literacy learning needs of the lowest individuals. Marie Clay's stance that Reading Recovery 'cannot specify how a classroom programme for children of wide-ranging abilities should be mounted' and that 'one would not design a satisfactory classroom programme by studying only the needs of the hardest-to-teach children' (Clay, 2005, p. i) served to deflect debates about Reading Recovery from the ebb and flow of curriculum trends and emphases.

In Northern Ireland, EEC funding for educational development has now (2008) almost ceased, with approximately one thousand fewer children receiving Reading Recovery annually. The numbers of teachers and Tutors/Teacher Leaders have reduced accordingly. As Openshaw, Soler, Wearmouth, & Paige-Smith (2002, p. 25) have stated,

> the development of Reading Recovery in New Zealand and England illustrates how it is not simply the efficacy of individual programmes, but a combination of that efficacy and the political context at the micro and macro levels which establishes, expands and eventually de-stabilises new reading initiatives.

It was almost certainly Marie Clay's awareness of the political and fiscal context within which an educational enterprise has to be located that led her consistently and persistently to avoid aligning Reading Recovery with any particular literacy curriculum style.

'Every Child a Reader' initiative

Reading Recovery professionals had continued to lobby intensively for the early literacy intervention's wider acceptance in England. The immediate outcome was dedicated funding for a 3-year pilot (2005–2008) in 625 inner city schools; it included the training of Tutors/Teacher Leaders and teachers. The pilot's success led the national government to commit funds to provide Reading Recovery for 30,000 lowest achieving children annually until 2011.

Several converging initiatives contributed to the Reading Recovery campaign to launch the newly expanded Every Child a Reader initiative. Three were powerfully influential.

- Investment from the charitable trust of a major international financial institution (KPMG) was committed, confidence grew, and other major funders became involved. Their high-powered networks continued pressure on government to invest.

- An economic assessment of the return on investment of early intervention to address literacy difficulties was commissioned by the trust fund.

- A research evaluation was commissioned to compare the impact of Reading Recovery with other early interventions in use in poor, inner-city schools serving multi-ethnic communities.

Two studies are discussed in more detail here.

The long term cost benefits of early literacy intervention

Straw's 1992 comment, 'Reading Recovery is expensive,' has been repeated continually. The 2006 KPMG economic assessment commissioned financial experts to

- review the research on long term consequences of literacy difficulties for individuals and society,

- estimate the costs to the public purse that results, and

- estimate the return on investments in early intervention to address literacy difficulties.

The analysts' review showed 'very poor literacy' to be linked to costly educational special needs provision, truancy, exclusion from school, reduced employment opportunities, increased health risks, and greatly increased risk of involvement in the criminal justice system (KPMG, 2006). These increased risks operate over and above those associated with social disadvantage in general and those associated with lack of qualifications. Costs were attached to each of these risks and summed over the life course to the age of 37, the last point at which longitudinal survey data were currently available (Feinstein, 2002; Parsons & Bynner, 2002).

Based on a moderate Reading Recovery success rate that posited 79% of children taught reaching sustainable literacy levels, the analysts predicted a return on investment in the range of 14- to 17-fold for every pound (£) spent on Reading Recovery over the period between 2006–2008 and 2037–2039, when the children involved in the Reading Recovery 3-year Every Child a Reader pilot will have reached the age of 37. Their conservative estimates did not include savings that could not readily be quantified, such as the economic effects of reduced spending power, social housing costs, the costs of generally poor health, the costs of substance abuse over the age of 18, and the costs of inter-generational effects of poor literacy skills. In the overall figures, employment-related costs form the largest category of potential savings, with costs to the education system and the costs of crime providing the next largest categories (Bynner & Parsons, 1997; Parsons, 2002).

One striking finding showed the estimated costs of providing Reading Recovery (£2.398 in 2006) to each 6-year-old needing it, to be very close to the average costs of learning support/Special Education Needs provision for similar children throughout their primary years (age 5–11 years). Primary schools in England are therefore already spending approximately the same amount on each child with literacy difficulties whether they provide Reading Recovery at 6 years or a range of other interventions. The choice between Reading Recovery provision and a sequence of less effective interventions is not a cost issue, but a question of *when* to spend that money. The major difference is Reading Recovery's ability to prevent reading and writing failure, whereas struggling readers who have had no access to Reading Recovery are typically entering secondary schools at 11 years of age, reading at the level of a 7- or 8-year-old. The approach, structure, and thoroughness of the KPMG financial analysis adds a cost benefit argument to Marie Clay's claim that 'in the first three years of school, educators have their one and only chance to upset the correlation between intelligence measures and literacy progress' (Clay, 2005, p. 16). Provision of Reading Recovery in the second year of schooling to prevent later reading failure has now been shown in England to be economic good sense as well as a moral imperative.

Supporting evidence has come from Brooks (2007) who reviewed and re-analysed some 48 different literacy intervention schemes implemented in UK, including 121 separate studies. Brooks argued that ordinary classroom provision doesn't work for children with literacy difficulties. He shows that 'good' schemes can deliver at least twice the normal rate of progress, and it is reasonable to expect this. For nonreaders at 6–7 years, at least four times the rate of normal progress is necessary to catch up to literacy levels of their peers. Only Reading Recovery has been shown to deliver this outcome; the Reading Recovery national report for 2006–2007 (Douëtil, 2007b) on 5300 children in Reading Recovery showed average gains of 21 months in reading accuracy in 4–5 months, and continued standard rate of progress over the next 6 months.

Brooks' review asks of literacy interventions: 'How do we know it will work here?' (2007, p. 13). There is ample evidence that Reading Recovery works 'here' in the UK and Ireland for children with most difficulty.

Comparison study of literacy progress of young children in London schools

Reading Recovery annual data reports show outstanding literacy progress for children already failing, but one remaining question is still raised by sceptics: 'How do we know these children would not have got under way with literacy without provision of costly Reading Recovery intervention?' The London evaluation study (Burroughs-Lange & Douëtil, 2007) explored this question.

Adopting an unusual, naturalistic approach, this comparison study was designed to evaluate the impact of early literacy intervention on children in London schools in the course of 1 school year (2005–2006). Children receiving Reading Recovery were matched with low-achieving 6-year-olds in similar schools that offered other kinds of literacy interventions. The researchers did not participate in the work in the schools, nor did they manipulate any features of the schools' provision (Burroughs-Lange & Douëtil, 2007). The study evaluated

- the effectiveness of Reading Recovery in raising the literacy achievement of struggling readers (aged 6),

- the impact of Reading Recovery on other aspects of children's behaviour and attitudes to school, and

- the impact of Reading Recovery on literacy levels of 6-year-olds' classrooms, through their weakest peers having access to the effective early intervention (Reading Recovery).

The London boroughs selected for Reading Recovery and comparison samples were amongst the lowest achieving in England. Forty-two of these schools in 10 London boroughs and districts participated in the study. They were similar in size, economic disadvantage, and numbers of children learning English as an additional language. All of the schools offered some children extra tuition as well as classroom literacy teaching. Reading Recovery operated in half of these schools.

A comparison was made of the literacy progress of the lowest achieving 6-year-olds and of their Year 1 classes at the beginning and end of the 2005–2006 school year. The lowest achieving children were assessed at both times using An Observation Survey of Early Literacy Achievement (Clay, 2002) and a word-reading test, British Ability Scales II Word Reading (Elliott, 1996). It was not known at the beginning of the year which children, if any, would go on to enter which intervention scheme. Their whole classes (1166 Year 1 children in all), including these lowest groups, were also assessed on the Word Recognition and Phonic Skills Test (Moseley, 2003).

What worked?

At the beginning of the 2005–2006 school year, the 292 lowest achieving children were unable to read even the simplest texts, could only recognize a few letters, and write about six words correctly. At the end of the year, the study showed that most of these children had made very little progress. The exception was the group of children who received Reading Recovery. From similarly low starting points, children who received Reading Recovery gained on average 14 book levels, 20 months reading age, and could write 45 words correctly (within a 10-minute time limit). At about age 6-and-a-half, they had now successfully caught up with their peers.

Results for the 87 Reading Recovery children were not separated out into children who achieved the goal of independent readers (discontinued) and those who had not 'caught-up' by the time their lessons ceased (referred). The mean literacy group results are reported for *all* children's progress across the year in which they received some Reading Recovery lessons or any other intervention.

For this lowest achieving group, Table 1 shows the literacy progress of 147 children in schools without Reading Recovery provision (Comparison Group) compared with the progress of 87 children who received Reading Recovery during the year. Measures were tasks of the Observation Survey (Clay, 2002) and the British Ability Scales II Word Reading (Elliott, 1996). At the end of the year in July 2006, on all measures, Reading Recovery children were doing significantly better and had reached age-appropriate literacy levels.

Table 1: **Mean Scores of Reading Recovery Children and Comparison Children at Beginning and End of the Year (September 2005 – July 2006)**

Time	Group	Number of Children	Book Level	Concepts About Print	Letter Identification	Hearing and Recording Sounds in Words	Writing Vocabulary	BAS II Reading Age
Sept 2005	Reading Recovery	87	< 1	10	38	12	6	4y 11m
	Comparison	147	< 1	10	35	13	6	4y 10m
July 2006	Reading Recovery	87	15	19	53	35	45	6y 7m
	Comparison	147	4	15	46	26	21	5y 5m

Some evidence of the wider impact of Reading Recovery beyond those children receiving the intervention was provided by the intact class measure (Word Reading and Phonics Skills) shown in Table 2. At the beginning of the school year, September 2005, both groups of classes had an average reading age of just over 5 years.

Table 2: **Year 1 Class Scores on Word Reading and Phonics Skills (WRAPS) in Reading Recovery and Non-Reading Recovery Schools at Beginning and End of Year (September 2005 – July 2006)**

	Children in Schools with Reading Recovery (N = 600)				Children in Schools with No Reading Recovery (N = 566)			
	Beginning of Year		End of Year		Beginning of Year		End of Year	
	Mean	S D	Mean	S D	Mean	S D	Mean	S D
WRAPS Age in Months	61.7	8.7	77.5	11.5	61.4	8.6	73.5	11.5

Significant difference between groups $p < .05$.

At the end of the year, on average, children in classes in schools with Reading Recovery were 4 months ahead of similar children in similar classes without access to Reading Recovery early intervention. Overall, this mean difference in achievement is slightly greater than might be expected by merely lifting the competence of the lowest few. As part of this evaluation, the Year 1 class teachers were asked to report on the progress during the year of the lowest achieving group in literacy, oracy, mathematics concepts, work habits, social skills, and other learning related attitudes (Quay, Steele, Johnson, & Hortman, 2001). The children who had received Reading Recovery during the year were reported by their teachers as having made greater progress across the range of learning and social behaviours such as self-confidence and ability to follow directions, as well as in literacy skills (Burroughs-Lange & Douëtil, 2007).

After demonstrating that Reading Recovery works even in the most difficult schooling contexts, and that there are long-term cost benefits from effective literacy intervention, one key question remains: Do the benefits of early intervention last?

Follow-up studies of Reading Recovery in England

To consider the evidence that could address this question, reviewed here are (a) a well-reputed study on children, some of whom received Reading Recovery intervention (Hurry & Sylva, 2007); (b) a study of ex-Reading Recovery children in England followed up in national testing at ages 7 and 11 (Douëtil, 2004); and (c) a 1-year follow-up on the London comparison study (Burroughs-Lange, 2008).

Marie Clay advises caution when talking about what effective early intervention can achieve: 'A few children are trying to learn complex tasks with multiple counts against them' (Clay, 2005, p. 13). Many other factors in children's lives impinge on their being able to continue to thrive and progress in their learning (Mortimore & Whitty, 1997; Wade & Moore, 1996). Most of these other factors do not go away once they have learned to be independent readers and writers at 6 years of age. However, a schooling system needs to be able to rely on two things: (a) early intervention that brings even the most disadvantaged children up to age competency and (b) knowledgeable teaching teams who can support the education of children who have had multiple life and learning challenges impact on their early schooling — challenges that could continue to upset children's early gains.

The first comparison study (Hurry & Sylva, 2007)

This early study relates to interventions in 1992–1993, followed up 1 year later in 1994, and again 4 years after the intervention in 1996. This work was partly re-analysed and newly presented in 2007 but with no new data added. The research design compared

- children in the first year of implementing Reading Recovery in six London boroughs (all Reading Recovery teachers in training) and in Surrey (1992–1993),

- children who received a Phonological Training delivered by the research team based on work of Bradley and Bryant (1985), and

- control groups drawn from schools in both early intervention settings.

At the end of the 1992–1993 and 1993–1994 school years, assessments of both Reading Recovery and Phonological Training showed significantly improved aspects of children's reading, 'with Reading Recovery having a broader and more powerful effect' (Hurry & Sylva, 2007, p. 1).

Three-and-a-half years after intervention (September 1996), there were no differential significant effects between the groups on reading overall. However, Reading Recovery showed a significant positive effect for a subgroup of children who were complete non-readers at 6 years old.

In response to Marie Clay's active development of Reading Recovery and its international dissemination, and to constant review of local data, several changes are evident in Reading Recovery teaching in 2008. In England, these changes take the form of (a) children's younger entry into Reading Recovery, (b) more attention to school and home liaison, (c) higher levels of literacy competency before Reading Recovery lessons cease, and (d) more attention to phonemic awareness and phonological knowledge in both discrete teaching components and embedded within reading and writing tasks in Reading Recovery lessons. Replication of Hurry and Sylva's evaluation could be expected to show considerable differences between 1992–1994 and 2006–2008. In England, the simultaneous extension of Reading Recovery and the strong push for greater phonics teaching in early years' classrooms would be an interesting context in which to reassess those very early findings.

The long-term effects of Reading Recovery on National Curriculum tests at end of key stages 1 and 2 (Douëtil, 2004)

Data were collected on ex-Reading Recovery children in national assessments at 7 and 11 years. In 1999, of the children who had received Reading Recovery in the 1997–1998 school year, 64% were in the Level 2 band (meeting age expectations) and 1% at Level 3 (above age expectations), while 35% were still below average levels. So two-thirds of the lowest achievers were sustaining average rates of progress 1 to 1½ years after intervention.

Of that same cohort of children when aged 11 in 2003, 41% were still at average levels and 10% above average (51% average or above). A further 28% were at Level 3 in reading, which is below age expectations of 11-year-olds, but well above an average 7-year-old. So comparisons between lowest achieving children who received Reading Recovery at 6 and their age peers showed robust effects of Reading Recovery through to age 11.

The Reading Recovery follow-up study in London schools (Burroughs-Lange, 2008)

Coinciding with re-publication of the early Hurry and Sylva study (2007), the London follow-up study is important. It looked at schools in poor, inner city areas, in the light of several years of National Literacy Strategy implementation and recent developments in Reading Recovery, including responses to new research on the functioning of the brain, the role of phonological knowledge in early literacy acquisition, and the data-led UK decision to intervene sooner, in Year 1.

In the London comparison study (described earlier) of 21 schools with Reading Recovery and 21 schools without Reading Recovery, children in the lowest attaining groups had begun the year (2005–2006) at similar low literacy levels. By the end of the year (July 2006), most children who had received Reading Recovery were in line with their chronological age in literacy. The Comparison Group (low-achieving children in schools without Reading Recovery) was on average 14 months behind.

A year later in July 2007, the literacy achievement of those same children remaining in the same 42 schools was again compared. Word reading measures (Word Reading and Phonic Skills and British Ability Scales II Word Reading) and word writing measures (Writing Vocabulary from the Observation Survey) were repeated along with a new reading comprehension measure (Progress in English 7).

As shown in Table 3, follow-up assessments favoured the ex-Reading Recovery Group in word reading (British Ability Scales II Word Reading). Children who had Reading Recovery in Year 1 had an average Reading Age of 7 years 9 months at the end of Year 2 while the Comparison Group without Reading Recovery had an average Reading Age of 6 years 9 months.

Table 3: Word Reading Age in Months on British Ability Scales II Word Reading: Lowest Literacy Groups (Follow-up in July 2007)

Group	N	Mean	SD
Comparison	108	81.18	16.23
Ex-Reading Recovery	77	93.21	14.26

Significant difference $p < .0001$, Effect size 0.74.

By the end of Year 2, children in the ex-Reading Recovery Group were still, on average, 8-and-a-half months ahead of the Comparison Group in word recognition and phonic skills as well. When viewed as standard scores (Table 4), the ex-Reading Recovery Group achieved the norm for their age group while the Comparison Group fell 10 standard points behind.

Table 4: Word Recognition and Phonics Skills (WRAPS) Standard
Scores: Lowest Literacy Groups (Follow-up in July 2007)

Group	N	Mean	SD
Comparison	109	90.17	12.81
Ex-Reading Recovery	77	100.32	10.86

Significant difference $p < .001$, Effect size 0.79.

In the more global assessment on reading accuracy, comprehension,
grammar, and spelling (Progress in English 7), change over time
comparisons cannot be made, but standard scores served to compare
the ex-Reading Recovery Group with the normally distributed group
standardization (see Table 5).

Table 5: Standard Scores for Progress in English 7: Lowest
Literacy Groups (Follow-up in July 2007)

Group	N	Mean	SD
Comparison	104	85.56	11.56
Ex-Reading Recovery	74	95.77	13.25

Significant difference $p < .001$, Effect size 0.88.

At the end of Year 2 (age around 7+), National Curriculum Assessments
(SATs) are undertaken. These results were collected for children who
had been in the lowest groups at start of Year 1. More than 86% of those
children in the study who received Reading Recovery in Year 1 went on
to achieve age-appropriate level in reading (Level 2), compared with 57%
in comparison schools.

Significant long-terms effects of the Reading Recovery intervention
were also found on the Writing Vocabulary Test of the Observation Survey
(see Table 6). Low-achieving children in non-Reading Recovery schools
were compared with Reading Recovery children at the end of Year 2.

Table 6: Writing Vocabulary Means for Lowest Achieving
Children (Follow-up in July 2007)

Group	N	Mean	SD
Comparison	114	34.1	17.4
Ex-Reading Recovery	77	65.1	28.1

Significant difference $p < .001$, Effect size 1.77.

Children who received Reading Recovery could, on average, write around 6 words correctly at the start of Year 1 and more than 65 words at the end of Year 2 (within a 10-minute time limit). Children without access to the Reading Recovery intervention during Year 1 could write correctly only around half that number of words at the end of Year 2.

National Curriculum Assessments (SATs) in writing showed that at age 7+, over 83% of the lowest achieving group children who had received Reading Recovery in Year 1 were now achieving the average level for their age, compared with 57% of groups in comparison schools.

Finally, progress in classroom literacy was followed up at the end of Year 2, repeating the Word Reading and Phonics Skills (WRAPS) and Progress in English 7. Table 7 compares WRAPS scores for classrooms in Reading Recovery schools and classrooms in schools without Reading Recovery at three points in time (beginning of Year 1, end of Year 1, and end of Year 2). Although analyses showed no significant differences between schools at the start of Year 1, differences were significant at the end of Year 1 ($p < .001$) and at follow-up at the end of Year 2 ($p < .001$).

Table 7: **Word Reading and Phonics Skills (WRAPS) Raw Scores in Year 1 and Year 2 Classrooms (September 2005, July 2006, July 2007)**

	Group	N	Mean	Std Deviation	Std Error Mean
Sept 2005	Comparison Schools No Reading Recovery	532	15.04	8.73	.38
	Schools with Reading Recovery	630	14.74	9.24	.37
July 2006	Comparison Schools No Reading Recovery	494	26.98	11.64	.52
	Schools with Reading Recovery	591	30.57	11.73	.48
July 2007	Comparison Schools No Reading Recovery	398	40.32	13.44	.67
	Schools with Reading Recovery	457	43.40	12.04	.56

Similarly, Table 8 reveals that classes in schools with Reading Recovery achieved higher follow-up scores on the Progress in English 7 assessment in July 2007.

Table 8: Raw Scores for Progress in English 7 by Classroom
Groups at End of Year 2, July 2007

	Group	N	Mean Score Range 0–35	Std Deviation	Std Error Mean
End Year 2 July 2007	Comparison Schools No Reading Recovery	381	21.09	8.88	.45
	Schools with Reading Recovery	455	24.61	8.38	.39

Significant difference *p* < .001.

In summary, the children who had received Reading Recovery in 2005–2006 were achieving, on average, within or above their chronological age band on all measures and were still around a year ahead of the comparison children in schools where Reading Recovery was not available. Whatever the measure used, it is clearly demonstrated that low-achieving children who had access to Reading Recovery went on to attain a far higher level than matched groups, and continued to progress with their age cohort a year later. Having Reading Recovery in their schools brought benefits to the literacy levels of class groups as well as low achievers, benefits that a year later were also shown to have been sustained.

The resurgence of 'faith' in phonics

There have been brief references in this chapter to the responsiveness of Marie Clay's theory to new research in the fields of cognitive neuroscience and into the role of phonemic awareness and phonological knowledge in the acquisition of reading and writing. These fields of research have largely served to confirm her work, particularly advances in understanding the brain's activity in relation to memory and learning. Their implications for Reading Recovery teaching have been incorporated into the training of teachers and Tutors/Teacher Leaders (see, for example, Clay, 2005).

In the UK, the continuing debate over the role of phonics in literacy learning has figured prominently in issues of diagnosis and treatment of dyslexia (Elliot, 2005). The Reading Recovery community has adopted the stance that the successful intervention of Reading Recovery prevents many children being labelled 'dyslexic.' For the very few children found to need further specialist help, the period of Reading Recovery teaching uncovers that need. Both outcomes are positive. (See Clay, 2005, Part One, pp. 55–56.)

Over the last 20 years in particular, there has been extensive growth of research and design of interventions centred on word-reading and decoding theories. Research has moved through a focus on reading progress predicted by phonemic awareness (e.g., Goswami & Bryant, 1990); the role of onset and rime (e.g., Bryant, MacLean, Bradley, & Crossland, 1990; Goswami, 1990); the awareness of 'letter neighbourhoods' that comes from reading mileage (De Cara & Goswami, 2003); benefits of study of morphology (e.g., Nunes, Bryant, & Olsson, 2003), and a host of studies claiming the benefits of teaching children to synthesize sound in decoding words in order to read text (e.g., Ellis, 2007; discussion of Johnston & Watson, 2005; and Dias & Juniper, 2002). Marie Clay's (2005) teaching guidance referred to children's awareness of syllables early, prior to phoneme awareness. But like Clay, Goswami (2000) points out that whilst awareness of syllables, of onset and rime, of phonemes, of synthetic and analytic phonics, all have an impact on reading progress, (e.g., Torgeson, Morgan, & Davies, 1992), importantly these are all amenable to impact from teaching, including any determination of developmental progression.

In England a major review (Department for Education and Skills, 'The Rose Review', 2006), in spite of favouring 'a balanced approach' to the teaching of reading, has been presented largely as demonstrating a pressing need for early and better teaching of 'synthetic phonics.' The 'searchlights' metaphor used by the National Literacy Strategy to represent the complex cognitive activity of reading and the need for flexibility in teaching has been replaced by the 'simple view of reading' intended to assist teachers assess and teach children (see Gough, Hoover, & Peterson, 1996, on their 'simple view').

Marie Clay observed that accurate reading in early acquisition is very unlikely without the young reader's considerable reliance on meaning as both the goal of the activity and a tool for checking probability. The simple view separates comprehension from decoding. Its authors present it as a 'conceptual framework' with 'clear definition between the two dimensions' of language comprehension and word recognition (see Oakhill, Cain & Bryant, 1999, on dissociation of word reading and comprehension). Four different 'patterns of performance' categorise readers as either good or poor in combinations of these two dimensions. Readers in the strongest quadrant will have good word recognition and good comprehension; those in the weakest quadrant will exhibit poor word recognition and poor comprehension. The rest will have either good or poor comprehension coupled with poor or good word reading — one strength and one weakness. As to how poor readers become good, few agree.

Marie Clay described the 'simplest' way to help young children become literate like this:

> The goal of teaching is to assist the child to construct effective networks in his brain for linking all strategic activity that will be needed to work on texts, not merely to accumulate items of knowledge. (Clay, 2005, p. 44)

That calls for the

> astute judgement of the teacher about when to slow up and attend to detail and how soon to call for ... quick responding to letters, words, and print features that are known. (Clay, 2005, p. 43)

By contrast, the English curriculum 'simple view' places the *initial* focus of teaching on letter-sound associations and using that knowledge to synthesize sounds across words in order to read text by decoding (see, for example, Dixon, Stuart, & Masterson, 2002). A few challenges from comparison studies across other languages (e.g., Goswami, 2005) raise questions about 'synthetic phonics' as a simple way into reading English, given the language's orthographic irregularity and syllabic complexity. In the dyslexia field, Snowling and colleagues (Bowyer-Crane, Snowling, Duff, Fieldsend, Carroll, Miles, Gotz, & Hulme, in press) have drawn attention to oral language as a neglected component in studies of poor reading progress. In short, researchers' questions derive from their prior assumptions about the primary goal of early literacy acquisition.

Research horizons

With Marie Clay no longer here to be the quiet voice and intellectual power behind an educational revolution, the challenge for future research into early literacy learning and effective teaching seems to fall into three areas of continued enquiry:

- early literacy acquisition,
- teacher learning, and
- effecting educational change in ephemeral political contexts.

Research in the field of learning and teaching generally takes one of two forms. Either it is

(a) *clinical* — focused on an experimental design which narrows down on particular aspect(s) of learning to read or write and tries to determine the cognitions involved in those processes in responses to controlled stimuli in out-of-classroom learning contexts; or

(b) *comparative* — focused on the teaching content/style of differing approaches, often based on differing theories about the reading process and its sub-skills. In many cases the researchers themselves teach or provide professional development for individuals/groups/classes in the practice they have developed.

Both forms of research are needed. Clinical/experimental research refines our theories of cognitions involved in learning to read and write, but reports of successful research can dishearten teachers uncertain whether the processes described would work for regular teachers in real schools. Powerful systemic and pedagogic change is likely only when these two strands of research inform each other. Exploratory research, monitored in detail, short and long term, can advance teaching of children and teachers' professional learning provided it includes research to establish infrastructures for implementing teaching protocols with inbuilt mechanisms for ongoing quality assurance.

Marie Clay's exemplary work with Reading Recovery shows what can be achieved when theoretically grounded teaching stays responsive to new clinical research, in an education system simultaneously attending to and valuing practitioner learning. In each new setting Reading Recovery has established an implementation infrastructure able to balance quality assurance and processes for revision, at levels of learner, teacher, and leadership. This maintains the relevance of an education enterprise whilst sustaining achievement of its declared goals.

Furthering understandings of early literacy acquisition

The legacy of Marie Clay to early literacy researchers is an absolute insistence on evidence-based practice. As she ensured with Reading Recovery, well-designed research always involves collection of the detailed quantitative and qualitative records that underpin educational decision-making. 'Assessment for learning' remains a much-used phrase in UK education. In the one-to-one setting, Reading Recovery's daily practice of recording observations of teaching and learning settings embodies fundamental assessment principles. More research is merited into how those principles might apply in broader settings. Teachers' observation data on struggling readers would have pertinence to the growing body of research on plasticity in the functioning of the brain.

Hobsbaum, Peters, & Sylva (1996) explored how Reading Recovery teachers use cognitive scaffolding of children's learning in writing. Further research is warranted on the role of reciprocity in early literacy learning, particularly on how teachers' shaping of activities operates on the learners' cognitive constructions.

Marie Clay (2005) stressed the importance of the learner developing speed and fluency in cognitive operations in order to strengthen pathways in the brain. Reading Recovery has few examples of medical and educational researchers working together. Her later work indicates the potential value of such collaboration.

In England, a research project is planned with the small group of children referred for post-Reading Recovery specialist help. Further intervention programmes for randomized samples of children will use either (a) refined Reading Recovery teaching or (b) dyslexia-trained teachers' largely phonics-based practice. Given the UK political context, these comparisons may prove counter-productive; Marie Clay's evidence-based approach using detailed observations of children's learning, teachers' rationales, and interactions within the learning environment would have the potential to yield much more powerful outcomes, furthering understandings through a depth of contextual knowledge.

Researching teacher professional learning

Teacher professional learning in Reading Recovery practice offers a rich field of research, with abundant anecdotal evidence of the transformational effects of Reading Recovery professional development on Trainers, teachers, and Tutors/Teacher Leaders. The effectiveness of teaching and learning at all Reading Recovery's levels is apparently founded on the common theoretical assumption that learning is individually constructed. Perkins (1992, 2006), in the legacy of Dewey and his interpreters, discusses the challenges of constructivist theories for troublesome learning when the goal moves from training memories to educating minds.

Clay and Cazden (1990) have shown the compatibility of Clay and Vygotsky theories of teaching and learning. The application of Vygotsky's 'zone of proximal development' is evident whenever Reading Recovery teachers, Tutors/Teacher Leaders, or Trainers assist the child or adult student by scaffolding new learning. The ways in which professional learning is scaffolded in Reading Recovery is worthy of researchers' attention. Taylor (2006) studied a 'spiral curriculum' in the initial professional development course for Tutors/Teacher Leaders at the University of London Institute of Education. Bodman (2007) developed a grounded, theoretical model of feedback/feed-forward in complex professional learning. These studies raise important questions about course design and management when the goal is growth of critically reflective, independent, self-developing, professionals. An earlier study (Lange & Burroughs-Lange, 1994) explored the relationship between professional uncertainty and growth.

Effecting educational change

Arguably, Marie Clay with Reading Recovery and Jerome Bruner with 'Man: A course of study' (Bruner, 2006) are the only theorists with strong personal research bases to have successfully transformed their learning theories into holistic educational activity that teachers could use successfully. Reading Recovery has been the longer-lived and more extensive in its large international take-up. Although lauded by curriculum developers, 'Man: A course of study' soon came under attack for the demands it placed on teachers. Juxtaposition of new research into management of change in education, with further research on the layers of activity involved in Reading Recovery implementation, could prove highly informative to both fields of study. It is significant that both Bruner and Clay worked from closely allied assumptions about learning which their own research furthered.

Whitty (2006) highlighted the difficulties governments encounter when establishing consistently and exclusively evidence-based policy. New Labour proclaimed its commitment not only to evidence-informed policy but also finding out and disseminating what works. In the last decade, UK governments have commissioned three searches for 'what works' evidence in early intervention. In recent years, the UK Reading Recovery evidence base has been enlarged, in particular through (a) the cost benefit study (KPMG, 2006); (b) the SATs follow-up to age 11 (Douëtil, 2004); and (c) the London Reading Recovery evaluation and follow-up (Burroughs-Lange, 2008). The complexities of informing policy by means of this particular collection of evidence have been suggested by reference to the quantity of research on literacy learning that has focused on psychological explanations at the level of word and sub-word reading (e.g., Oakhill, Cain, & Bryant, 1999).

The tension between national directives and an autonomy-seeking teaching profession is considerable. In the United Kingdom, where the government also commissions research, the balance tips in favour of national control. Reading Recovery could play a key role to furthering knowledge in the field. Hargreaves (1996) called for research that

> (a) demonstrates conclusively that if teachers change x for y there will be a significant and enduring improvement in teaching and learning and (b) has developed an effective

method of convincing teachers of the benefits of, and means to, changing from x to y. (p. 5)

The research that Marie Clay undertook, fostered, and supported goes well beyond Ball's (2001) requirement for research to provide at least 'accounts of what works for unselfconscious (teacher) drones to implement' (p. 266).

Educational advancements impact on all learners. When change lacks a sound research base, is idiosyncratic and poorly managed, and includes no detailed evaluation, the most vulnerable learners suffer most. Marie Clay and the history of Reading Recovery in the United Kingdom and Ireland, as elsewhere, have much to offer future generations. The robustness of Reading Recovery in navigating political floods and droughts carries interesting messages about the strength provided by a powerful research foundation and the consistency of focus drawn from it. Responsiveness, tentativeness, evidence-based action, and adoption of strategic approaches may not seem to sit well together. And yet the story told here shows how Marie Clay's valuing of all those, her communication of their significance, and her empowering of others to use them, have left a unique legacy. The hundreds of thousands of changed lives, adult and child, can continue to expand if the research baton she passed on is grasped firmly by the educational community she led and worked alongside.

References

Ball, S. J. (2001). You've been NfERed! Dumbing down the academy, National Educational Research forum 'a national strategy-consultation paper', a brief and bilious response. *Journal of Education Policy, 16*(3), 265–268.

Bickler, S., Baker, S., & Hobsbaum, A. (1998). *Book bands for guided reading* (1st ed.). London: UK Reading Recovery National Network.

Bodman, S. (2007). *The power of feedback in professional learning.* Unpublished doctoral thesis. London: Institute of Education, University of London.

Bowyer-Crane, C., Snowling, M. J., Duff, F. J., Fieldsend, E., Carroll, J. M., Miles, J., Gotz, K., & Hulme, C. (in press). Improving early language and literacy skills: Differential effects of an oral language versus a phonology with reading intervention. *Journal of Child Psychology and Psychiatry.*

Bradley, L., & Bryant, P. (1985). *Rhyme and reason in reading and spelling.* Ann Arbor, MI: University of Michigan Press.

Brooks, G. (2007). *What works for children with literacy difficulties: The effectiveness of intervention schemes, research report 380.* London: Department of Education and Skills.

Brooks, G., Pugh, A. K., & Schagen, I. (1996). *Reading performance at nine.* Slough: National Foundation for Educational Research.

Bruner, J. S. (2006). *In search of pedagogy, Volume 1: The selected works of Jerome Bruner, 1957–1978.* Chapter 8 — Man: A course of study. New York: Routledge.

Bryant, P., MacLean, M., Bradley, L., & Crossland, J. (1990). Rhyme and alliteration, phonemic detection and learning to read. *Developmental Psychology, 26,* 429–438.

Burroughs-Lange, S. (2008). *Comparison of literacy progress of young children in London schools: A follow up study.* London: Institute of Education.

Burroughs-Lange, S., & Douëtil, J. (2007). Literacy progress of young children from poor urban settings: A Reading Recovery comparison study. *Literacy Teaching and Learning, 12*(1), 19–46.

Bynner, J., & Parsons, S. (1997). *It doesn't get any better: The impact of poor basic skills on the lives of 37 year olds.* London: Basic Skills Agency.

Clay, M. M. (2002). *An observation survey of early literacy achievement* (2nd ed.). Auckland: Heinemann.

Clay, M. M. (2005). *Literacy lessons designed for individuals, Parts one and two.* Auckland: Heinemann.

Clay, M. M., & Cazden, C. (1990). A Vygotskian interpretation of Reading Recovery. In L. Moll (Ed.), *Vygotsky and education* (pp. 206–222). Cambridge, UK: Cambridge University Press.

De Cara, B., & Goswami, U. (2003). Phonological neighbourhood density effects in a rhyme awareness task in 5-year-old children. *Journal of Child Language, 30*, 695–710.

Department for Education and Skills (2006). *Independent review of teaching of early reading: Final report, 'The Rose Review.'* London: Department for Education and Skills.

Department of Education and Employment (DfEE) (1998). *The National Literacy Strategy: Framework for teaching.* London: DfEE.

Department of Education and Science (DES) (1988). *Report of the Committee of Enquiry into the Teaching of the English language* (The Kingman Report). London: Her Majesty's Stationery Office (HMSO).

Dias, K., & Juniper, L. (2002). Phono-Graphix — Who needs additional literacy support? An outline of research in Bristol schools. *Support for Learning, 17*(1), 34–38.

Dixon, M., Stuart, M., & Masterson, J. (2002). The role of phonological awareness and the development of orthographic representations. *Reading and Writing, 15*, 295–316.

Douëtil, J. (2004). *The long-term effects of Reading Recovery on National Curriculum tests at end of Key Stages 1 and 2.* London: Institute of Education, University of London. (Mimeograph)

Douëtil, J. (2007a). Influence of Marie Clay in Europe. *Journal of Reading Recovery, 7*(1), 127.

Douëtil, J. (2007b). *Reading Recovery™ annual report for UK and Ireland 2006–2007.* London Institute of Education, University of London.

Earl, L., Watson, N., Levin, B., Leithwood, K., Fullan, M., & Torrence, N. (2003). *Watching and learning 3. Final report of the external evaluation of England's National Literacy and Numeracy Strategies.* Ontario: Ontario Institute for Studies in Education, University of Toronto.

Elley, W. B. (1992). How in the world do students read? *I. E. A. study of reading literacy.* Hamburg: The International Association for the Evaluation of Educational Achievement.

Elliot, J. (2005). The dyslexia debate: More heat than light? *Literacy Today, 45*, 8.

Elliott, C. D. (1996). *British ability scales II word reading.* London: NFER Nelson.

Ellis, S. (2007). Policy and research: Lessons from Clackmannanshire Synthetic Phonics Initiative. *Journal of Early Childhood Literacy, 7*(3), 281–297.

Feinstein, L. (2002). *Quantitative estimates of the social benefits of learning, 2: Health (Depression and Obesity).* London: Centre for Research on the Wider Benefits of Learning.

Gardner, J., Sutherland, A., & Meenan-Stain, C. (1998). *Reading Recovery in Northern Ireland: The first two years.* Belfast: The Blackstuff Press.

Goswami, U. (1990). Phonological pruning and orthographic analogies in reading. *Journal of Experimental Child Psychology, 4*, 323–340.

Goswami, U, (2000). *Phonological and lexical processes.* In M. L. Kamill, P. B. Mosenthal, P. D. Pearson, & R. Barr, *Handbook of reading research: Vol. III* (pp. 251–268). Mahwah, NJ: Lawrence Erlbaum.

Goswami, U. (2005). Synthetic phonics and learning to read: A cross-language perspective. *Educational Psychology in Practice, 21*(4), 273–282.

Goswami, U., & Bryant, P. E. (1990). *Phonological skills and learning to read.* Hillsdale, NJ: Lawrence Erlbaum.

Gough, P. B., Hoover, W. A., & Peterson, C. L. (1996). Some observations on the simple view of reading. In C. Cornoldi and J. V. Oakhill (Eds.), *Reading comprehension difficulties: Processes and remediation.* Mahwah, NJ: Lawrence Erlbaum.

Hargreaves, D. (1996). *Teaching as a research-based profession.* London: Teacher Training Agency.

Hilton, M. (2006). Measuring standards in primary English: Issues of validity and accountability with respect to PIRLS and National Curriculum test scores, *British Educational Research Journal, 32*(6), 817–837.

Hobsbaum, A. (1997). Reading Recovery in England. In S. L. Swartz & A. F. Klein (Eds.), *Research in Reading Recovery* (pp. 132–147). Portsmouth, NH: Heinemann.

Hobsbaum, A., & Clay, M. M. (1993). *A training scheme for the Reading Recovery programme: The pilot years 1991–93.* Unpublished report. Institute of Education, University of London.

Hobsbaum, A., Peters, S., & Sylva, K. (1996). Scaffolding in Reading Recovery. *Oxford Review of Education, 22*(1), 17–35.

Hurry, J., & Sylva, K. (2007). Long-term outcomes of early reading intervention. *Journal of Research in Reading, 30*(2), 1–22.

Johnston, R., & Watson, J. (2005). *The effects of synthetic phonics teaching on reading and spelling attainment: A seven year longitudinal study.* Edinburgh: Scottish Executive Education Department.

KPMG Foundation (2006). *The long term costs of literacy difficulties.* London: KPMG Foundation.

Lange, J. D., & Burroughs-Lange, S. G. (1994). Professional uncertainty and professional growth: A case study of experienced teachers. *Teaching and Teacher Education, 10*(6), 617–631.

Literacy Task Force (1997). *A reading revolution: How can we teach every child to read well?* London: Institute of Education, University of London.

Moore, M., & Wade, B. (1998). Reading Recovery: Its effectiveness in the long term. *Support for Learning. 13*(3), 123–128.

Mortimore, P., & Mortimore, J. (1999). The political and the professional in education: An unnecessary conflict? In J. S. Gaffney and B. J. Askew (Eds.), *Stirring the waters: The influence of Marie Clay* (pp. 221–238). Portsmouth, NH: Heinemann.

Mortimore, P., & Whitty, G. (1997). *Can school effectiveness overcome the effects of disadvantage?* London: Institute of Education, University of London.

Moseley, D. (2003). *Word recognition and phonic skills* (2nd ed.). Abingdon: Hodder & Stoughton.

Munn, P., & Ellis, S. (2005). Interactions between school systems and Reading Recovery programmes: Evidence from Northern Ireland. *The Curriculum Journal, 16*(3), 341–362.

Nunes, T., Bryant, P., & Olsson, J. M. (2003). Learning morphological and phonological spelling rules: An intervention study. *Reading and Writing, 7*, 298–307.

Oakhill, J. V., Cain, K., & Bryant, P. (1999). *Reading development and the teaching of reading: A psychological perspective.* Oxford: Blackwell.

Office of Standards in Education (1992). *Reading Recovery in New Zealand: A report from the Office of Her Majesty's Chief Inspector of Schools.* London: Her Majesty's Stationery Office (HMSO).

Office of Standards in Education (1998). *The National Literacy Project: An HMI evaluation. A report form the Office of Her Majesty's Chief Inspector of Schools.* London: Her Majesty's Stationery Office (HMSO).

Openshaw, R., Soler, J., Wearmouth, J., & Paige-Smith, A. (2002*).* The socio-political context of the development of Reading Recovery in New Zealand and England. *The Curriculum Journal, 13*(1), 25–41.

Parsons, S. (2002). *Basic skills and crime: Findings from a study of adults born in 1958 and 1970.* London: Basic Skills Agency.

Parsons, S., & Bynner, J. (2002*). Basic skills and social exclusion.* London: The Basic Skills Agency.

Perkins, D. (1992). *Smart schools: From training memories to educating minds.* New York: Free Press.

Perkins, D. (2006). Constructivism and troublesome knowledge. In J. H. F. Meyer & R. Land (Eds.), *Overarching barriers to student understanding: Threshold concepts and troublesome knowledge.* Abingdon: Routledge Faber.

PIRLS (2006). *Progress in international reading literacy study in primary schools in 40 countries.* Report by Ina V. S. Mullis, Michael O. Martin, Ann M. Kennedy, and Pierre Foy (2007). Chestnut Hill, MA: TIMSS & PIRLS International Study Center, Boston College.

Quay, L., Steele, D., Johnson, C., & Hortman, W. (2001*).* Children's achievement and personal and social development in a first year Reading Recovery program with teachers in training. *Literacy Teaching and Learning, 5*(2), 7–25.

Raban, B. (1990). Reading research in Great Britain 1988. *Reading, 24*(3), 107–127.

Stainthorp, R. (2000). The National Literacy Strategy and individual differences. *Journal of Research in Reading, 23*(3), 299–307.

Stannard, J., & Huxford, L. (2007). *The literacy game: The story of the National Literacy Strategy.* Abingdon, Oxford: Routledge.

Straw, J. (1992). *The Daily Telegraph,* 4 January 1992, page 1.

Taylor, S. (2006). *An advanced professional development curriculum for developing DEEP learning.* Unpublished doctoral thesis. London: Institute of Education, University of London.

Torgeson, J. K., Morgan, S., & Davies, C. (1992). The effects of two types of phonological awareness training on word reading in kindergarten children. *Journal of Educational Psychology, 84,* 364–370.

Wade, B., & Moore, M. (1996). Home activities: The advent of literacy. *European Early Childhood Educational Research Journal, 4*(2), 63–76.

Warnock Report (1978). *Special Educational Needs.* London: Her Majesty's Stationery Office (HMSO).

Whetton, C., Twist, L., & Sainsbury, M. (2007). Measuring standards in primary English: The validity of PIRLS — a response to Mary Hilton. *British Educational Research Journal, 33*(6), 977–986.

Whitty, G. (2006). Education(al) research and education policy making: Is conflict inevitable? *British Research Journal, 32*(2), 159–176.

Wright, A. (1992). Evaluation of the first British Reading Recovery programme. *British Educational Research Journal, 18*(4), 351–367.

Part Three
The Capacity to Reach Beyond

7

Implementing Reading
Recovery Internationally

Marie M. Clay

As Reading Recovery expanded to other countries from the mid-1980s into
the new century, Marie Clay wrote several articles to guide its international
implementation. It seems fitting to bring her ideas together in one compilation
to ensure the theoretical perspectives and rationales of Reading Recovery will
be retained.

This chapter draws on five of Marie Clay's implementation publications
listed at the end of the chapter. An organizational structure for this chapter
evolved as the publications were reviewed. Excerpts from each of these works
were selected to highlight Marie Clay's attention to the implementation of
Reading Recovery as a systemic intervention. Alterations to original sources
were limited to necessary transitions, issues of style, readable formatting,
and adjustments of terminology to reflect changes that Marie Clay made
over time. A brief overview follows.

In an introduction to literacy learning, Marie Clay explains the
opportunity Reading Recovery creates for young learners who are the
lowest achievers in literacy in their second year of school. Then, reasons for
the success of Reading Recovery in very different international settings are
identified. Crucial factors are clustered in five areas:

> guidelines for delivery,
> the training of teachers,
> the lesson components,
> the complex theory of literacy learning, and
> theories about children's development.

A systemic view of change is an exploration of the critical notion that systems
must change and adapt to support an educational innovation. This is
followed by an explanation of the way Reading Recovery was constructed —
as a problem-solving approach to an unstructured problem. Represented
as three concentric circles, each encompasses a particular area of problem-
solving, namely implementing, teaching, and learning.

- *The outer circle is the challenge of making Reading Recovery work in different education systems. Particular implementation issues are discussed.*

- *The second circle is the training of teachers to be problem-solvers; it explores the changes that take place in teachers' thinking and practice during their year of in-service training. The roles and training of Trainers and Tutors/Teacher Leaders also are explored.*

- *The inner circle is the problem-solving inherent in children's learning. By having a short period of individual help, children learn to construct effective processing systems and so become successful readers and writers.*

The chapter ends with some remarks from Marie Clay about the implementation of Reading Recovery internationally.

Introduction and compilation by Barbara Watson

Educational programmes are designed for particular settings, historical times, and cultures. They are not expected to transplant readily to other educational systems. However, Reading Recovery has responded to the needs of children and the administrative values of many education systems. Through local initiatives it has spread throughout New Zealand, to many of the Australian states, to remote and urban areas within Canada, to numerous states in the USA, to the United Kingdom and the Republic of Ireland, to Denmark, and to island territories like Anguilla, Jersey, and Bermuda. This early intervention is like a standard boat tossed into several turbulent rivers and struggling to master the rapids and stay afloat in each of them.

Central tenets of Reading Recovery have been tentativeness, flexibility, and problem-solving. These qualities have surfaced in the ways in which the teaching addresses individual patterns of strengths and weaknesses in children, and in how the teachers are trained to design a lesson series for individual children, and again in the solutions people have found for implementing this literacy intervention. Somehow Reading Recovery professionals have learned how to hold fast to principles, practices, and rationales while at the same time allowing for variability in the educational practices and beliefs and change over time in society.

The opportunity

Reading Recovery addresses a problem of concern to most Western education systems. It is an early literacy intervention designed for children who clearly show that they have already become at risk in literacy learning in their classroom programme. It takes young children who have the lowest achievement in reading and writing and tries to bring them to average bands of performance in a relatively short time. Any child entering Reading Recovery is taken from where that child is to somewhere else, working up from what the child already knows, using his or her strengths and what he or she does well. The special situations that allow the lowest achievers to learn quickly and catch up with their classmates involve teaching them one at a time, and not in a prescribed sequence such as occurs in class or group instruction. The lessons are individually designed, differ from day to day, and emphasise change according to individual needs across a series of lessons.

Reading Recovery targets the lowest achieving children in reading and writing by the end of the first year at school, not excluding any child for any reason in an ordinary classroom, a challenging position adopted to ensure reliability of teacher judgement. It also takes care of other values like children's rights, fairness and equality, and social, cultural and linguistic inequalities (Sylva & Hurry, 1995). The Reading Recovery teachers, trained in systematic observations of reading and writing behaviours, identify potential Reading Recovery students in consultation with other school staff. The children are simply the lowest performers in their particular schools.

An attractive feature of Reading Recovery is the way in which it feeds back information on success to all participants from the beginning. Children who are turned off reading and writing take only a few weeks to show that they feel in control of their work tasks. Teachers who doubt the intervention's claims need about 8 weeks to recognize the surprisingly good responses of some of their students; administrators come round when the first children's lessons are discontinued and they are able to survive back in their classrooms. It has been the enthusiasm of the teachers and the joy of the children at having some control over their own success that has been most surprisingly replicated in each country worked in.

Reading Recovery was designed for implementation in New Zealand and had many features that were consistent with instruction in that country, but it has now been used with children from a variety of ethnic, language, and ability groups. It is delivered by some very well trained and dedicated professionals in each of its many different settings. Designed to be a system intervention, it has the potential to be cost effective as at least two-thirds of those who entered Reading Recovery are returned to average levels of performance in all the countries it is in. Another 25% can succeed in a well-resourced, high-drive, highly efficient programme. Having cleared 90% of the poorest performers from the classrooms, the system is then freed to devote special resources to the residual group with reading and writing difficulty.

Success in international settings

What enables Reading Recovery to work successfully in a variety of educational settings internationally? The important answers probably cluster in five areas, in each of which the need for tentativeness and flexibility is great. The five areas are guidelines for delivery, the training of teachers, the lesson components, the complex theory of literacy learning, and theories about children's development.

Guidelines for delivery

The Reading Recovery guidelines guard against shifts towards ineffective practices. Shifts can occur so easily for many reasons, and monitoring research has indicated ways in which changes can limit the potential for success. Adaptations may arise because it makes someone's life easier to do standard things in a standard way, and adopt less demanding objectives.

When operated with tentativeness and flexibility, Reading Recovery's guidelines guard against prejudicing any child's chances of learning. Research and experience support the conclusions that the guidelines lead to the best outcomes for the most children. Let me give one example. There are recommendations about how many children a Reading Recovery teacher should teach each day. A minimum of four is suggested in the training year, and wherever this is possible in subsequent years. Many people cannot understand why an experienced teacher should not work with as few as two children each day. Well, Reading Recovery teachers are decision-makers; they design an individual series of lessons to suit individual children. When they meet only two children each day over the period of a year they are not challenged to make enough varied decisions and their teaching tends to drift away from the innovative. Enter an exceptionally challenging child and the teacher is not ready for the task ahead.

Reading Recovery has been able to work in systems that are large and small, church and secular, public and private, in state education departments and in private universities, small and remote or large and urban. It prepares children for very different classroom programmes, to achieve much the same level of outcomes, and to do this in English, Spanish, and French. Education systems differ and at any one time they are changing in different ways depending on their social and educational histories. Reading Recovery has to acknowledge and work with those differences. Problem-solving it into different education settings is one essential feature of this early intervention.

The long period of training prepares teachers to be decision-makers

Neither a practical apprenticeship nor an explicit text was considered satisfactory for training Reading Recovery professionals. It was assumed that teachers could understand a new approach in a short course but would they change their daily practice in appropriate ways? An apprenticeship might create some inspired teaching but would teachers be able to put what they did and why they did it into words to share with others? What were needed were new understandings, new practices, different decisions for different children, and a means of sharing new insights and unsolved problems with colleagues. The professional networks of expertise would be very important in Reading Recovery. From the Trainers, who train the Tutors/Teacher Leaders, to the Tutors/Teacher Leaders who train the teachers, to the teachers who make decisions minute by minute in their individual lessons with children, everyone has to understand the child, the possibilities, and the potential of the intervention to reach its goals for individual children.

Reading Recovery training of teachers is thorough wherever it occurs, a year-long training designed as a supervised apprenticeship in which teachers must change their practices, as well as their understanding. They must learn to articulate the rationales for children's observed behaviours and for the teaching that must follow, learning to learn from children, and from colleagues.

Lesson components support perceptual/cognitive processing

In spite of limitations in individual profiles teachers find ways around the children's problems in most cases. Reading Recovery lessons must be relatively short (30 minutes), streamlined, brisk, varied, with scope for established skill and knowledge to be consolidated, responses produced at speed without too much attention, but time to work on new challenges which lift competency to higher levels. We tend to give tasks in a Reading

Recovery lesson simple labels (the economy of words) but a couple of examples may illustrate their complexity.

> Rereading several familiar texts achieves a number of things: it increases the amount of reading done, it results in much successful processing so that children 'orchestrate' the complex set of things they already do well, it allows for independent problem-solving, recognition is speeded, phrasing is possible, there is attention to print detail, and the stories are enjoyed. Teachers may be working on several of these goals in one lesson.

> Writing one or two sentences or a 'story' requires the child to take the first steps towards composing. Initially, the production is shared between teacher and child; there is a gradual lift over time in the amount, quality, and independence of the child's writing. The child comes to know how texts are compiled from letters and words, that writing involves segmentation of speech, is related to the sounds of speech, can be read, and that there are different ways to construct new words.

These are simple tasks that call for complex learning. A great deal of learning is being achieved in the 30-minute lesson, and much of it is clearly learning how to do 'literacy things', which should be useful for more independent work in classrooms. The teacher attends to many aspects of literacy learning. The results should provide an insurance of success whatever the demands of the classroom programme.

The utility of a complex theory of learning

In contrast to a simple theory of learning, such as one which rates the learning of phonemic awareness or some other single variable as the first significant thing to learn about literacy, Reading Recovery's complex theory of literacy learning supports the view that there are many parts of literacy processing which can be difficult for children. Different children have different strengths and weaknesses, and there may be many causes of difficulty varying from child to child. One child may have a single difficulty or a cluster of several difficulties. The challenges for the teacher come in making teaching decisions that adapt to each child's idiosyncratic patterns of competencies. Using a complex theory, Reading Recovery hopes to be able to serve both children with one kind of problem and children with several problems. Some children find that bringing one competency into a working relationship with another competency is nearly impossible, making this integrating of complex behaviours of literacy activities an important part of what Reading Recovery teachers attend to.

Reading Recovery theories face the issue of multiple causes head on: the need for help arises for multiple reasons (causes) across children in the treatment group, but the individual learner is challenged by multiple causes within his or her individual functioning. While that position is realistic, it is also theoretically frustrating for many people.

A theory about constructive individuals independently pushing the boundaries of their own knowledge, rather than groups led through each step by a teacher

This applies to the low achievers as much as to the proficient ones. Independence is encouraged in simple ways to allow children to solve the problems. Reading Recovery theory assumes that the goal of early literacy learning is to have children who can, in time, read silently and compose and write relatively independently and who teach themselves more by engaging in these activities. The constructive child is one who makes something of the instruction and becomes a fluent processor of printed messages.

How do these five things explain Reading Recovery's success in a variety of settings? If we assume that we need constructive children in classrooms who can independently solve many literacy learning problems for themselves, then by the end of the series of lessons a successful Reading Recovery child should be able to use the activities of the classroom to push his own knowledge even further. The well-trained teacher will be tentative and flexible in her interactions with a range of children, each of whom presents somewhat different problems. The cognitive processing and the wide range of competencies developed in the children should prepare them for performance in almost all classroom programmes. But here comes another qualification: there must be minor adjustments to tune in a particular child to the special demands of his classroom teacher in the last few weeks of the Reading Recovery lessons.

At the level of the education system the intake, teaching, and discontinuing procedures are easy to manage, the progress of every child is monitored, and quality control measures operate whatever the administrative structure. The ex-lowest achievers must be able to learn within the classroom without special programming, but with an attentive teacher.

A systemic view of change

Problems of educational change are often equated with problems of getting teachers to change, summed up in the cry 'If only we could find and train the teachers to . . .' when in fact what is missing is a pedagogical plan to support the innovation so that the system learns what is required and how to get it into place (Dalin, 1978).

Organized systems maintain their integrity through a strategic balance of vital processes. They are not free to learn, adapt, or change in any way. They can only be modified in some way that is consistent with that vital strategic balance (White, 1976, 1979). It may be hard to achieve a policy change but it is harder to achieve and sustain a change to the operating system itself. One can approach both child learning and education system learning in this way. The child who is to be taught reading and writing already has a functioning spoken language system that operates productively and concepts, however primitive, about literacy. This pre-existing organization interacts with the reading and writing instruction just as the pre-existing organization in the education system interacts with the ideal model of the innovative intervention.

This is the perspective of my own field of study, developmental psychology. So my personal orientation in developing Reading Recovery was to take account of the complex interdependence among parts of the system. I knew that older children were hard to teach as failing readers, and that their return to average levels of performance was rarely achieved. A new attack on this problem was needed, and it called for more than an analysis of the counter forces that could be operating when a new intervention is tried. In an effective intervention the interdependence of variables demands a systemic plan, for an innovation cannot move into an education system merely on the merits of what it can do for children.

Because an education system is designed to maintain itself and because it does this by existing laws, regulations and other control mechanisms, taking an innovation aboard involves a change process that will require problem-solving as each new response to the innovation appears in the system. Advocacy for change can occur as a conflict with what exists and this potential must be recognized. Conflict with existing provisions, regulations, beliefs, or professional roles is likely to be continuous in an innovating system so that neither consensus nor conflict is an indicator of success or failure (Dalin, 1978). When an innovation is taken over by another education system from the one in which it originated, it must allow for a problem-solving period while the receiving system makes its adaptations. The art in the change process is that changes should not distort or diminish its payoff and any changes made should be explicitly referred to theories of what is occurring. Compromise or unthinking adaptations can readily change the impact of the innovation and reduce its capacity to deliver effective results. During periods of expansion every effort should be made to ensure that the parts of the intervention retain their cohesion and links with other parts of the intervention.

According to Dalin, programme developers must see change as a problem of institutional linkage in which there is likely to be conflicts about issues that will affect survival of their programmes. The implications of a new intervention at the level of an education system must be clear. The goals and benefits must be stated — in the case of Reading Recovery they are to reduce the number of children unable to work at average levels in their classrooms and to do this for a high percentage of such children, and as a result of this process to identify early those who will need continuing help. There are both human and economic values in this saving of time, effort, and resources that appeal to different stakeholders.

Because of my own background in developmental psychology, many aspects of the innovation were planned on suppositions about behaviour change in children and in teachers. Within that discipline framework one could conceptualize forces that facilitate, or block, or modify the innovation and direct it back to old practices and procedures, or leave it prey to the whim of current advocacy. One useful concept is that the individual and the system are in a process of learning to operate and understand the innovation. The origins of progress would lie in the child-teacher interactions but the success of Reading Recovery would also depend on many other variables.

Such systemic relationships make an innovation that is likely to survive: one that is cohesive both internally (in terms of theory, training, programme design, evaluation) and with the host system (i.e., it must be workable, contributing, cost-effective, and a winner with the stakeholders).

Support at several levels of the education system is necessary for an effective implementation. A teacher may work superbly with children but a principal may reorganize resources in the next year and call a halt to the good work. The Reading Recovery Tutor/Teacher Leader must urge the teachers to accelerate their pupils' progress, for this determines the cost-effectiveness of the intervention.

The idea is simple but the intervention is complex. It calls for shifts in thinking of those who train to be Reading Recovery teachers and Tutors/Teacher Leaders, and it is hard for researchers and evaluators to understand an early literacy intervention that breaks with so many established parameters. Reading Recovery aims to get rid of literacy difficulties, to accept an hypothesis of multiple causation, and has a theory to explain why it succeeds even when it flies in the face of much experience and established practice.

Reading Recovery professionals have to solve problems — about children's learning, about teachers' learning, and about making Reading Recovery work in education systems — which I graph in three concentric circles. Trainers and Tutors/Teacher Leaders train to become specialists in these three areas of problem-solving.

Three concentric circles:
Implementing, teaching, and learning

Education studies of new educational developments do not necessarily arise from a theoretical hypothesis. Discovering what was workable in Reading Recovery led to the construction of a theory to explain this, the reverse of academic enquiry. On the one hand teachers had children they could not teach, and on the other, educational psychologists had too many referrals and few effective treatments for the hard-to-teach literacy problems. I worked with a team to find a research-based solution to these problems. Reading Recovery was constructed by a problem-solving approach to an unstructured problem [although Robinson's (1993) authoritative work in this area is critical of the path we took]. Theory did not drive practice; rather there was a circle of influence from practice to theory and back to practice, informed and altered by data from day-to-day documentation of changes in children and an imperative that it must be workable in schools.

No particular school of thought on literacy learning drove the exploration, but new work at the time included Bruner (1957, 1973), Cazden (1972), Chomsky (1972), Donaldson (1978), Graves (1978), Miller (1967), Read (1975), Smith (1971), the Russian school of developmental psychologists, and information processing psychologists like Rumelhart (1994).

A typical research review assumes that theory comes first, and it is subsequently applied to practice, and we gamble on whether teachers and education systems can work from a theoretical account. I recommend that a critique of Reading Recovery should reverse the cycle, start with the outer circle and ask:

1. Can this education system put this intervention in place? and

2. Can teachers be trained to teach children and achieve change? before asking the question from the inner circle,

3. What theoretical assumptions do the data on children's learning support or challenge?

Critiques usually try to answer question 3, but this is only relevant if the first two questions can be answered affirmatively. Readers of reviews should first be assured that the conditions in questions 1 and 2 have been met.

The outer circle: Working in school systems

A sampling of some of the implementation issues in Reading Recovery will illustrate why a sound approach to evaluating the children's learning would be to start an evaluation by satisfying oneself and one's readers that the implementation of Reading Recovery to be studied was an effective one.

Age at entry

At what age should Reading Recovery be available? The general statement should be that selection should occur as soon after entry to school as we can reliably identify children falling behind their same age peers in the new classroom, and the timing has to be problem-solved in each education system. In New Zealand it is after 1 year of school (i.e., around the sixth birthday), after a fair chance to settle into the school, to adjust to demands, and to begin to learn. Two reasons for this timing are that

- reviews of research reiterate that we cannot predict literacy problems well enough before instruction begins, and

- a 'multiple causation' theory includes lack of learning opportunities in life or school contexts as well as problematic learning histories, and does not relate only to a child's potential for learning. Reliable prediction of which individuals will fail or succeed is not achieved before the onset of instruction.

Across the world further questions are raised. Should entry be earlier in places in the United Kingdom where the school entrant could enter school at just over 4 years of age? Or do we wait until after 7 years for the child who begins schooling at 6 years? What could be recommended for countries that begin school at 7 years? In the United States does the kindergarten count as school, and what about half-day kindergarten?

Age of entry is an example of how implementation of Reading Recovery must be problem-solved into every country because of the differences in societies, in populations, and in education systems, as well as politics, economic theories, social problems, and religions. On the other hand a country's theories of child development and learning, of literacy learning, and of early intervention must be taken into account. Surprisingly, about 6 years of age is a practical compromise and we have enough experience on the ground to show that this works. The factors to be weighed are age, time at school, general preparedness, and some things about child development. We had to have learners with two qualities: first, what they knew had to be woven into a fabric of interacting response systems which they controlled (for islands of knowledge about specific aspects of literacy processing would not make an effective reader or writer), and secondly, the learners had to become relatively independent of teachers so they could work well in classrooms.

The negative consequence of starting too early is giving individual teaching that would not have been needed if we had waited longer, and the negative result of waiting too long is that the time it takes to deliver an effective series of lessons increases the longer the children have been in formal instruction, and therefore fewer children can be served for the same teaching resource.

Daily lessons

The absence of teacher or learner from the daily lessons threatens the accelerative learning needed for children to catch up with their classmates. The difficulty of getting children to school every day requires attention, but obtaining parental permission for the child to join Reading Recovery offers an opportunity to negotiate for special help from the family to have the child at school. After several research studies the variable 'teacher not available to teach' emerged as a bigger problem than child absence.

Despite excellent reasons why the trained teacher should perform other duties in school or in society, it is absolutely necessary for the Reading Recovery children to receive a lesson each day. This frequent contact allows yesterday's responding to be still clear in the minds of both teacher and child. For schools this means release of an effective teacher for 2 hours a day (varied according to training status and the school's need) and without pulling that person from their allotted task. The potential for accelerated learning is reduced if the teacher is not available to teach daily. The lessons must occur in an intensive series and the same number of lessons spaced out over time is a poor substitute resulting in poorer learning.

The length of the school year

This determines how many days the teacher has to teach. Different models for 3 or 4 terms, and all-year-round schools can create difficulties with the 'a lesson every day' demand.

The learning needs of individual children do not align with the school year of teaching. In New Zealand schools, for the children who were not yet ready to leave Reading Recovery when the school year ended in mid-December, it was easy to resume their lessons in February when the next school year began, continuing to teach them until they reached one of two outcomes, discontinued or referred. An incomplete series of lessons occurs only when a child leaves the school and attends a new school that does not provide Reading Recovery assistance. In some other countries like the United States with a shorter school year and different promotion possibilities, it is often unworkable to continue Reading Recovery help into the next school year, but solutions to this problem are being formulated.

How long does Reading Recovery take?

The time of supplementary help is surprisingly brief. With consistency across the world the time in an efficient implementation averages from 12 to about 20 weeks thus providing a guideline within which to shape our expectancies and policies. The fact that individuals spend different lengths of time in Reading Recovery is irritating for researchers and administrators; they would like a fixed number of treatments for all, a prescribed turnover point, 'all change here,' but the discontinuing criteria require a teacher to ensure, as best she can, that a child is now sufficiently independent to survive in the classroom without further help. Reviewers also find it difficult to understand the flexibility with which Reading Recovery adapts to individual learners so that time in the intervention was reported as 15 weeks for research convenience in one study (Center, Wheldall, Freeman, Outhred, & McNaught, 1995) and 20 to 26 weeks in another (Sylva & Hurry, 1995). Unfortunately, figures in reviews can become the reference for new research or implementations. The capacity of Reading Recovery to adapt to the learning needs of individuals is critical to (a) learning and (b) effective implementation.

Discontinuing rates across different countries

Comparison of the rate at which children leave Reading Recovery at average band levels of performance can be made within an education system but they must be made cautiously across countries. It is now clear that they depend on implementation delivery factors such as the average number of children passing through a half-hour teaching slot in the year, the length of the school year, and whether daily lessons are delivered. In each 30-minute teaching 'slot' New Zealand teachers tend to get two children out of Reading Recovery and take a third child in, to be continued in the next school year. This is considered 'best practice' and results in about 67% discontinued in the calendar year! The Ministry of Education Research Division's annual figures (published and available on request) show that in New Zealand 0.2–1.5% of the age cohort is referred for longer-term assistance in a calendar year.

The second circle:
Training teachers for problem-solving

The training for Reading Recovery teachers is a year-long period of change. Change during that year is a unit of learning in itself. Geekie (1992) reported a shift over a year from widespread scepticism to obvious commitment among Reading Recovery teachers and among schools. Teachers in Reading Recovery are trained to make effective decisions on the evidence of the child's responses during the individual teaching sessions. They decide where to direct the child's attention next to further his particular cluster of abilities. They initiate and design the lessons and there is no package of teaching materials. How do these changes in teacher behaviours come about?

Peer support

Goodlad (1977) recommends a network of peers to build a necessary support system for information sharing and problem-solving. The experiences of trusted colleagues matter in the adoption of new practices. This model of training worked well for Reading Recovery. It generated high interest, effort, and dedication in the face of difficulties and an air of curiosity and surprise that something different was occurring.

Teachers begin training on the assessment observations of reading and writing behaviours. These procedures allow for records of behavioural change in the reading and writing process in day-to-day lessons. Observational procedures overcome the limitations of standardized tests for monitoring if, how, and when behaviour is changing.

Teachers observe exactly what children are doing and make these observations more explicit by analysing Running Records of text reading daily. Teachers write an observation summary report of the useful responses that the child controls before they begin teaching. This careful analysis leads the teacher to design particular lessons for a particular child. Teachers discuss perplexing points or alternative interpretations at in-service sessions and they submit their analyses for review by Tutors/ Teacher Leaders. Before they begin teaching children, teachers write predictions of what changes they would expect to see in children's reading and writing as they improve. This helps them to specify particular goals for each child and to grapple with some of the conceptual issues.

To minimize feelings of insecurity that teachers might initially feel about changing their teaching patterns they are invited to teach according to their best judgement. They are reminded that they are experienced teachers and urged to draw on their experiences of working with children. It is considered economical to move teachers from the full strength of their present competencies rather than to demand at the outset new behaviours that might cause confusion and disrupt established and efficient responses.

Novel learning

New concepts and procedures gradually became part of the teachers' repertoire. As they learn to use the new teaching procedures, each knows that she is a learner and so are her peers. If the demonstration child of the day 'plays up' and makes the teacher's task harder, the audience of peers are the most sympathetic a teacher could have. By the end of the training year teachers acquire new theories of how their pupils perform and how they should respond. They are able to question, challenge, discuss, work out a course of action, and explain their decisions in ways they can all understand because these new ideas are shared and explicit and in relation to children whose presenting problems are particularly challenging. While training is delivered during 2-hour training sessions at 1 or 2 weekly intervals over the period of a year, teachers are working with children and carrying out other teaching duties throughout the period they are in training. In many schools, staff have supported a school organization which frees the Reading Recovery teacher to continue working in this way because the intervention is seen as one designed to reduce the number of reading and writing problems in the age group and eventually in the school as a whole.

The quality of the Reading Recovery teachers' instruction following the training year has also received attention. It is believed that Reading Recovery has to be run with little variation from the functionally effective procedures studied to date. Twice every term teachers return to an ongoing professional development session conducted by the Reading Recovery Tutor/Teacher Leader. They discuss two lessons by peers, and their own teaching. Teaching improves after training and more children's series of lessons are discontinued in less time. Research reports need to record how long Reading Recovery has been in place together with details of experience beyond training.

Challenging assumptions: New alternatives

In all countries, teachers bring assumptions to their teaching, sometimes country-specific and sometimes more general. Such assumptions call for small adjustments in training courses in each country, but because Reading Recovery must not limit the progress of any child by its practices and policies, all teachers are required to open up their local clusters of assumptions to new alternatives.

1. Some assumptions are about *curriculum sequences* that should occur, including inflexible beliefs that a child must know (A) before she or he can try to do (B)! Assumptions like this underpin programmes which teach a letter a day for a whole year in some kindergartens, or require children to know all letter-sound relationships before they try to read, or insist that children read before they try to write.

2. Some assumptions are about *task difficulty* and the *assumed limitations for learning that children have.* There are assumptions about '*hard things*' that must be left until later (such as comprehension), or '*things that must come first*' or '*things that will require many repetitions.*' Teachers think, 'It will be hard and I will have to help you,' or 'I will have to simplify it for you,' or 'I will have to instruct you until you can learn for yourself.' A Reading Recovery teacher must invite learners to deal with *complex texts,* to *learn at a faster rate than average,* and become independent learners who initiate, process, monitor, and self-correct expanding their own literacy processing system while reading and writing independently.

   These assumptions of curriculum sequence or teaching sequence are inappropriate in Reading Recovery; they are assumptions devised for group instruction, and are not suited to individual learning, looking for a fast track to success and taking different paths to common outcomes. To accelerate the progress of a child with a low repertoire, a teacher must find any route to the desired outcome and allow for the entire range of idiosyncratic competencies to support the struggling learner. A teacher must monitor her own assumptions about learning and about an individual child to take advantage of every incipient opportunity to 'leap forward.'

3. On the other hand there are sets of assumptions which limit progress because they take for granted that all competencies needed for literacy behaviours will emerge in some natural way when the learner is ready, causing a teacher to wait for these emerging competencies to reveal themselves. Some teachers do not want to govern the amount of

challenge in a reading text, nor consider a gradient of difficulty, nor think about how a new competency can be helped to emerge from what is already known. This is not the place to debate this matter in relation to classroom learning but these things are not true for those learners who, by definition and selection, are finding learning extremely difficult.

The challenges in the training of teachers lie in uncovering hidden assumptions made by teachers in each country that are antagonistic to the progress of hard-to-teach children. We need them to become more flexible and tentative, to observe constantly and alter their assumptions in line with what they record as the children work. They need to challenge their own thinking continually. Such change begins during their training year but teachers discontinue the series of lessons for more children in the next 2 years as they become more familiar with Reading Recovery and how it can work. They learn to use the rationales for decision making which make the teaching and the organization of the intervention run more effectively. Owing to the complexity of what is being learned, the individual learning trajectories of the children, and the incomplete theory out of which the teachers work, there will always be problems to solve. Teachers need to recognize that they start with diverse assumptions about learning to read and write and these differences are a strength within their collegial network.

In different countries there have been differing degrees of willingness to consult peers, and for Tutors/Teacher Leaders or Trainers to form networks, to seek a second opinion, and to overcome the unreliability of one person's decision by pooling knowledge in network decision-making. Such consultation is self-correction behaviour aimed at catching the errors in individual judgements; it is essential.

Sometimes the emphasis during training sessions behind the one-way screen is on putting what you see into words, but equally important is the articulation of how what you see conflicts with what you had assumed. Bringing the implicit, whether observed or assumed, into verbal form that allows discussion and revision is an essential part of training in each country. As a College of Education Dean said to his peers,

> Reading Recovery has managed to operationalise that vague notion that teachers ought to reflect on their own practice. That behind the glass play by play analysis and the collegial debriefing with the teacher after her teaching session represents some of the best teacher education I have witnessed in my 28 year history in the field. (Pearson, 1994)

Who provides this quality training and support for Reading Recovery teachers?

Reading Recovery Tutors/Teacher Leaders

Tutors/Teacher Leaders in Reading Recovery are key people. They have a complex role that requires a wide range of skills obtained in a full year of training. They are what Goodlad (1977) calls 'a redirecting system.' A redirecting system, according to Goodlad, must be insistent, persistent, and sustained over continued crises. With that I concur.

The Tutors/Teacher Leaders are seen as leaders in their local districts. They have, during their training, been expected to learn to explain Reading Recovery to those who need to know about it, to answer criticisms, to argue for retention of its basic principles, and to write letters to the local papers or use local media to correct misunderstandings about the intervention. They have an important leadership role in their own districts where they train teachers for the local schools over the period of a year, maintain contact with past trainees operating independently in their schools, and are able to deal with the public and professional education about Reading Recovery at the district level.

As part of the year's full-time training, Reading Recovery Tutors/Teacher Leaders train as Reading Recovery teachers and work through the experiences of a trainee group. Only by observing the operation of Reading Recovery over a whole year can Tutors/Teacher Leaders become aware of the shifts in teachers' understandings, their questioning, and their in-service needs as their skills increase.

Reading Recovery Tutors/Teacher Leaders are required to test practice against theory. They need an academic understanding of the theoretical concepts upon which Reading Recovery is based and yet they require a flexibility to consider new concepts and practices. They must have a sensitive awareness of the organizational, professional, and child development issues associated with the innovations in the intervention and extensive teaching experience in the first 2 years of school. They have to analyse continuously what they are doing in order to weigh up in theoretical terms any proposals to change Reading Recovery.

They need to collaborate with teachers whose work they observe and discuss. They must be skilful in helping teachers to grow and develop and in working supportively with them, even though it is their role to also criticise and evaluate the teachers' performance.

Tutors/Teacher Leaders develop a thorough knowledge of the whole operation of Reading Recovery in an education system and of the development and history of the project. The organization and administration of the teachers' training course, from the introductory talk to the research evaluation at the end of the year, is studied in detail by Tutors/Teacher Leaders during their training. Critical appraisal of Reading Recovery's strengths and problem spots, and of competing explanations for its success, provide them with practice in discussion. Trainee Tutors/Teacher Leaders observe trained Tutors/Teacher Leaders on visits to teachers in their schools, talking over teaching techniques, answering questions, observing the teacher at work. Late in training, trainee Tutors/Teacher Leaders make similar visits to teachers and practise communicating with other professionals or with the public in print and in discussions.

The selection of people to train as Tutor/Teacher Leaders is important. They need to have been effective classroom teachers, and they must become competent Reading Recovery teachers. They need to be able to help teachers change while supporting them through such change. Concurrent with their training courses they take university courses about theoretical issues and recent research on reading and writing processes and issues with literacy difficulties. When such courses are closely related to theories which support and challenge this particular programme, they prepare the Tutors/Teacher Leaders to respond to analyses and evaluations of competing and controversial ideas in related fields such as prevention, early intervention, individual teaching, clinical approaches, and evaluations of programmes.

The involvement of a tertiary institution with a research capability is an important factor supporting the Tutor/Teacher Leader course. On the one hand it was important for the survival of the original programme that the academic development team should relinquish ownership of it and their hold on it. In New Zealand, the education system has assumed responsibility for training the teachers and the Tutors/Teacher Leaders, except for the contribution from university course work.

However, in other settings, ways have been found for tertiary institutions to play an important role in sustaining quality control over the professional development and implementation aspects of Reading Recovery, to prevent massive change so that it no longer fulfils its promise. In the USA, a federal agency, the National Diffusion Network, selected Reading Recovery as an exemplary educational intervention and provided a small amount of funding to support well-controlled dissemination through training and monitoring grants. It was also necessary to bring the intervention in the USA under trademark law to protect it from creative and uncreative substitute programmes that appeared. This move has been misunderstood by some who failed to see how destructive unlimited variants and poor training could be to an intervention which had demonstrated that children who were hard to teach could succeed under a special set of conditions.

Collectively, Reading Recovery Tutors/Teacher Leaders exemplify Goodlad's 'redirecting system' because they teach children, train teachers, educate the local educators, negotiate the implementation of the intervention, act as advocates for whatever cannot be compromised in the interests of effective results, and talk to the public and the media, correcting misconceptions. Without a redirecting system for an innovation, the established or traditional system may gradually take the innovation and transform it back to old practices.

How do these key people receive their training and ongoing support?

Reading Recovery Trainers

In Reading Recovery there are cycles of change in children, a year's cycle of change in teachers, and a year's cycle of different changes in the Tutors/ Teacher Leaders-in-training across four major areas of learning. The Trainer of Tutors/Teacher Leaders must have full knowledge of what it means to bring about all these cycles of change on the ground in practice, but in ways that are consistent with the academic theories that support Reading Recovery. A Trainer must bring these several areas of expertise together in an ongoing way, as the intervention is problem-solved into an education setting.

It is a feature of the Reading Recovery training that teachers do not graduate to be Tutors/Teacher Leaders, and Tutors/Teacher Leaders do not become Trainers of Tutors/Teacher Leaders. This is because at each successive level of training, the roles of the professionals, and the theories they need to use, are different. A teacher can do an excellent job without the theoretical understanding that a Tutor/Teacher Leader must have of the reading and writing process, so that preferably that Tutor/Teacher Leader can engage in the debates at the cutting edge of current knowledge. A Tutor/Teacher Leader may carry out excellent local teacher training and support a local implementation of quality, without needing to know how to train others to carry out this role.

So where do the Trainers who must prepare Tutors/Teacher Leaders for many roles come from? These professionals typically are from or become attached to tertiary institutions as members of staff. Trainers complete the requirements of (a) becoming a successful teacher of Reading Recovery children, and (b) becoming a Tutor/Teacher Leader within their training. They must stay in close contact with how teachers are learning to deliver Reading Recovery and they must be able to ensure that both teachers and Tutors/Teacher Leaders gain a working knowledge of how to act in ways that are consistent with a theory of the task and a theory of learning (Wood, Bruner, & Ross, 1976). A Trainer needs to be able to think integratively about theory, bringing diverse areas of current theoretical and practical knowledge together into working relationships but, in addition, Trainers must be successful in educating other professional educators to do this.

Trainers also help to develop and coordinate Reading Recovery in their own education system. They need to advise administrators on how the quality of the implementation can be sustained over time, achieving high rates of discontinuing and so maintaining the cost-effectiveness of the intervention. They need to know the range of research that has been reported and to advise administrators on research needed to monitor the implementation.

When Trainers are being prepared to work in new education systems which are taking on Reading Recovery for the first time, this is particularly challenging, because the differences in educational cultures and practices call for problem-solving the theory of the early intervention into the beliefs, practices, and academic literature of a new education system.

The inner circle: The learning of the children

Children's learning has not shown clear differences across countries, except for those created by different classroom programmes (i.e., different learning opportunities) or associated with age. Culture and language have created interesting questions but no big problems.

Independent reviewers from the United States and the United Kingdom, who are not involved in devising or delivering Reading Recovery, provide the following characteristics of the intervention's background theory. Both reviews say that Clay (1979) describes reading as a 'message-gaining, problem-solving activity which increases in power and flexibility the more it is practised.'

Wasik and Slavin (1993) list the components of the reading model as perceptual analysis, knowledge of print conventions, decoding, oral language proficiency, prior knowledge, inference making, reading strategies, metacognition, and error detection and correction strategies. They omit 'visual' from perceptual analysis, translate phonemic awareness into decoding, and create an unexplained metacognition component, all of which are imprecise and could mislead. They select three major theoretical principles for mention:

- Reading is considered a strategic process that requires the integrating of letter-sound relationships, features of print, and language which is derived from the interaction of the reader's unique background and the print;

241

- Reading and writing are interconnected and the child must make the connections; and

- Children learn to read by reading and only reading frequently can the child come to detect regularities and redundancies present in written language.

I would not quarrel with the words above or with the following. 'There is no systematic presentation of phonics, yet during the reading and writing activities letter-sound relationships are taught as one of the basic strategies for solving problems' (p. 183).

Sylva & Hurry (1995) reiterate the message-getting, problem-solving activity quoted above and add that children make use of a variety of strategies to help them in this problem-solving activity, the most central of which are

- their understanding of the concepts of print,

- their phonological awareness of sounds in words and letters and letter strings on the page,

- their understanding of the meaning of the text, and

- their knowledge of syntax.

> Meaning is not derived from the print alone but also from the knowledge of the world that readers bring to the task, for example their knowledge of the language of books and of language in general, their prior knowledge of the subject matter of the text, their ability to make inferences. (p. 7)

The goal of Reading Recovery is to help children to use all the skills and strategic activities that they have at their disposal (and to) 'encourage children to monitor their own reading, detecting and correcting errors by checking responses against all possible strategies.' This improves children's reading and writing 'over a wide range of skills,' described as a broad-spectrum approach.

Against this reporting one can set less accurate accounts of Reading Recovery's theory given by Center et al. (1995), Hiebert (1994), Iversen and Tunmer (1993), Razinski (1995) and Shanahan and Barr (1995). Center at al., for example, report the theory in this way: 'reading is viewed as a psycho-linguistic process in which the reader constructs meaning from print,' and most readers would then place Reading Recovery in the wrong theoretical camp with psycholinguistics rather than information processing.

Variants within the learning theory

To be an effective intervention, Reading Recovery must be responsive to the discourse of new research and theory and not be locked into the theory of the late 1970s when it was developed (Pearson, 1994). In the early 1970s, its practices may have appeared ahead of research in some areas but as more information and new theory becomes available, areas of uncertainty should be informed and practices should change.

The dynamically changing theory is concerned with how we understand the sequence of changes in ways in which children process complex arrays of information as they learn to read and write. A multivariate theory of such changes (rather than a single causal theory) forces an openness to new knowledge. If 'Reading Recovery helps children to integrate a wide range of skills involved in reading and writing' (Sylva & Hurry, 1995), then there are a myriad of unknowns hidden in the verb 'to integrate' when it is combined with a developmentalist's interest in 'change over time.' Much of it has to do with how and what the constructive learner learns from his own decision processes when problem-solving continuous text. What is challenging for theory construction is that during the time of reading and writing acquisition, each one of the multivariate processes is in a formative stage.

New editions of teachers' text covering theory (Clay, 1991, 2001), assessments (Clay 2002, 2006), and teaching procedures (Clay, 2005) are essential for an intervention that is evaluating and responding to shifts in available knowledge.

Children with English as a second language

It has been reported that these children are, or should be, excluded from selection (Hiebert, 1994). This does not happen in the five countries where their progress has been watched. They are probably the group of children who derive most benefit in subsequent years from having had this supplement early, because language was the major block to their learning and they had 30 minutes every day with a teacher who increased their time for talking and personalized their instruction. Hobsbaum's study (1995) from England reported satisfactory progress for children who spoke more than one language.

Reading Recovery in another language

If special care is taken to redevelop the observation (assessment) tasks and the instructional procedures, then the 'window of opportunity' for an early intervention in literacy learning appears to be able to cross language barriers and remain effective. For children learning to read and write

English, no important differences appear in what it is the children need to learn to do in different countries. However, since teaching began in Spanish (Escamilla, 1994) we have had to consider that there is more involved than theoretical concepts and assessment tasks. The timing in acquisition and the emphases during instruction for effective processing in another language might change. An early discovery in studies of early writing was that English-speaking children hear the consonants of the language easily and have problems with hearing the vowels and, by contrast, Spanish-speaking children hear the vowels and miss out the consonants at first (Ferreiro & Teberosky, 1982). Current questions are about

- the role of the syllable in Spanish literacy acquisition,

- whether the linguistic discovery of onset and rime applies to Spanish,

- how to help beginning readers cope with so many long words in their first books, and

- for languages with much more regular letter-sound relationships than English (Spanish, Maori, and German, for example), how might Reading Recovery teachers tell whether the learner who has become a rapid decoder of regular phoneme-letter relationships is taking full account of meaning and language structure?

These aspects of processing may be more readily observed in the oral reading of English than in more regular languages.

Possible neglect of writing

Progress in Reading Recovery is measured in terms of both reading and writing progress, and the child is expected to survive back in the classroom in both curriculum areas. A large body of research shows that readers and writers have to develop phonemic awareness, and build the use of the sound system of their spoken dialect and language into their developing networks of strategies for two similar but different processing systems, reading and writing. Researchers who continue to separate reading and writing and their respective theories do not model the actual or potential links between these two activities, and reviewers tend to skip over the writing in Reading Recovery and its contribution. If children can use their knowledge about reading and writing to support each other then these two activities have reciprocal effects on each other. Teachers with very different assumptions can retard the progress of children if they skip the writing or give it minimal attention, assuming that they should and can give priority to reading and attend to writing as a later learning task.

Conclusions

A good review will be referred to when the original studies are forgotten. It summarizes the position to date and acts as a bulwark, saving readers from the need to return to original sources. Reviewers therefore have a responsibility to understand and report previous research accurately before biasing the subsequent course of practice, research, and theory with their conclusions. Whether we like it or not, Herber (1994) has shown that we do not usually review back more than 21 years. While this is not the place for a meta-analysis of reviews it is important to stress that, internationally, accurate reviewing is very important and seldom achieved.

Success is relative and time-limited. The biggest threat to survival follows the success of a new intervention. An innovative programme that is getting good results has many supporters in the growth stage. Once it is in place it is taken for granted. More than that, it is a well-known fact that preventive programmes, once implemented and effective, destroy the evidence that they are needed and after a time without the evidence before it the public, politicians or educators may gradually reduce the intervention's resources and effectiveness. However, there will be a lag time before the systemic effects of the innovation are noticed and a further period before they can be ignored.

One-to-one tutoring as reviewed by Allington (1994), Pikulski (1994), and Wasik and Slavin (1993) is a potentially effective means of preventing reading failure. It deserves an important place in discussions of reform in preventive, compensatory, remedial, and special education strategies.

> If we know how to ensure that students will learn to read in the early grades, we have an ethical and perhaps legal responsibility to see that they do so. Preventive tutoring can be an alternative for providing a reliable means of abolishing illiteracy among young children who are at risk of school failure. (Wasik & Slavin, 1993, p. 158)

High rates of success for Reading Recovery have encouraged a frequent error in education: the error of over-extension of its potential, and consequential misapplications. It would be unfortunate to lose the specialist solution because of this. No one claimed that Reading Recovery would be an effective solution to anything but the learning problems of the lowest achievers in the second year of school; no one claimed that it would improve the *mean scores* of the age cohort; no one claimed that it would provide the answers to all literacy difficulties; no one claimed its theory to hold for all literacy learning.

The exploration of teacher training and support, the delivery of teaching, and the management at the school, district, and state/country level of Reading Recovery demonstrate that any further research should, for economy's sake, study the outcomes in learning only in places where it can be established that

- the teachers are in or beyond their second year of teaching after training and are part of the recommended support system offered by Tutors/Teacher Leaders, and

- Reading Recovery is implemented according to state or national guidelines. The schools should follow the local guidelines for the delivery of the intervention and the implementation should be in its fourth year. I am still inclined to the opinion that a follow-up study should follow children over time, together with the age/class group in their school for that is the valid comparison group against whom their entry and exit criteria are judged. Under the above conditions it would be good judgement to carry out a cost effectiveness study.

In this early intervention 6-year-olds become competent 7-year-old readers and writers. It will not help older children become anything but 7-year-old readers and writers. Therefore sound school programmes for 8–18-year-olds are still necessary to take full advantage of the foundation skills that Reading Recovery establishes.

There has to be a reason why we have high rates of success across each of the countries we work in. The consistency, despite vast differences in educational practices, policies, and provisions, implies that (a) the teaching procedures must be appropriate for the children's learning needs and (b) there must be scope for a large range of individual differences to be addressed. In general, Reading Recovery gets close to what is needed in an early intervention.

The challenge for the future is to hold fast to these quality features, for the pressure to be less demanding threatens the tentativeness, flexibility, and problem-solving principles that have contributed to our current success. Across the world Reading Recovery is a target for copyists who want to help more children. These innovators modify, simplify, and design cheaper versions that make the very compromises that have led to weak solutions to this problem in the past. They advocate but they do not observe, develop, try out, research, check, or provide data. They live by assurances or single demonstrations with a case or small group. It seems that few people are prepared to consider 'a different programme for every child' in this hard-to-teach group. Respect for individual learning should apply to seemingly low achievers when the foundations of later learning are being laid down.

Reading Recovery designs individual solutions from its theory and research to its delivery and daily instructions, and results appear in a relatively short period of time. One-to-one teaching is not merely a convenient or privileged delivery tactic. It is the only delivery system that could arise from a theory that says that the causes of the difficulties are multiple, they differ from child to child, and each child has a different profile of strengths. This is heretical in an academic world that spends much energy in searching for one explanation for reading difficulties; therefore Reading Recovery's approach stands somewhat in isolation. Many who admit it works do not accept explanations of why it works, and the practice will not survive unless the supporting theories are understood.

However, there is one thing we have learned internationally. Children do not have to be slow learners. We have created and categorized slow-learning children by the ways in which we package and deliver our age-bound cohort structure for instruction. Reading Recovery set out to deliver learning opportunities differently.

The following publications were drawn on for this chapter:

- Clay, M. M. (2001). *Change over time in children's literacy development* (pp. 298–301). Auckland: Heinemann.

- Clay, M. M. (1997). International perspectives on the Reading Recovery program. In J. Flood, S. B. Heath, & D. Lapp (Eds.), *Handbook of research on teaching literacy through the communicative and visual arts* (pp. 655–667). Old Tappan, NJ: Simon and Schuster. (Reprinted in *Journal of Reading Recovery*, 2007, 7(1), 16–34).

- Clay, M. M. (1992). Reading Recovery: The wider implications of an educational innovation. In A. Watson & A. Badenhop (Eds.), *Prevention of reading failure* (pp. 22–47). London: Ashton Scholastic.

- Clay, M. M. (1992). A second chance to learn literacy: By different routes to common outcomes (The Reading Recovery Programme). In T. Cline (Ed.), *The assessment of special education needs* (pp. 69–89). London: Routledge.

- Clay, M. M. (1987). Implementing Reading Recovery: Systemic adaptations to an educational innovation. *New Zealand Journal of Educational Studies, 22*(1), 35–58.

References

Allington, R. L. (1994). The schools we have. The schools we need. *The Reading Teacher, 48*(1), 14–29.

Bruner, J. S. (1957). On perceptual readiness. *Psychological Review, 64,* 123–152.

Bruner, J. S. (1973). Organization of early skilled action. *Child Development, 44,* 1–11.

Cazden, C. (1972). *Child language and education.* Cambridge: Harvard University Press.

Center, Y., Wheldall, K., Freeman, I., Outhred, L., & McNaught, M. (1995). An evaluation of Reading Recovery. *Reading Research Quarterly, 30,* 240–263.

Chomsky, C. (1972). Stages in language development and reading exposure. *Harvard Educational Review, 22,* 1–33.

Clay, M. M. (1979, 1985). *The early detection of reading difficulties: A diagnostic survey with recovery procedures.* Auckland: Heinemann.

Clay, M. M. (1991). *Becoming literate: The construction of inner control.* Auckland: Heinemann.

Clay, M. M. (2001). *Change over time in children's literacy development.* Auckland: Heinemann.

Clay, M. M. (2002, 2006). *An observation survey of early literacy achievement* (2nd ed.). Auckland: Heinemann.

Clay, M. M. (2005). *Literacy lessons designed for individuals.* Auckland: Heinemann.

Dalin, P. (1978). *Limits to educational change.* Basingstoke: Macmillan.

Donaldson, M. (1978). *Children's minds.* Glasgow: Fontana.

Escamilla, K. (1994). Descubriendo la lectura: An early intervention literacy program in Spanish. *Literacy, Teaching and Learning: An International Journal of Early Literacy, 1*(2), 77–90.

Ferreiro, E., & Teberosky, A. (1982). *Literacy before schooling.* Portsmouth, NH: Heinemann.

Geekie, P. (1992). Reading Recovery: It's not what you do, it's the way that you do it. In M. Jones & E. Baglin Jones (Eds.), *Learning to behave: Curriculum and whole school management approaches to discipline* (pp. 170–188). London: Kegan Paul.

Goodlad, J. I. (1977). *Networking and educational improvement: Reflections on a strategy.* Washington, DC: NIE.

Graves, D. (1978). *Balance the basics: Let them write.* New York: Ford Foundation.

Herber, H. (1994). Professional connections: Pioneers and contemporaries in reading. In R. B. Ruddell, M. R. Ruddell, & H. Singer, (Eds.), *Theoretical models and processes of reading.* (4th ed.) (pp. 4–21). Newark, DE: International Reading Association.

Hiebert, E. (1994). Reading Recovery in the United States: What difference does it make to an age cohort? *Educational Researcher, 23*(9), 15–25.

Hobsbaum, A. (1995). Reading Recovery in England. *Literacy, Teaching and Learning: An International Journal of Early Literacy, 1*(2), 21–40.

Iversen, S. J., & Tunmer, W. E. (1993). Phonological skills and the Reading Recovery program. *Journal of Educational Psychology, 85,* 112–126.

Miller, G. (1967). *The psychology of communication.* New York: Basic Books.

Pearson, P. D. (1994). Notes on Reading Recovery opportunities and obligations. Speech to Deans of Colleges of Education with Reading Recovery training programmes. Personal communication.

Pikulski, J. J. (1994). Preventing reading failure: A review of five effective programs. *The Reading Teacher, 48*(1), 30–39.

Razinski, T. (1995). Commentary on the effects of Reading Recovery: A response to Pinnell, Lyons, DeFord, Bryk, and Seltzer. *Reading Research Quarterly. 30*(2), 264–270.

Read, C. (1975). *Children's categorization of speech sounds in English.* Urbana, IL: National Council of Teachers of English.

Robinson, V. (1993). *Problem-based methodology.* Oxford: Pergamon Press.

Rumelhart, D. (1994). Toward an interactive model of reading. In R. B. Ruddell, M. R. Ruddell, & H. Singer (Eds.), *Theoretical models and processes of reading* (pp. 864–894). Newark, DE: International Reading Association.

Shanahan, T., & Barr R. (1995). Reading Recovery: An independent evaluation of the effects of an instructional intervention for at-risk learners. *Reading Research Quarterly, 30*(4), 958–997.

Smith, F. (1971). *Understanding reading.* New York: Holt, Rinehart & Winston.

Sylva, K., & Hurry, J. (1995). *Early intervention in children with reading difficulties: An evaluation of Reading Recovery and a phonological training* (Short and Long Reports). London: Thomas Coram Research Unit, University of London. Reprinted in *Literacy Teaching and Learning: An International Journal of Early Literacy,* 1996, *2*(2), 49–68.

Wasik, B. A., & Slavin, R. E. (1993). Preventing early reading failure with one to one tutoring: A review of five programs. *Reading Research Quarterly, 28,* 179–200.

White, S. H. (1976). Developmental psychology and Vico's concept of universal history. *Social History, 43,* 659–671.

White, S. H. (1979). Old and new routes from theory to practice. In L. B. Resnick & P. A. Weaver (Eds.), *Theory and practice of early reading, vol 2* (pp. 285–298). Hillsdale, NJ: Erlbaum.

Wood, D., Brunner, J. S., & Ross, G. (1976). The role of tutoring in problem-solving. *Journal of Child Psychology and Psychiatry, 17,* 89–100.

8

Every Child Counted: Evaluating Reading Recovery Around the World

Marie Clay's early Reading Recovery research sought answers to questions about possible outcomes if instruction were delivered in a different way and end results were compared with ordinary classroom instruction (see Chapter 2). As Reading Recovery has expanded internationally, outcomes for all children who have received the intervention, whether in trials or systematic implementations, have been collected and reported. To date, outcomes have been documented for approximately 2.5 million children around the world.

Ways of evaluating outcomes are remarkably similar. All countries with Reading Recovery use information from An Observation Survey of Early Literacy Achievement *(Clay, 2002, 2006) to identify children for Reading Recovery and to monitor change over time. In addition, some external measures are systematically used in all countries except the United States where currently pilot studies are trialling possible instruments for this purpose.*

Differences generally relate to educational context. For example, the school year in the Northern Hemisphere usually begins in September and ends in May/June, while Southern Hemisphere schools operate across the calendar year. The varied length of school year influences decisions made on outcomes for many children. Political and educational priorities at the local, state/province, and national levels may influence some aspects of the information collected.

While descriptions of child outcomes may differ slightly, most countries use the following general categories:

- *successfully completed (lessons discontinued after child reaches class level expectations),*

- *recommended/referred for further assessment and possible specialist support after around 20 weeks of lessons,*

- *moved/transferred from the school while receiving Reading Recovery,*

- *unable to continue lessons because of unusual circumstances such as a child's long-term illness, and*

- *lessons carried over to next school year (in all countries except the United States where 'incomplete intervention' describes the status of children who are unable to continue lessons because the first-grade school year ended).*

Some general trends are consistent across evaluation systems. All countries report consistency of child outcomes across time. With shifts to include more process data, education agencies are now also able to study the impact of implementation decisions on child outcomes. The evolution of technology has expedited and enhanced data collection, analysis, and reporting. With most countries now using web-based technology, additional data can be collected more easily to address specific questions in a timely fashion.

In this chapter, evaluation processes and trends are reported for New Zealand, Australia, the United States, Canada, and the United Kingdom and Ireland. Presentation is based on the chronological order of the implementation of Reading Recovery.

Introduction by Billie Askew

Monitoring Reading Recovery in New Zealand
Christine Boocock

The evolution of data collection and reporting

Annual monitoring and national reporting of individual school participation and outcomes for children has been a key feature from the beginning of Reading Recovery as a government supported and funded early literacy intervention in New Zealand. The Ministry of Education, formerly the Department of Education, carries out the annual analysis and reporting of these data on state and state-integrated primary schools[1] for the whole country. In collaboration with the national Trainers, Reading Recovery Tutors/Teacher Leaders work in regionally based

---

1 A state-integrated school is a school with a special (religious) character, which has been integrated into the state system. State and state-integrated schools total 96% of all primary and secondary schools in New Zealand.

teams assisting the Ministry with collecting annual data from schools and checking that these data are complete. A number of additions to the data gathered and changes in the procedure have taken place over time. National monitoring and reporting indicates that over the past 25 years, about 250,000 New Zealand children have received individual help in Reading Recovery. This has been achieved through the dedicated work of approximately 1400 teachers annually, 30 to 35 Tutors/Teacher Leaders, and a small team of Trainers.

Central responsibility for monitoring the implementation

Building on Marie Clay's early research, reported in Chapter 2, a system was created for monitoring the outcomes for children in Reading Recovery across the country. This system provided a framework for other countries to adapt as Reading Recovery spread across the world.

During the early expansion of Reading Recovery from 1984 to 1988, the Department of Education called for information on the delivery of Reading Recovery each year, including the outcome status of children across the country. This annual survey was the responsibility of the Schools Division at central office. Late in each school year, data collection forms (End-of-Year Summary forms) were forwarded to the 10 Education Board district Liaison Inspectors and passed on to Tutors/Teacher Leaders, who distributed them to teachers in the schools operating Reading Recovery.

Data were collected on the number of children who entered Reading Recovery in each year and whether (a) they reached average levels (Discontinued), (b) they were referred for specialist help (Referred), or (c) their lessons were to be continued in the next school year (Carried Over). This information was collated and analysed by Department personnel and although it was not published it provided an accountability check on the operation of Reading Recovery, informed decisions on the placement of Tutor/Teacher Leader positions, and assisted in the distribution of resources.

A steady increase in the number of children entering Reading Recovery over the first 5-year period reflected the gradual expansion of the intervention in New Zealand. Marie Clay considered such strong evidence of the feasibility of the national implementation of an early literacy intervention to be of interest both in New Zealand and overseas and gained the Department's permission to publish these data. The article 'National Monitoring 1984–1988: Coverage, outcomes and Education Board figures,' was published in the *New Zealand Journal of Educational Studies* (Clay, 1990) and later reprinted in *Reading Recovery: A Guidebook for Teachers in Training* (Clay, 1993). (See Chapter 2.)

Changes to the administration of education

In 1989, a major educational reform in New Zealand known as 'Tomorrow's Schools' created self-managing schools by disestablishing regional Education Boards and renaming and restructuring the national Department of Education to create a Ministry of Education. Following this change, the newly designated Ministry of Education's Research and Statistics Division (renamed the Research Division in 1993) assumed responsibility for the Reading Recovery data collection, analysis, and reporting. Reading Recovery Tutors/Teacher Leaders, employed until this time by Education Boards, became employees of regional Teacher Training Colleges (now merged with universities), funded by the Ministry of Education to provide Tutor/Teacher Leader services. Tutors/Teacher Leaders continued to be professionally responsible to the Trainers at the National Reading Recovery Centre.

These changes affected the procedure for gathering data. The End-of-Year Summary forms for data collection were now sent annually from the Ministry of Education to the Trainers, who forwarded them to Tutors/Teacher Leaders for distribution to schools by Reading Recovery teachers. Schools returned the completed forms to Tutors/Teacher Leaders for checking; the National Reading Recovery Centre then received and examined the forms, finally sending them on to the central Ministry of Education for collation, analysis, and reporting. This procedure ensured the data were as reliable as possible.

Changes in data collected

Over the years a number of changes have been made in the nature of the data gathered and the form in which the information is collected.

Additional information. Initially schools submitted an End-of-Year Summary form that recorded the number of Reading Recovery teachers working in a school, the number of children entering Reading Recovery and their outcomes, and the average duration of the lesson series for both the Discontinued and Referred groups of children. From 1992, an interest in gathering more specific details led to the collection and reporting of child gender data.

From 2000, the ethnicity of children was included, adopting the system of recording used by Statistics New Zealand in which children are assigned to one ethnic group only. Information is documented on children from a total of 14 ethnic groups, but for some analyses children are clustered into five major groups: Maori, Pasifika, Asian, NZ European, and Other.

Individual student data. A major shift occurred in 2001 with the introduction of Individual Student Report forms to be completed in addition to a School End-of-Year Report form. Since that time, schools have been required to supply information on individual outcomes for all children who enter Reading Recovery. Number of lessons and calendar weeks are reported for those children whose series of lessons have been discontinued or who have been referred for specialist help. In addition, initial and final entry data and shifts in instructional text levels (Clay, 2002, 2006), Burt Word Reading Test scores (New Zealand Council for Educational Research, 1981), and Writing Vocabulary task scores (Clay, 2002, 2006) are reported for these two groups of children.

Online data collection. Consistent with its commitment to information technology, the Ministry of Education has changed the way data are collected. In 2002, the Ministry of Education piloted a website for online data collection in one region of New Zealand, and from 2003 all schools nationwide were able to enter data online. Electronic data collection has allowed Reading Recovery teachers to enter data on an Individual Student Report at any time during the year. When the Reading Recovery teacher(s) have completed all Individual Student Reports, the principal or a delegated staff member is asked to complete the School End-of-Year Report and confirm the information entered earlier. Reading Recovery Tutors/Teacher Leaders then check the data electronically to ensure complete reporting. The Ministry of Education and Trainers liaise regularly about data collection procedures and analysis for quality assurance purposes.

Publication of reports

Since 1989, the Ministry of Education has published annually a summary of the national data. Initially the reports appeared in the New Zealand Ministry of Educational Research Division's publication *The Research Bulletin.* From 2001 onwards, the reports have been made available electronically through the Ministry of Education website or, on request, as a hard copy. Annual reports from 1999 are currently available on Education Counts www.educationcounts.govt.nz.

A valuable summary of the data from 1984 to 1998 was published in *The Research Bulletin* (Kerslake, 1999). This brief report reviewed data over 14 years of national implementation including data presented by Marie Clay (1990) and reported 'a steady ongoing demand for Reading Recovery and a consistent pattern of outcomes for students' (p. 77).

These readily available, annually published reports on Reading Recovery have played very important roles. They have provided the

Ministry of Education with systematic data on the continued effectiveness of Reading Recovery. They have facilitated access for researchers and practitioners in New Zealand and throughout the world to investigate aspects of the delivery of Reading Recovery. One example is seen in a recent major research project commissioned by the Ministry of Education from the independent New Zealand Council for Educational Research. This group undertook further in-depth statistical analysis of the child outcome data for 2003 in conjunction with a wide range of other research methods, including interviews, case studies, and focus groups (McDowall, Boyd, Hodgen, & van Vliet, 2005). The analysis of the child outcome data led to findings related to the achievement of Maori and Pacific children in Reading Recovery, a key focus of the study.

Notable trends in the data over time

Data on the national implementation of Reading Recovery in New Zealand have now been collected for almost 25 years. Despite changes in the type of data collected and method of reporting, many remarkably consistent trends can be discerned. The increasing amount of data now collected means that some trends have been observable for a longer time than others.

Child data

A major trend, consistent over the whole period of data collection to date (1984–2007), is the number of children whose series of lessons are discontinued each academic year. Sixty per cent of children successfully complete their series of lessons each year, with between 23% and 25% reported as expected to complete a series in the following year. (In New Zealand, children with an incomplete series of lessons continue to receive help after the 6-week summer break when they enter a new class level.) Since 1993, the Ministry has made statistical estimates of the proportion of children who have gone on to successfully complete Reading Recovery based on the data from each current year. This has been consistently between 83% and 87% over the last 15 years.

A second remarkably consistent trend is noted for the group comprising the children who have not reached levels of achievement in reading and writing high enough to enable them to continue to learn in the classroom without further specialist help. These children, classified as 'Referred on,' have made up between 8.2% and 9.2% of those in Reading Recovery over the last 5 years.

The gender ratio of students is also a consistent feature of the national data. Since this information was first gathered in 1992, it has been reported annually that two-thirds of the children in Reading Recovery are boys. However, the data show very little difference in literacy outcomes for boys and girls.

School data

A trend noted from the mid-1990s in school data was the increase of Reading Recovery participation in rural schools (Kerslake, 1999). The comparatively large number of rural schools in New Zealand that serve communities of less than 1000 people (33%) has been an important factor in the national distribution of Reading Recovery. In 1991, 31% of all rural schools had Reading Recovery. By 1994, 51% reported implementing Reading Recovery. This figure remained steady through until 1997 when this information was last reported. The increased availability of Reading Recovery in rural schools can be attributed to the development of a pragmatic organizational scheme, Reading Recovery 'clusters.' When small schools form a 'cluster,' the Ministry of Education can direct funding to one school to enable a Reading Recovery teacher based there to also teach in other reasonably close, small schools each day as the need arises.

A further interesting and consistent trend has been observed through the reporting of school and child data by decile ranking in the last 5 years. This system, calculated to reflect the socio-economic status of the school community, was introduced in the late 1990s to provide an index on which to base differential Ministry of Education funding for schools. Decile 1 schools are the 10% of schools with the highest proportion of schools of children from low socio-economic communities. Decile 10 are the 10% of schools with the lowest proportion of children from these communities. Whilst Reading Recovery is available in slightly more high decile schools annually than low decile schools, those low decile schools that implement Reading Recovery have a greater number of children entering Reading Recovery.

Conclusion

In her summary of the first five years of national data gathering, Marie Clay made this claim:

> The results challenge much accumulated wisdom about literacy problems; clearly they are alterable variables for many children. (Clay, 1990, p. 69)

New Zealand now has an impressive history of evaluation data available on the implementation of Reading Recovery as a 'second wave of teaching effort' as part of a comprehensive approach to learning and teaching in schools. These results demonstrate that Reading Recovery has had a major effect on the literacy achievement of New Zealand children.

Significantly, it is the Ministry of Education that undertakes this important evaluative role and produces the annual comprehensive reports that are essential for monitoring the ongoing success of the intervention in New Zealand. The interest and commitment of many people over time has ensured the ongoing availability of this valuable information.

Monitoring Reading Recovery in Australia
Janet Scull

Reading Recovery commenced in Australia in 1984 with a training group of 14 teachers in Bendigo, Victoria who worked with 121 children (Wheeler, 1986). Since that time, Reading Recovery has expanded to six Australian states and one territory, with various education systems supporting the implementation based on the principle of equity provision; the lowest achieving children, after one year of schooling are given a second chance for literacy learning.

Consistent across each implementation is a commitment that every child be counted to ensure responsible and transparent fiscal accountability and intervention evaluation. Hence, we continue as we started, with all Reading Recovery children's data collected, analysed, and reported by the responsible bodies in each locality.

Australia with its federalized system of government has granted states and territories authority for education. Consequently, various state government departments of education and Catholic diocesan school systems have assumed responsibility for the introduction and implementation of Reading Recovery in Australia, largely independent of each other. State budget allocations are always associated with high levels of public accountability and reporting to ensure gains in return for the financial investment. Reading Recovery has not been exempt from this intense level of examination. Furthermore, those responsible for Reading Recovery implementation use data to monitor and evaluate the effectiveness of the intervention on children's early literacy learning, a mechanism for quality assurance processes. Reading Recovery data have been collected and reported systemically across 14 education authorities.

Australia's commitment to counting every child is demonstrated in the sections that follow through an exploration of some exemplar

Reading Recovery data collection processes that have ensured the intervention's accountability.

Data collection processes

The first processes for annual data collection in Australia were modelled on the New Zealand experience. 'Hard copy' paper data collection commenced in Victoria in 1984, with other implementations adopting this form of collection in the first instance. In New South Wales, where statewide Reading Recovery implementation commenced in 1996, student data continues to be collected in this way. Other states and systems have moved to electronic data collection following Victoria's lead in 2000. Despite the various mechanisms available for data collection, consistency in the data collated and analysed is evident.

Across the various implementations, the number of schools, teachers, and children accessing Reading Recovery teaching are collated annually. From 121 children in 1984 it is calculated that in 2006, a total of 27,243 children participated in Reading Recovery nationally in government and non-government schools.

Marie Clay's 1990 comments about the expansion of Reading Recovery in New Zealand can also be applied to Australia.

> ... the results of Reading Recovery in numbers of children discontinued show that this is a programme which schools and teachers have been able to mount and deliver. They have seen a high proportion of the children who have immense difficulty making the transition into formal literacy brought to a fair measure of independence in classroom work in a relatively short period of time. (Clay, 1990, p. 69)

While the number of children participating in Reading Recovery indicates the breadth and expansion of Reading Recovery coverage in Australia, the success of the intervention is best measured by the impact on children's literacy learning. Children's learning outcomes are based on scores on Observation Survey tasks (Clay, 2002, 2006) and in some systems on additional word tests, most prominently the Burt Word Reading Test (New Zealand Council for Educational Research, 1981) and the Duncan Word Test (Duncan & McNaughton, 2001).

Uniformly, children's data are recorded upon entry to and exit from Reading Recovery and at the end of the school year. Teachers enter a status outcome for each child to indicate whether the child's lessons were discontinued (able to work within average achievement band of their class); referred to other services for additional literacy support; had lessons carried over into the following year to complete their series of lessons; or transferred, leaving the school prior to the completion of the intervention. The children's time in Reading Recovery in weeks and lessons is also recorded. In addition, background information is collected, as teachers indicate if a child is from a non-English speaking environment, is Aboriginal, and/or from the Torres Strait Islands.

Data collected systemically reveal the pre- and post-intervention measures of children's literacy achievement. As many children complete the Reading Recovery intervention prior to the end of the school year, end-of-year testing is completed on all children whose series of lessons have been discontinued to monitor progress without the additional one-to-one support of the Reading Recovery teacher. Importantly, this aggregated data set shows the continued growth in children's text level reading beyond the intervention.

Examination of the rich data sets allows for close analysis of the efficacy of the Reading Recovery intervention. In combination, demographic and children's outcome data are used to monitor intervention effectiveness across differentiated cohorts, by gender, background, school district, and intake.

Of critical concern are the educational opportunities and outcomes of Australia's indigenous population. In 2000, the Ministerial Council on Education, Employment Training and Youth Affairs in their *National Statement of Principles and Standards for More Culturally Inclusive Schooling in the 21ˢᵗ Century* stated that appropriate curriculum

> . . . allows indigenous students to share in the same educational opportunities experienced by other Australian students and at the same time allows them to be strong in their own culture and language and reposition their cultures, languages, histories, beliefs and lifestyles in a way which affirms identity and the ability to operate in cross-cultural situations.

Unfortunately, educational outcomes of indigenous children continue to fall below those of their non-indigenous peers. National and state data consistently report the lower levels of educational attainment of this cohort (Department of Education and Training, Victoria, 2005b; Ministerial Council on Education, Employment Training and Youth Affairs, 2005). However, Reading Recovery data report strong outcomes for this group of children; given the opportunity to participate in an intense early intervention, outcomes equivalent to non-indigenous groups are achieved.

In Queensland, relatively high numbers of indigenous children have participated in Reading Recovery (Department of Education and the Arts, Queensland, 2006). And most recently Reading Recovery has been introduced in the Kimberley region of Western Australia to provide some of Australia's most geographically isolated children access to opportunities offered to children in other locations. The majority of children in Reading Recovery in Kimberley in 2006 were indigenous Australians; student gains in text reading level were impressive with an average gain of 13 text levels reported (Scull & Bremner, 2007).

Data sets have also been used to analyse child outcomes by date of entry to the intervention. Children who enter Reading Recovery early in the school year enter with lower text levels, and the series of lessons is longer (Department of Education and Training, Victoria, 2003–2007a). These data have particular implications for teaching practices and resource allocation.

Similarly, exemplary data from the diocese of Wollongong reveal that more children with entry to Reading Recovery during the first half of the school year were referred for additional support (Catholic Education Office, Diocese of Wollongong, 2007). Data acknowledge the two positive outcomes of Reading Recovery, as stated by Clay (2005): 'One positive outcome is for the child to be successful and for lessons to be discontinued. The second positive outcome is to be referred for further assessment, for long-term assistance and for specialist help' (p. 55). However, 'the more effective the education system is at delivering an early literacy intervention, the fewer children will need to be referred for further intensive help' (p. 56).

The reduction of referral rates is considered to be a further measure of the effectiveness of Reading Recovery teaching with improvement in outcomes for students over time critical to the long-term efficacy of the intervention. Wollongong data sets prompted strategic action to reduce referral rates and to specifically target additional support programmes to areas of identified need (Catholic Education Office, Diocese of Wollongong, 2004).

Continuous monitoring

The electronic and web-based data collection processes now adopted by a number of educational systems assist with the ongoing monitoring of Reading Recovery's effectiveness. The available technology allows for the continuous entry of children's data. At any time, site administrators are able to assess the progressive totals of children whose lessons were discontinued or who were referred to additional support services, children's entry levels and exit levels as indicated by test measures, and time in Reading Recovery by weeks and lessons. Additional to aggregated data, individual children are closely monitored throughout their participation in the intervention. Children's text level progress and writing vocabularies are regularly reviewed. A number of education systems monitor the daily teaching of children as teachers submit graphs of lesson attendance for analysis.

Tracking children into the next school year

A small percentage of children who entered late in the year remain on Reading Recovery at the end of the school year and continue their series of lessons in the subsequent school year. The 5- to 6-week vacation break over the months of December and January is not seen as prohibitive to a successful outcome. To ensure these children are included in end-of-year data collection processes, children with an incomplete series of lessons at the end of the school year are accounted for with an 'in programme' outcome. Since the introduction of electronic data collection, for example, Victoria has successfully tracked children with an 'in programme' outcome into the following school year. This has provided a high level of transparency ensuring that outcomes for all children are recorded and accurately reported. A high percentage of the children who complete the intervention in the following school year reach class standards and lessons are discontinued (Department of Education and Training, Victoria, 2003, 2004, 2005a, 2006, 2007a).

Students' outcomes beyond Reading Recovery

Acknowledging the success of the Reading Recovery intervention in supporting children's early literacy learning, educational authorities are seeking long-term solutions to complex problems such as low levels of literacy performance. As such, systems are looking to analyse Reading Recovery children's outcomes beyond the year of implementation.

The Department of Education and Training in New South Wales pays close attention to the long-term literacy outcomes of Reading Recovery children, mapping their progress against this state's Basic Skills Test (a systemic assessment in Years 3 and 5 to target assistance for children who achieve lower results so that the requirements set by the syllabus in English and Mathematics are met). The expected achievement bands for Year 3 and Year 5 are Bands 2 and 3, respectively. In 2006, 75% of all former Reading Recovery students whose lessons were discontinued demonstrated acceptable literacy skills in their Year 3 Basic Skills Test (that is, they were placed in Band 2 or higher). Moreover, 4 years after the Reading Recovery intervention, 87% of students in Year 5 in 2006 were achieving at an acceptable level, being placed in Band 3 or higher (New South Wales Department of Education and Training, 2007).

Reporting processes

The reporting of child data remains with individual state and territory systems. Hence, means of reporting Reading Recovery outcomes vary. Australian states with large Reading Recovery implementations and high levels of public funding account for Reading Recovery in annual education reports where aggregated data are used to show key outcomes of the intervention. The annual reports of various Departments of Education are available electronically via government websites (Department of Education and Training, Victoria, 2007b; New South Wales Department of Education and Training, 2007).

Alternatively, specific Reading Recovery reports can be accessed via departmental websites (Department of Education, Tasmania, 2007; Government of South Australia Department of Education and Children's Services, 2007). In addition, detailed analysis and reporting of data is undertaken by Reading Recovery Trainers and Tutors/Teacher Leaders and disseminated to interested stakeholders, including reports and presentations to school administrators, principals, and teachers.

Notwithstanding the diligence of personal responsibility for implementation and attention to accountability processes, a coherent reporting process is desirable to indicate the full extent of the impact of Reading Recovery on children's early literacy learning in Australia.

Conclusion

The theme of this chapter — every child counted — resonates well with the Australian implementations of Reading Recovery. Importantly, data collection and analysis processes reflect the intent of educational systems to work to maximize the overall effectiveness of the intervention and ensure that optimal opportunities are provided for each child to 'discover things for himself, work out some possibilities, and extend his own processing skills in both reading and writing . . . and enjoy the challenge of doing this' (Clay, 2005, p. 62).

Monitoring Reading Recovery in the United States

Francisco Gómez-Bellengé

Data have been collected for every Reading Recovery child in the United States since the first implementation in 1984. With the rapid growth of Reading Recovery in this country, data collection and reporting had to become institutionalized and has, over the years, evolved to Internet data collection and automated reports provided to all stakeholders. The evaluation of student outcomes is a condition for granting use of the US Reading Recovery royalty-free trademark to participating sites, ensuring the continuing quality of services to children.

Reading Recovery and Descubriendo La Lectura[2] data in the United States are collected, analysed, and reported by the National Data Evaluation Center (NDEC) at The Ohio State University. To date, the Center has processed data for more than 1.8 million US Reading Recovery children plus thousands of children representing a national random sample of first-grade literacy achievement.

History

In 1984–1985, Marie Clay and Barbara Watson introduced Reading Recovery to faculty at The Ohio State University and teachers in the Columbus City Schools (Lyons, 1998). Successful results led the Ohio General Assembly to fund teacher training sites in Ohio, and in 1987, the US Department of Education's National Diffusion Network recognized Reading Recovery as an exemplary research-based intervention and made funding available to school districts in other states. By 1996–1997, Reading Recovery was operating in 48 states and some Department of Defense schools.

At the conclusion of the pilot year, calculators were used to compute means and standard deviations of Observation Survey scores. Then for several years, data collection was staffed by graduate students working with Ohio State faculty. National Diffusion Network funding created the National Data Evaluation Center and the beginning of formalized data collection through optical scan forms. Data collection for Descubriendo la Lectura began in 1993–1994. Throughout the evolution of the data evaluation process, a methodology committee (comprising Reading

---

2 Descubriendo la Lectura is the reconstruction of Reading Recovery in Spanish for children whose language of instruction is Spanish.

Recovery Trainers, Tutors/Teacher Leaders, university researchers, and school/district administrators) has worked with the Center staff to inform decisions about data collection and reporting.

The first optical scan forms in use until 1997 reported only child-level data. A second generation of scan forms including both child and teacher data were in use from 1998–1999 to 2001–2002. Data collection moved to the Internet exclusively in 2002–2003; data submission is now web-based over a secure site.

Evaluation methodology

When Marie Clay granted the US trademark for Reading Recovery to The Ohio State University, the university assumed responsibility for a data collection centre to evaluate outcomes across the country. The annual evaluation of Reading Recovery allows for replication across time and space, providing both systematic and simultaneous replication. Evaluation procedures for Descubriendo la Lectura (Reading Recovery in Spanish) are identical to those used in Reading Recovery. Nine questions guide the annual evaluation:

Required

1. How many children were served and who was served in Reading Recovery?

2. What was the intervention status of children served by Reading Recovery? How many had their series of lessons successfully discontinued?

3. What was the progress of the Reading Recovery children on literacy measures?

4. What proportion of Reading Recovery students scored in each national achievement group for each measure of the Observation Survey?

5. What were the gains from exit to year-end testing of Reading Recovery children whose lessons began in fall (beginning of school year) and were successfully discontinued?

Optional

6. Was there a change in the performance placement of Reading Recovery children from beginning to end of the school year?

7. What percentage of Reading Recovery children were referred and placed in special education?

8. What percentage of Reading Recovery children were considered for retention and retained in first grade?

9. What informal responses to Reading Recovery did teachers, administrators, and parents make?

Additional process data are collected and reported in a statistical appendix, primarily for evaluation of local implementation factors. The methodology allows for summative (outcome) and formative (process) evaluation as well as internal and external evaluation.

Every child who receives at least one Reading Recovery lesson is included in the evaluation. Data are also collected for a random sample consisting of two Grade 1 students drawn at random from each participating school. Because of the large number in the random sample, it is considered representative of the population of US first graders. Data about characteristics of Reading Recovery schools and teachers are also collected.

An Observation Survey of Early Literacy Achievement (Clay, 2002, 2006) is administered to Reading Recovery students at the beginning of Grade 1, at entry to the intervention, at exit, and at year-end. The Survey is administered to random sample students at the beginning of the school year, at mid-year, and at year-end.

Reading Recovery is evaluated using a pre-test–post-test two-group quasi-experimental research design, a strong design for a very large-scale annual evaluation. The random sample is a non-equivalent comparison group. Through factor analysis, an equivalent comparison group can be drawn from a subset of the random sample. Reading Recovery students can therefore be compared to both students that represent the general population (non-equivalent group) and students who were also very low readers at the beginning of first grade but did not receive Reading Recovery (equivalent group). This allows for the computation of a quasi experimentally derived treatment effect.

Current US norms were derived from the random sample taken in 2002–2003 using stratified proportional random sample methods (Gómez-Bellengé & Thompson, 2005). These norms are published in Marie Clay's 2006 edition of *An Observation Survey of Early Literacy Achievement*.

Procedures for data collection and reporting

At the beginning of each school year the National Data Evaluation Center, in collaboration with Reading Recovery Trainers, updates rosters of teachers, schools, and school districts and ties them to the federal National Center for Education Statistics (NCES) numbering system. This allows the National Data Evaluation Center to incorporate NCES data into its reports.

Typically, data collection occurs year round. As teachers enter data, the website verifies entries for completeness and accuracy and prevents entry of impossible data values or warns of improbable values. At the end of the school year, Tutors/Teacher Leaders verify entries and submit the data to the National Data Evaluation Center. Upon submission of a site's data, an automated process creates teacher training site reports, school district reports, and school reports and notifies Tutors/Teacher Leaders to log on to secure web pages to download or email the reports.

The National Data Evaluation Center provides each University Training Center with a report including information about all sites affiliated with the centre. State reports are available to university Trainers upon request. A national report is published annually by the National Data Evaluation Center (see website: www.ndec.us).

Changes to reports over time

Early reports were created at the level of a teacher-training site. The first major change in reporting was the introduction of University Training Center reports, followed by state reports, district reports, and finally school reports. School reports were designed with the support of the methodology committee; the focus is on individuals, not trends.

Another major change to the reports came with the advent of the federal No Child Left Behind legislation in 2002, which required states to report school and district data disaggregated by race, gender, English Language Learner status, and Special Education status. Because Reading Recovery was eager to demonstrate that it contributed to closing achievement gaps, the National Data Evaluation Center began producing disaggregated data reports.

Major findings of the evaluation process

Reading Recovery serves a large and diverse population in the United States. About 75% of students who receive a complete series of lessons reach grade-level expectations and lessons are discontinued. These children begin first grade well behind other children and end the year within an average range of grade-level performance.

The progress of Reading Recovery students accelerates in relation to average students during the intervention, and they maintain their gains in the months following the intervention. Those whose lessons are discontinued by mid-year are highly likely to be rated average readers at year-end by their classroom teachers and highly unlikely to be subsequently placed in special education or retained in grade for reading-related reasons.

Looking at the years 1998–2007, several trends are in evidence:

- Remarkably consistent results over the years

- Increasingly higher text reading levels at the beginning of the year, higher gains during the school year, and higher reading levels at year-end for the general population

- Larger achievement gaps at the beginning of the year for Reading Recovery students relative to the general population, followed by faster acceleration and higher reading levels at year-end

- Fewer interventions lasting longer than 20 weeks in the first part of the school year, with an increasing number of interventions lasting exactly 20 weeks

- A decrease in the proportion of interventions starting at the beginning of the year that are discontinued, accompanied by an offsetting increase in the proportion of interventions beginning around mid-year that are discontinued.

These trends merit close monitoring. The increasing success of early literacy classroom instruction is creating a new challenge for Reading Recovery because the initial achievement gap is increasing and the level of acceleration required to close that gap is also increasing. This trend validates Marie Clay's prediction:

> *Lifting the average scores in schools will increase rather than decrease the need for early intervention* ... Higher general levels of achievement will create larger gaps between the average and the lowest achievers in literacy acquisition unless special measures are put in place. (Clay, 2001, p. 216)

Research evolving from evaluation data

With sufficient resources to process and analyse data, the National Data Evaluation Center supports the research of university Trainers. Many of the examples listed below are available on the National Data Evaluation Center website (www.ndec.us/Documentation.asp).

- The Center facilitated the work of Reading Recovery Trainer Robert Schwartz, whose randomized experimental trial was used as evidence by the What Works Clearinghouse (Schwartz, 2005).

- The Center is currently facilitating data collection for a group-size study by Dr Schwartz and colleagues through a custom-designed website.

- A collaborative team used existing data to explore primary predictors of reading (Lose, Gómez-Bellengé, & Ye, 2006).

- A series of sub-group studies have demonstrated that Reading Recovery reduces or closes achievement gaps between different demographic groups (Rodgers, Gómez-Bellengé, & Wang, 2004; Rodgers, Gómez-Bellengé, Wang, & Schulz, 2005).

- Evaluation data demonstrated that outcomes for English Language Learners taught in Reading Recovery are essentially similar to those of native English speakers (Kelly, Gómez-Bellengé, Chen, & Schulz, 2008).

- A study found that the Observation Survey correlates well with the Iowa Test of Basic Skills (ITBS), with both batteries identifying the same children as low readers and showing significant progress on literacy measures for Reading Recovery students (Gómez-Bellengé, Rodgers, Wang, & Schulz, 2005).

- Another examination of the Observation Survey and the Iowa Test of Basic Skills concluded that the Survey is a valid and reliable instrument that can be used for programme evaluation (Tang & Gómez-Bellengé, 2007).

- A method of measuring a treatment effect for Reading Recovery using the six measures of the Observation Survey, none of which have normal distributions, was described (Ye & Gómez-Bellengé, 2006).

- A study of the Dynamic Indicators of Basic Early Literacy Skills (DIBELS) and the Observation Survey brought into question the use of the DIBELS for identifying learners' levels of literacy proficiency and 'at-riskness' at the beginning of first grade (Doyle, Gibson, Gómez-Bellengé, Kelly, & Tang, 2008).

- Refinement of the National Data Evaluation Center methodology and technical reports led to recognition of Reading Recovery evaluation in the scientific community (see for example Denton, Ciancio, & Fletcher, 2006).

The future

The evaluation of Reading Recovery in the United States continues to establish the effectiveness of this intervention. The infrastructure that has been developed to monitor Reading Recovery is leading edge. Yet the need for an active and forward-looking programme of research continues. While few now question the effectiveness of Reading Recovery, issues of cost and long-term effects merit further study. Additional research related to the influence of implementation factors on outcomes could provide process data for Reading Recovery leaders.

The United Kingdom and the Republic of Ireland have been contracting data processing services from the National Data Evaluation Center for the last few years. The Center was recently renamed the International Data Evaluation Center (IDEC) and invites international Reading Recovery colleagues to join forces to maintain the scientific credibility of Reading Recovery effectiveness.

The vision of Marie Clay was extraordinary in its depth, breadth, and reach. She recognized that a concept, no matter how good, needs fertile ground and adequate support to thrive. She also recognized the unique nature of individual contexts. The power of technology now allows Reading Recovery to share a common platform for data collection and processing customized for local settings and a common forum for the International Reading Recovery Trainers Organization (IRRTO) to conduct and disseminate research on Reading Recovery.

Monitoring Reading Recovery in Canada
Irene Huggins

A brief history

Systems to document and evaluate the implementation of Reading Recovery at all levels have been established in Canada. The data collected are reflected in annual national, provincial, training centre, and school reports.

Although Reading Recovery has been implemented in Canada since 1988, data for students included in Reading Recovery have been collected and reported nationally since 1995–1996. Prior to that time, Reading Recovery student data were sent to The Ohio State University and reported at the local Training Centres.

Established in 1992, The Canadian Institute of Reading Recovery (CIRR) began to create a national process for collecting and reporting

269

Canadian evaluation data. A CIRR research team developed a National End-of-Year Summary form used for the first time during the 1995–1996 school year. Modelled after the New Zealand Ministry of Education's Reading Recovery End-of-Year Summary form, this form allowed for the collection of data from every school implementing Reading Recovery across Canada (445 schools in 1995–1996). The form has been modified during each of the data collection periods from 1995–1996 to 2007–2008.

The Board of Directors of the Canadian Institute of Reading Recovery continues to support the collection of national data from all Reading Recovery schools. This annual project has two primary objectives: (a) to describe the Canadian Reading Recovery implementation, and (b) to document the growth of the intervention in each of the provinces as well as nationally. To support schools and sites (Training Centres), the Canadian Institute supported research to establish Canadian norms for *An Observation Survey of Early Literacy Achievement* in 2008. Canadian norms have also been established for the French version of the Observation Survey, *Le sondage d'observation en lecture-écriture* (Clay & Bourque, 2003).

National data: The process

The Canadian Institute of Reading Recovery National End-of-Year Summary forms are distributed to Tutors/Teachers Leaders in April. They then distribute one form to each of the Reading Recovery schools in their jurisdiction. Reading Recovery/Intervention préventive en lecture-écriture teachers (in both English and French implementations of Reading Recovery) complete these forms by the middle of June and return them to the Tutors/Teacher Leaders by the end of June. The forms are checked for accuracy by the Tutors/Teacher Leaders and sent to the Trainer responsible for completing the Regional Institute (Western, Central, and Eastern) Report. The forms are checked again and data are entered and analysed.

Data from all three Regional Institutes are compiled in a preliminary National Report. The report is reviewed by the Canadian Trainer Team in September and by the Canadian Institute Board of Directors at their October/November meeting. Provincial data reports are reviewed with the Tutors/Teacher Leaders in the region affiliated with a Regional Training Institute so that local trends can be analysed and discussed. Executive summaries of the provincial and national data are prepared and distributed to the Reading Recovery schools during the first term of school.

National data: What is collected

The National End-of-Year Summary Form includes information about Reading Recovery schools, teachers, and students. These data provide information concerning the growth of Reading Recovery in terms of

- the number of schools implementing Reading Recovery,

- the number of teachers providing Reading Recovery instruction,

- the number of instructional hours allocated for Reading Recovery,

- the number of students receiving Reading Recovery instruction in each school, and

- the proportion of Grade 1 students included in Reading Recovery in any given year.

The National End-of-Year Summary form also includes information on the outcomes for students participating in Reading Recovery for that school year. Literacy outcomes are reported in three categories determined by the children's entry to Reading Recovery: (a) carried over from the previous school year, (b) entered Reading Recovery in the current school year, or (c) moved in from a different school. The average number of weeks and lessons is also reported within these three categories for the students who are discontinued or referred.

Provincial and national reports

Data have been reported at the provincial and national levels since 1995–1996. The national report includes the number of Training Centres, Tutors/Teacher Leaders, schools, teachers, and students included in Reading Recovery in a school year. This documents the annual growth of Reading Recovery in each of the provinces and in the country. Since 1995–1996, over 130,000 students have been included in Reading Recovery across Canada.

Outcomes for students in Reading Recovery are reported each year. Trends (including the number of students who successfully completed their series of lessons) are evaluated by the Reading Recovery teachers, Tutors/Teacher Leaders and Trainers in order to improve the quality of the implementation of Reading Recovery provincially and nationally.

Trends and observations

The number of Reading Recovery Tutors/Teacher Leaders, teachers, schools, and students increased steadily from 1995–1996, and has remained relatively constant since 2001–2002. While there is variation from province to province on the proportion of students included in Reading Recovery, the overall implementation rate for schools offering Reading Recovery has remained constant at approximately 20.5%.

Student outcomes have been very consistent over the past 10 years, varying by a maximum of 6.2 % since 1995–1996. The greatest variation in the progress data over time is observed in the proportions of children whose Reading Recovery lessons were *successfully discontinued* and the proportions of those who were *recommended for longer term support*. The proportions varied in the former by 4.9 % and by 6.9% in the latter over the 10 years of the data collection.

While there has been only a small amount of variation over time in the proportions of students *recommended as requiring specialist help or long-term literacy support*, the proportion had increased slowly but steadily since the early years of the National Data Collections (i.e., from 17.8% in 1995–1996 to 25.5% in 2006–2007). However, the percentage of students who completed their series of lessons has increased from 86.5% in 1995–1996 to a high of 92.6 % in 2005–2006.

Site (Training Centre) reports

The Tutors/Teacher Leaders from each Training Centre across Canada complete an Annual Site Report that includes information from all the Reading Recovery teachers and schools implementing Reading Recovery in their region. The Tutors/Teacher Leaders report the number of teachers, schools, and students included in Reading Recovery. Outcomes for all students, as well as long-term monitoring data are reported for each school. Tutors/Teacher Leaders set annual goals for improving the implementation based on the results collected from the schools and their records of the work in these schools.

Trends and observations

Training Centre reports have shown results consistent with those in other countries. Reports on rates of implementation, outcomes for students, and longitudinal monitoring show that most students entering Reading Recovery are able to merge into the average group within the classroom and maintain their gains until the end of Grade 3, the final year of monitoring.

School reports

Each year the Reading Recovery teachers, together with the other members of the school team, prepare reports that show the effectiveness of the intervention in their school. These reports guide future implementation decisions and inform administrators in the school district about what has been achieved with Reading Recovery in the school.

These reports are designed to inform the administrators in the school district about the implementation of Reading Recovery in the school, what has been achieved, and information to guide the decisions on the future implementation.

The school report includes the following information: number of children included in Reading Recovery in the current school year, characteristics of these children including evidence that the lowest achieving students were included in Reading Recovery, outcomes for these students, results of long-term monitoring of students up to the end of Grade 3, and the impact on reading and writing achievement levels in the school. The Reading Recovery School Team sets goals for continuous improvement based on a review of the school data.

Trends and observations

School reports have increased in detail and diligence in reporting the results of monitoring former Reading Recovery students to the end of Grade 3. As implementations have matured, teachers have been able to increase the effectiveness of the school team as they use data to inform instructional practice.

Training group data

Each year the teachers who are completing their year of training are required to submit information on all the students they have taught in Reading Recovery for the school year. All children are reassessed using the tasks in An Observation Survey of Early Literacy Achievement (Clay, 2002, 2006) and the Burt Word Reading Test (New Zealand Council for Educational Research, 1981). Student data are recorded on the End-of-Year Survey Record for Training Teachers form and sent to the Tutor/Teacher Leader who then summarizes the information, analyses the results, and sends a summary to the Regional Trainer. These data are analysed for trends and issues that relate to the implementation of Reading Recovery. The report of the Training Group data is shared with all Tutors/Teacher Leaders and changes to the In-service Course for Teachers may be recommended and monitored by the Trainer team.

Final observations and evaluation trends

There has been an increase in scores for Reading Recovery students in all tasks of An Observation Survey of Literacy Achievement and the Burt Word Reading Test over the last 10 years. At entry, there have been variations in scores, with a greater number of children entering Reading Recovery at higher instructional text levels and with higher scores in both the Writing Vocabulary and Hearing and Recording Sounds in Words tasks. Exit scores have also increased with the most notable results in instructional text levels, Writing Vocabulary and Burt Word Reading Test. In particular, scores for students who had their lesson series carried over from the previous year have been discontinued at levels that match the increasing scores of average classroom achievement.

The Canadian Institute of Reading Recovery National Implementation Data Reports are available from The Canadian Institute or from the any of the Regional Training Institutes.

Monitoring Reading Recovery in the United Kingdom and Ireland
Julia Douëtil

Systematic annual national monitoring and evaluation has been a part of the Reading Recovery intervention in the United Kingdom and Ireland since 1994. Initially a paper exercise, by 2003 national monitoring moved to a completely web-based data management system supported by the National Data Evaluation Center (NDEC) in Ohio. This huge shift, requiring many teachers to use the Internet for the first time, was achieved with surprising ease, thanks to a user-friendly web design closely matching pre-existing systems and a hugely supportive Tutor/Teacher Leader network.

The cost and effort involved in the annual monitoring exercise has proved its worth. Not only has it provided evidence of Reading Recovery's effectiveness but also it has enabled us to refine our understanding of how to make this complex system intervention more efficient and effective in our context. This has given rise to certain distinctive features of the implementation in the United Kingdom and Ireland.

The UK and Ireland Reading Recovery database

National monitoring data are collected every June (in Ireland) and July (elsewhere) and reports compiled at national, district, and school levels. School level data include the school's government identifier code, contact details, name of teacher or teachers, and the number of children in an average year group (to assist in determining the level of coverage in the school). Teacher level data include the year in which the teacher trained in Reading Recovery, additional responsibilities in the school, the number of teaching slots available, the number of children taught in the year, and the number of days the teacher was available to teach Reading Recovery during the year.

At the level of the child, where possible, a Unique Pupil Number (a government-issued personal identifier that enables us to follow children's progress in future years) is recorded. Background information on each child includes date of birth, sex, entitlement to free school meals, year group, and first language. Additional information includes ethnicity and membership in special cohort groups deemed to be especially at risk, such as children in the care of local authorities, refugee or asylum seekers, and traveller children. An attempt is made to identify whether children are recognized as having Special Educational Needs (SEN), although this is complicated by the fact that different systems have different SEN descriptors and protocols. Although limited, the information has enabled us to demonstrate that hundreds of children each year can be removed from registers of SEN or moved to lower levels of concern, with related cost implications.

Information collected for each child includes entry and exit date, intervention outcome, and the number of lessons and weeks in Reading Recovery. Information about 'lost lessons' can be an important indicator of risk to an implementation from the erosion of daily teaching.

Children's entry and exit scores on all six Observation Survey assessments are collected, plus the British Ability Scales II Word Reading (Elliott, 1996), an independent word reading assessment. Follow-up assessments are recorded after 3 months and again after 6 months on book level, writing vocabulary, and British Ability Scales II Word Reading. Finally, results of national assessments at the end of Year 2 (age 7) are collected where administered, although for some children this may be a year after the end of their Reading Recovery lessons.

With the expansion of Reading Recovery in England beginning September 2008 as part of a wide-scale government funded initiative, new demands will be made on data collection and reporting. Where possible teachers will be asked to indicate how Reading Recovery is funded in their school and to list other literacy interventions used in the school. The database will also be expanded to collect basic information about children in the same age group who received literacy interventions other than Reading Recovery.

An exciting development is a 'diary' system whereby teachers will be able to enter certain assessments (e.g., book levels, writing vocabulary, lesson number, and week number) onto the website at intervals throughout the child's series of lessons. The diary can be downloaded in the form of a simple graph, providing schools with a simple and flexible way of communicating about a child's progress.

Consistency and change

Over more than a decade of monitoring, certain features of our implementation have remained remarkably constant. Boys have consistently been over-represented among the lowest attaining group identified for Reading Recovery by approximately two to one. Each year around half of the cohort comes from the least well off 18% of families, identified by entitlement to free school meals. The proportion of the cohort learning English as an additional language fluctuates, ranging from 0% to more than 90% in individual districts and from 9% to 20% of the national cohort.

Entry levels of the lowest attaining children identified for Reading Recovery provide a barometer of changes in classroom literacy programmes. Since 1997, an increased emphasis on phonics-based teaching methods in primary schools, especially in England, has been accompanied by children with higher scores on some assessments.

However, text reading levels for these same children have remained consistently low, around 60% at book levels 0 or 1 on entry, after a full year in formal literacy teaching. The most recent monitoring (July 2008) showed a drop in scores on Concepts About Print for the second consecutive year, evidence which backs up concerns expressed by Reading Recovery teachers in the field. This early warning has enabled us to alert colleagues in National Literacy Strategies and spurred action to investigate and address the issue.

Timing of the intervention

When Reading Recovery was introduced in England in 1990, the New Zealand model was adopted, screening between the ages of 6 years and 6 years 3 months to identify children needing intervention. British law requires that children start formal education in the school year (September to August) in which they reach the age of 5, but at what point in that year they start is governed by local policy and can vary enormously. Early monitoring revealed that many children in the given age band had already been involved in literacy learning for considerably more than a year, compromising the premise of early intervention. Evidence from national monitoring in 1999–2000 suggested that the delay was indeed detrimental.

In consultation with Marie Clay it was decided to allow schools and districts to elect to target a lower age group, 5 years 9 months to 6 years, in order to provide the intervention at the most opportune moment for the child. Subsequent evidence (see English national tests, below) supports this change, demonstrating no ill effects on children's outcomes in Reading Recovery, and an advantageous effect for children receiving the intervention in Year 1 on outcomes of national (government) tests up to 5 years later.

Lesson series carried over from one year to the next

In the United Kingdom, children may begin their Reading Recovery lessons at any point in the school year, as a place becomes available. So at the point of data collection each year some children are still only partway through their lesson series and will continue in the next school year. Thus, data collection is complicated by the timing of entry and exit across school years and by the fact that age groups may be referred to by different names in each of the five countries within the implementation.

Follow-up

Given that children may enter Reading Recovery at any point in the year as places become available, it was recognized early in our implementation that a year-end reassessment of every child was unhelpful. Instead, informal follow-up procedures were augmented at 3 and 6 months following the end of each child's lessons using two measures from the Observation Survey — text reading level and writing vocabulary. Although these assessments may take place at any point in the year, their consistency in relation to the child's lesson series was more informative as to what typically happened to children after Reading Recovery. Results showed children progressing through two to four book levels and adding to their writing vocabulary as they adjusted to working independently after Reading Recovery. However, this effectiveness measure came into its own when an independent word reading measure (British Ability Scales II Word Reading below) was added in 2005.

English national tests

Because of political pressure in England to report the results for Reading

Recovery children using national tests at age 7, this information was added to routine national monitoring in 2000. The results proved to be a powerful answer to the challenge that the effects of Reading Recovery did not last. The 2002 monitoring report showed two out of three ex-Reading Recovery children (66%, n = 1018) operating at government national target levels at the end of Year 2 (Y2), age 7. It also showed that children's chances of reaching national targets improved to 77% if they had received Reading Recovery in Year 1 (Y1) and to 91% if they both received Reading Recovery in Y1 *and* reached levels for discontinuing lessons. A subsequent small-scale study demonstrated that the advantageous effect of receiving Reading Recovery in Y1, rather than Y2, continued 5 years after the end of Reading Recovery (Johnson, 2005).

British Ability Scales II Word Reading

Early criticism of Reading Recovery monitoring and reporting focused on the reliance on in-house assessment tools, and the lack of a standardized measure. A large body of evidence for the effectiveness of Reading Recovery was ruled inadmissible to a nationally influential report (Brooks, 2002). After searching for a measure sensitive enough to distinguish between children in the earliest stages of literacy learning, sufficient to track children in the years after Reading Recovery, and having persuasive authority in all UK and Irish contexts, permission was obtained to use the British Ability Scales II Word Reading assessment (Elliott, 1996). Scores were reported for the first time in 2005.

Reading age measures from this assessment tool have greatly enhanced national monitoring and the perceived credibility of that evidence. Children entering Reading Recovery were shown to have a nominal reading age of 4 years 10 months, the lowest possible score on the measure, effectively non-starters in literacy learning. Those whose lessons were discontinued reached an average reading age of 6 years 7 months, a reading age gain of 21 months during the 5 months of their series of lessons, around four times the normal rate of progress.

Scores on British Ability Scales II Word Reading also forcefully demonstrated that children referred for further support (recommended) did make progress, reaching an average reading age of 5 years 7 months. They gained on average 9 months reading age in the 5 months of their lesson series, close to twice the normal rate of learning, a degree of progress deemed a successful outcome for many other literacy interventions (Brooks, 2007).

Perhaps the most powerful finding, however, was use of the British Ability Scales II Word Reading to measure progress following the end of individual lessons. Children were shown to progress at a steady rate of 1 month in reading age as each month passed — they had learned how to learn as normal readers do. That this also held true for referred (recommended) children was testament to Marie Clay's insistence that Reading Recovery is never wasted on the child who does not achieve all its goals. These groundbreaking findings of 2005 were replicated in 2006, 2007, and 2008.

The data dilemma

The meticulous monitoring and reporting of Reading Recovery is both our strength and our Achilles heel. The quality, detail, and rigour of the evidence that we can present about Reading Recovery is unequalled in our education system and has been a significant factor in the acceptance of Reading Recovery as an effective and efficient solution to the problem of literacy difficulties on a national scale. But the value placed on monitoring and reporting can at times dictate the implementation instead of reporting it. National monitoring can inform teachers' professional judgement, but if their decisions are influenced by the consequences for their data rather than the best needs of the children in front of them, the monitoring process could well become a disservice to children.

Reading Recovery in the United Kingdom and Ireland currently faces an unprecedented level of support from governments and a period of phenomenal expansion. With that support will come increased scrutiny, within which our national monitoring will be crucial. Enabling administrators at every level in the system to interpret the results of that monitoring, in all its complexity, is an essential task for Reading Recovery professionals across the whole United Kingdom and Republic of Ireland.

References

Brooks, G. (2002). *What works for children with literacy difficulties: The effectiveness of intervention schemes.* London: DfES research report 380.31.

Brooks, G. (2007). *What works for pupils with literacy difficulties? The effectiveness of intervention schemes* (3rd ed.). London: DCSF research report 00688-2007BKT-EN. www.standards.dcsf.gov.uk

Catholic Education Office, Diocese of Wollongong (2004). *Reading Recovery implementation in a small system of schools.* Paper presented at the 5th International Reading Recovery Institute, Auckland, 2004.

Catholic Education Office, Diocese of Wollongong (2007). *2000–2006 Reading Recovery outcomes.* Wollongong: Catholic Education Office.

Clay, M. M. (1990). The Reading Recovery programme, 1984–88: Coverage, outcomes and Education Board district figures. *New Zealand Journal of Educational Studies, 25*(1), 61–70. Reprinted in Clay, M. M. (1993), *Reading Recovery: A guidebook for teachers in training.* Auckland: Heinemann (and in Chapter 2 of this book).

Clay, M. M. (1993). *Reading Recovery: A guidebook for teachers in training.* Auckland: Heinemann.

Clay, M. M. (2001). *Change over time in children's literacy development.* Auckland: Heinemann.

Clay, M. M. (2002, 2006). *An observation survey of early literacy achievement* (2nd ed.). Auckland: Heinemann.

Clay, M. M. (2005) *Literacy lessons designed for individuals: Part one:* Auckland: Heinemann.

Clay, M. M., & Bourque, G., Masny D. (2003). *Le sondage d'observation en lecture-écriture.* Montréal (Québec), Canada: Chenelière/McGraw-Hill.

Denton, C. A., Ciancio, D. J., & Fletcher, J. M. (2006). Validity, reliability, and utility of the Observation Survey of Early Literacy Achievement. *Reading Research Quarterly, 41*(1), 8–34.

Department of Education, Tasmania (2007). *Reading Recovery — Case studies.* Tasmania: Department of Education. Retrieved 4 January 2008, from http://wwwfp.education.tas.gov.au/literacy/readingrecovery.htm

Department of Education and the Arts, Queensland (2006). *Reading Recovery 2005 annual report.* Queensland: Department of Education and the Arts.

Department of Education and Training, Victoria (2003). *Reading Recovery data 2002.* Victoria: Department of Education and Training.

Department of Education and Training, Victoria (2004). *Reading Recovery data 2003.* Victoria: Department of Education and Training.

Department of Education and Training, Victoria (2005a). *Reading Recovery data 2004.* Victoria: Department of Education and Training.

Department of Education and Training, Victoria (2005b). *Years Prep — 10 curriculum and standards framework II — Benchmarks, 2005,* Victoria: Department of Education and Training. Retrieved 18 December 2007, from http://www.sofweb.vic.edu.au/standards/publicat/bench.htm

Department of Education and Training, Victoria (2006). *Reading Recovery data 2005.* Victoria: Department of Education and Training.

Department of Education and Training, Victoria (2007a). *Reading Recovery data 2006.* Victoria: Department of Education and Training.

Department of Education and Training, Victoria (2007b). *Department of Education and Training, Annual report 2005–2006.* Victoria: Department of Education and Training. Retrieved December 18, 2007, from http://www.education.vic.gov.au/about/publications/annualreport/default.htm

Douëtil, J. (2007). *Reading Recovery annual report for the UK and Republic of Ireland: 2006–2007.* London: Institute of Education.

Douëtil, J. (2008). *Reading Recovery annual report for the UK and Republic of Ireland: 2007–2008.* London: Institute of Education.

Doyle, M. A., Gibson, S. A., Gómez-Bellengé, F. X., Kelly, P. R., & Tang, M. (2008). Assessment and identification of first-grade students at risk: Correlating the Dynamic Indicators of Basic Early Literacy Skills and An Observation Survey of Early Literacy Achievement. In K. Youb, V. J. Risko, D. L. Compton, M. K. Hundley, R. T. Jimenez, K. M. Leander, & D. W. Rose (Eds.), *57th yearbook of the National Reading Conference* (pp. 144–159). Oak Creek, WI: National Reading Conference.

Duncan, S., & McNaughton, S. (2001, December). Research note: Updating the Clay Word Test. *New Zealand Journal of Educational Studies, 36*(1), 101–104.

Elliott, C. D. (1996). *British Ability Scales II Word Reading.* London: NFER Nelson.

Gómez-Bellengé, F. X., Rodgers, E., Wang, C., & Schulz, M. (2005). *Examination of the validity of the Observation Survey with a comparison to ITBS.* Paper presented at the annual meeting of the American Educational Research Association, Montreal, Quebec.

Gómez-Bellengé, F. X., & Thompson, J. R. (2005). *U.S. norms for tasks of An Observation Survey of Early Literacy Achievement* (NDEC Rep. No. 2005-02). Columbus: The Ohio State University, National Data Evaluation Center.

Government of South Australia Department of Education and Children's Services (2007). Reading Recovery DECS 1993–2006. Retrieved 18 December 2007, from http://www.earlyyearsliteracy.sa.edu.au/pages/cg0001086/19303/

Johnson, R. M. (2005). *Reading Recovery in Sheffield: A five year follow-up study.* Unpublished master's report. London: Institute of Education, University of London.

Kelly, P., Gómez-Bellengé, F. X., Chen, J., & Schulz, M. (2008). Learner outcomes for English language learner low readers in an early intervention. *TESOL Quarterly, 42*(2), 135–160.

Kerslake, J. (1999, October). Trends in Reading Recovery: Data between 1984 and 1998, *The Research Bulletin.* Wellington: Ministry of Education.

Lose, M. K., Gómez-Bellengé, F. X., & Ye, F. (2006, April). *Organizational factors and teacher characteristics of low repertoire students successfully served in an early intervention.* Paper presented at the annual meeting of the American Educational Research Association, San Francisco, CA.

Lyons, C. (1998). Reading Recovery in the United States: More than a decade of data, *Literacy Teaching and Learning, 3*(1), 77–92.

McDowall, S., Boyd, S., Hodgen, E., & van Vliet, T. (2005). *Reading Recovery in New Zealand: Uptake, implementation, and outcomes, especially in relation to Maori and Pasifika students.* Wellington: New Zealand Council for Educational Research.

Ministerial Council on Education, Employment Training and Youth Affairs (2000). *National statement of principles and standards for more culturally inclusive schooling in the 21st century.* Retrieved 4 January 2008, from http://72.14.253.104/search?q=cache:WVCx3U3cM4J:www.whatworks. edu.au/docs/principl.pdf+statement+of+principles+and+standards+for+ more+culturally+inclusive+schooling&hl=en&ct=clnk&cd=3&gl=au

Ministerial Council for Education, Employment Training and Youth Affairs (2005). *National report on schooling in Australia. Preliminary paper. National Benchmark Results Reading, Writing And Numeracy, Years 3, 5 & 7.* Canberra: Ministerial Council for Education Employment Training and Youth Affairs. Retrieved 4 January 2008, from http://online.curriculum. edu.au/anr2005/

Ministry of Education Research Division. Summary of the data on Reading Recovery, Published annually from 1989 to 1999, *The Research Bulletin.* Wellington: Ministry of Education.

Ministry of Education Research Division. *Annual monitoring of Reading Recovery: The data for 1998 to 2006.* Published annually on www. educationcounts.govt.nz

New South Wales Department of Education and Training (2007). *Annual report 2006 NSW Department of Education and Training.* Retrieved 18 December 2007, from http://www.det.nsw.gov.au/reports_stas/annual_ reports/report2006.htm

New Zealand Council for Educational Research (1981). *Burt word reading test.* Wellington: New Zealand Council for Educational Research.

Rodgers, E. M., Gómez-Bellengé, F. X., & Wang, C. (2004, April). *Closing the literacy achievement gap with early intervention.* Paper presented at the annual meeting of the American Educational Research Association, San Diego, CA.

Rodgers, E. M., Gómez-Bellengé, F. X., Wang, C., & Schultz, M. M. (2005, April). *Predicting the literacy achievement of struggling readers: Does intervening early make a difference?* Paper presented at the annual meeting of the American Educational Research Association, Montréal, Québec.

Schwartz, R. M. (2005). Literacy learning of at-risk first grade students in the Reading Recovery early intervention. *Journal of Educational Psychology, 97*, 257–267.

Scull, J. A., & Bremner, T. (2007). *Reading Recovery in the Kimberley: Report on the first year of implementation.* Broome: St Mary's College Broome.

Tang, M., & Gómez-Bellengé, F. X. (2007). *Dimensionality and concurrent validity of An Observation Survey of Early Literacy Achievement,* Paper presented at the annual meeting of the American Educational Research Association, Chicago, IL.

Wheeler, H. (1986). *Reading Recovery: Central Victorian field trials, 1984.* Bendigo: Bendigo College of Advanced Education.

Ye, F., & Gómez-Bellengé, F. X. (2006, April). *Propensity score adjustment in structural equation modeling for the analysis of treatment effects: Application to an early literacy intervention.* Paper presented at the annual meeting of the American Educational Research Association, San Francisco, CA.

Part Four

Envisioning the Way Forward

9

A Dynamic Future

Mary Anne Doyle

Marie Clay's search for the possible in children's literacy led to the development and global expansion of Reading Recovery. The unprecedented growth and success resulted from dynamic processes described as 'the best evidence yet of the direct link between good design and educational excellence' (Wilson & Daviss, 1994, p. 50). The important features of Marie Clay's efforts, conducted over time individually and with colleagues, remain vital to successful redesign processes. In particular, adhering to critical features of a redesign system, Reading Recovery

- has shaped its methods according to the results of its own and others' research,

- has tested and honed its techniques through years of trials and refinements,

- equips its specialists with a common body of proven knowledge and skills that allow instructors to tailor each lesson to each child's needs,

- maintains rigorous systems of self-evaluation . . . and offers ongoing training and support to the teachers and schools.
                                        (Wilson & Daviss, 1994, pp. 50–51)

These features, integral to establishing and sustaining this highly effective, research-based literacy intervention, provide a strong foundation for the future. Therefore, Marie Clay's design creates a pathway forward by adhering to research, self-study, and careful monitoring while safeguarding key components of its implementation and redesign system. This suggests stability and endurance as well as refinements, redevelopments, and exciting possibilities. This final chapter of *Boundless Horizons* details the dynamic future of Reading Recovery. It reviews foundational strengths and forecasts ways in which Marie Clay's design will sustain the effectiveness of Reading Recovery and support change and growth in response to new research in measured, thoughtful ways.

Establishing structures

Marie Clay gave judicious attention to planning the growth and evolution of Reading Recovery from the first opportunity to go beyond New Zealand in 1984. The educational system was in the state of Victoria, Australia, and she made the important decision not to be a primary, visible leader of its development (Clay, 1997). She therefore nurtured independence and leadership in those responsible for implementing Reading Recovery. In this decision Marie Clay demonstrated her wise commitment to sustaining an educational innovation by transferring leadership to others. This approach is a key component for securing successful, enduring implementations of educational programmes (Hargreaves & Fink, 2006) and became the model Marie Clay applied throughout the impressive expansion of Reading Recovery across Australia, Europe, and North America.

To ensure quality and effectiveness, Reading Recovery Trainers were prepared to work with administrators, educators, and others in establishing, monitoring, problem-solving, and extending Reading Recovery in their respective settings. At the same time, Trainers collaborated with the chief stakeholders, particularly key educational leaders, senior administrators, and financial decision-makers whose support and goodwill were critically important to the innovation.

In each national context, Trainers have assumed responsibility for ensuring the quality and effectiveness of the intervention for participating schools, teachers, and children. They have also addressed complex issues through study and research as detailed in previous chapters. Through their research, they have conducted not only the rigorous self-evaluations necessary to examine and confirm effectiveness, but also the investigations that have contributed to the development of new understandings. These efforts build the important evidence that impels the redirecting, redesign processes.

One outgrowth of this pattern of activity was the emergence of national and regional networks of Reading Recovery Trainers. These networks provide a forum and a collective strength for working on implementation issues, encouraging and designing research, and supporting the growth of the intervention in their nations, states, regions, and affiliated sites beyond their national borders. Current networks comprise the Australia and New Zealand Trainer Team, the European Trainer Group, the Canadian Trainer Team, and the North American Trainers Group encompassing the United States and Canada.

The global setting

Reading Recovery's global setting introduced new considerations for providing stability, sustainability, and advancement of the intervention and research. Mindful of the succession of leadership and guidance internationally, Marie Clay planned for the transfer of decision-making and intervention support from herself to an international body of Reading Recovery Trainers comprising all Trainers from each network. Her persistent efforts to facilitate international collaboration among this group and to develop an organizational structure designed to assume international responsibilities resulted in the establishment of the International Reading Recovery Trainers Organization (IRRTO) in 2001. With her guidance, IRRTO has developed structures and procedures that unite and empower international Reading Recovery professionals. Through a firm commitment to ongoing research, development, and quality of delivery wherever children receive Reading Recovery lessons, the future prospects of the intervention are assured.

Concurrent with her scaffolding of the International Reading Recovery Trainers Organization as a leadership entity, Marie Clay developed plans to maintain the permanent availability and relevance of her published texts. In 1997, she initiated the Marie Clay Literacy Trust as a non-profit, charitable foundation charged with supporting reading, literacy learning and teaching, and Reading Recovery internationally. At her request in 2007, the Marie Clay Literacy Trust became the authority responsible for her intellectual property. Future editions of her books and all international developments of Reading Recovery will involve both the International Reading Recovery Trainers Organization and the Marie Clay Literacy Trust working collaboratively.

Acknowledging international strengths

The international growth and success of Reading Recovery are unprecedented in the fields of literacy education and early intervention. As documented in earlier chapters of this book, Reading Recovery's effectiveness in differing national and educational contexts confirms both robust theory in relation to children's literacy development and profound, dynamic processes of implementation and growth.

With these observations in mind, it seems appropriate to identify the strengths unique to the international context. These are the key factors that will continue to inform and motivate the growing community of researchers, literacy educators, and policy makers of the benefits for children of this critical 'second chance' in literacy learning.

A shared theory of literacy processing

Those involved with Reading Recovery around the world share a theory of literacy processing arising from the research of Marie Clay. Unlike other reading researchers and theorists, Marie Clay focused her investigations uniquely on children's formative years of literacy learning. Using an unusual lens of systematic and controlled observation, she was able to describe young children's successful, early patterns of literacy behaviours. This had never been done before in this way, or with such clarity.

Key understandings, or principles, within Marie Clay's theory that guide the work of Reading Recovery educators internationally include the following.

- Literacy learning is a complex problem-solving process.

- Children construct their own understandings.

- Children's oral language is both a resource and a beneficiary of literacy learning.

- Children begin literacy learning with varying knowledge bases.

- Children take different paths to literacy learning.

- Reading and writing are interrelated and reciprocal processes.

- Literacy acquisition is about reading and writing continuous texts.

- Literacy learning is marked by a continuous process of change over time.

Around the world, teachers grounded in these understandings are empowered to change the learning trajectories of young readers and writers, bringing them in a short time to an acceptable level of literacy independence for their age. This is the heart of Reading Recovery wherever the intervention has taken root and come to fruition. Reading Recovery began with a focus on children, and it continues to serve them. Children's needs will always be implicit in every research project, every refinement of implementation, and every individual lesson. Ultimately, to ensure the important benefits of instruction, teachers' professional development is the key.

Commitment to ongoing professional learning

Reading Recovery provides an exemplary model of professional learning in an international context. Teachers who train to deliver the Reading Recovery intervention are valued for their prior experience of teaching young children and for their intellectual capacity for enquiry. They learn to observe children closely, to make astute decisions while in the act of teaching, and eventually to become independent problem solvers. This is achieved with the assistance of Tutors/Teacher Leaders.

In a supportive training environment, teachers build theoretical understandings throughout their first year of professional development while they work individually with children experiencing difficulty with literacy learning. Guided by close study of the professional texts of Marie Clay, they are trained by Tutors/Teacher Leaders in regular in-service sessions, or classes. Through a one-way viewing screen, Reading Recovery teachers observe and comment on their peers' teaching at each session. Group discussions help them to collaborate and problem-solve with colleagues. In their local schools, they continue to develop their instructional effectiveness through daily, individual teaching of diverse children. Systematic and sensitive observation informs their teaching decisions, and they learn to make children's learning easy by building on their strengths. Very importantly, all teachers participate in professional development as long as they remain in Reading Recovery.

Planned but flexible implementation processes

The New Zealand experience of the development and national implementation of Reading Recovery afforded Marie Clay and her colleagues a wealth of knowledge regarding systemic intervention. As they moved by invitation overseas, shepherding each new national implementation of Reading Recovery, their astute understandings ensured that Reading Recovery was instituted and delivered as it had been designed and evaluated in Marie Clay's original research (see Chapter 2). She concluded that the accomplishment of replicating Reading Recovery 'across settings and countries by many teachers under different educational policies is in itself an outcome to be valued' (Clay, 2001, p. 253). That success has made Reading Recovery a unique demonstration of what is possible in educational innovation. Furthermore, the processes now in place for initiating Reading Recovery in a new nation or reconstructing Reading Recovery in another language provide models for exciting future expansions in and beyond the English-speaking world.

Under Marie Clay's direction, the Reading Recovery model of systemic intervention was the motive power for dynamic processes of change (see Chapter 7). Marie Clay identified five important factors sustaining the strength of every Reading Recovery implementation. These include

- the guidelines for delivery of the intervention,
- the long period of training to prepare teachers to be decision-makers,

- lesson components that support perceptual/cognitive processing,

- the utility of a complex theory of literacy learning, and

- a theory about constructive individuals pushing the boundaries of their own knowledge, rather than groups led through each step by a teacher (Clay, 2001, pp. 299–301).

Within that framework, change follows four dimensions:

- behavioural change in children's reading and writing, achieved by teaching,

- behavioural change on the part of teachers, achieved by professional development delivered by Tutors/Teacher Leaders,

- organizational changes in schools, achieved by administrators and teachers,

- changes in system variables by controlling authorities (Clay, 1994, p. 122).

These dimensions of change are observed in all Reading Recovery contexts. They are supported by Trainers at national and regional levels; by Tutors/Teacher Leaders at the local level through ongoing attention to training, implementation, and advocacy; and above all by the teachers who work daily with children who previously struggled with literacy learning (see Chapter 7).

As she worked in international settings, Marie Clay applied her lens as a developmental psychologist keenly aware of the human processes inherent in changing national educational systems. Her attitude of tentativeness and flexibility eased the way to overcoming many initial difficulties. She encouraged a culture of collegial problem-solving that enabled administrators and educators to fit Reading Recovery into local contexts. She recognized that societal, cultural, and educational factors impact innovations over time and 'require the innovation to adjust through problem-solving in a continuous pattern of change' (Clay, 1994, p. 136).

The parallel with observing and teaching individual children is striking: it is equally important to be a good listener to such key players as administrators and educators. A sensitive observer can systematically and patiently identify organizational strengths that will prove invaluable as the implementation is developed. Marie Clay's astute direction respected each system's uniqueness. Using a process of accommodation, she found adaptive ways to implement Reading Recovery without lessening the high standards that lead to optimal results for both teachers and children. It remains a superb strategy for longevity.

Some of the adjustments permitted in response to local and national differences include (a) adjustments of the age of entry to the intervention to reflect practices of the various educational systems, (b) the use of alternative word tests to accommodate word frequencies in local reading programmes, (c) plans for transitioning children from their Reading Recovery lessons to their classrooms, and (d) solutions to a range of practical issues including the identification of story books for instruction. These minor modifications do not compromise the core features and goals of Reading Recovery which are non-negotiable, such as individual, daily instruction of children identified as the lowest-achieving readers and writers without exception, accelerated learning, and the prevention of later reading and writing failure.

Commitment to research: from evaluation to exploration

Around the world, on any school day of the year, young children can be found reading and writing in a mutually responsive one-to-one relationship with their Reading Recovery teachers. Their backgrounds are diverse, their needs wide-ranging. Some are being taught in Spanish, some in French, most in English. Some speak with the accent of the indigenous people of their land. Every child is making significant progress. Two-thirds of them will accelerate their learning and will be able to read and write at average levels of achievement, or more, for their age and grade level. These children will have shown that they have the basis of a self-extending system of literacy learning, able, in Marie Clay's phrase, to use literacy to build literacy. Given the careful monitoring that Reading Recovery requires of teachers, children's gains will be sustained. These results, documented annually and consistently in every international setting, suggest that Marie Clay's theory of literacy is robust: a unique strength.

It is the function of evaluative research to validate the effectiveness of an educational innovation. A major factor in Reading Recovery's success has been the rigour of its systems for monitoring and reporting children's progress. Each national authority maintains annual evaluations for every child taught (see Chapter 8). From country to country, across all education systems, these data confirm children's success and Reading Recovery's effectiveness.

Studies of specific subgroups of children across international settings show similar results. Reading Recovery has been a powerful intervention for English Language Learners, as confirmed by research findings in

New Zealand, the United Kingdom, and the United States.[1] The evidence goes further. Studies completed in New Zealand and the United States[2] show Reading Recovery to be effective in reducing the achievement gap for children of varying socio-economic groups and racial/ethnic backgrounds (see previous chapters for details of these studies and their outcomes).

Evidence of sustained effects further validates the effectiveness of Reading Recovery. While studies of subsequent literacy achievement presented in previous chapters suggest strong and positive trends, Marie Clay found Rowe's (1997) longitudinal study in Australia to be one of the most interesting and informative. Included in the large random sample of 5000 learners followed across grade levels were 147 former Reading Recovery participants. Marie Clay (2001) summarized the important evidence of sustained effects for the Reading Recovery students as follows:

> *Children* [former Reading Recovery students] *who would have been the lowest achievers clustered around the 0–10 percentile as six-year-olds were at nine, ten and eleven years of age spread across the achievement range in the same way as the main research sample, and the lower limits of their distribution tended to be higher than those of their non-Reading Recovery peers.* (Clay, 2001, pp. 264–265)

In other words, the Reading Recovery children were distributed through the range of achievement levels in the same way as their originally more-competent peers. Marie Clay concluded: 'That is as good as it gets . . . the best result we could expect from an early intervention without subsequent interventions' (Clay, 2001, p. 265). For Reading Recovery researchers, this study was an indication of the 'kind of outcomes it would be sensible to predict in future studies' (p. 265) of Reading Recovery students beyond their first-grade year.

Strengths to equip a dynamic future

Bringing all this evidence together reveals Reading Recovery as eminently well-positioned to enter an exciting future. At the same time there is great opportunity to deepen its influence and extend children's

---

1 Smith, 1994; Hobsbaum, 1997; Neal & Kelly, 1999; Kelly, Gómez-Bellengé, Chen, & Schulz, 2008.

2 Clay, 1993; Rodgers, Gómez-Bellengé, & Wang, 2004; Rodgers, Gómez-Bellengé, Wang, & Schulz, 2005.

access to its service in the countries with either established or newer implementations. The network of international Trainers, the wealth of institutional knowledge from experienced administrators and educators, and the extensive body of evaluation results and research reported by each country combine to form a vast resource of understandings and insights key to the dynamic future of Reading Recovery. This set of strengths includes the following:

- Reading Recovery is an optimal early intervention in literacy education confirmed by results published internationally.

- A systemic intervention, Reading Recovery can accommodate national needs through problem-solving in a continuous pattern of change.

- The theoretical base for Reading Recovery is robust: it includes understandings of how children learn, how teachers can teach, and how a delivery system can be designed and launched in a wide array of settings.

- Reading Recovery instruction and concepts reflect a complex theory of literacy processing shown to be advantageous in designing literacy instruction for struggling learners.

- One-to-one instruction, adhering to established guidelines validated by research and practice, makes a powerful contribution to national goals of equity for all learners.

- Individual instruction allows effective teaching for children of wide ranges of diversity, including learning difficulties, language differences, and special individual attributes.

- Reading Recovery assessment and teaching procedures can be redeveloped to offer early interventions in literacy for speakers of languages other than English.

- Initial and ongoing professional development for Reading Recovery educators enhances their abilities to observe closely and to make informed decisions about teaching.

- International exchanges provide beneficial opportunities for shared problem-solving, learning, and identification of new issues and research directions.

- Ongoing research, conducted internationally by Trainers and other researchers, continues to inform and direct new developments.

In summary, these strengths confirm the dynamic nature of Reading Recovery — its power to grow from within. They ensure the ongoing relevance of Reading Recovery for educational planning and the appropriateness of established procedures for new national settings and new languages.

The way forward

Without question, the future of Marie Clay's work will entail

- international expansions of Reading Recovery in English,

- redevelopments of the Observation Survey and teaching procedures in languages other than English to reach new populations,

- exploration of ways to individualize instruction for a wider audience of young children presenting quite different personal and learning histories, and

- examination of the complex questions about learning, literacy, and early intervention that arise continually.

New lines of enquiry will involve applications of current understandings as well as investigations of new issues and new questions. The result will continue the redesign processes that enrich and extend Marie Clay's original research and ensure ongoing excellence.

In keeping with her usual meticulous planning, Marie Clay established a way forward by charging members of the International Reading Recovery Trainers Organization (IRRTO) with the following related functions:

1. to support ongoing research in order to provide direction for change and growth in Reading Recovery through international collaboration and investigation,

2. to consider ramifications for IRRTO member countries of a significant body of research findings,

3. to consider recommendations for changes in policy, implementation, and/or practices of trademarked Reading Recovery on the basis of international collaboration and research,

4. to oversee developments including the introduction of Reading Recovery in a new country and/or redevelopment of Reading Recovery in another language (Clay, 2005a, p. *ii*).

International Reading Recovery Trainers Organization members and literacy colleagues have begun to address these functions by engaging in study, research, reflection, and sharing. Their commitment to research and development will remain a constant focus, forecasting a changing and vibrant future for Reading Recovery.

Broadening international horizons

New and broadening horizons for Reading Recovery are opening up unprecedented opportunities to study the particular characteristics and emphases of widely differentiated education systems, all interested in what Reading Recovery can offer their students and teachers. Within the last year (2007–2008), the Executive Board of the International Reading Recovery Trainers Organization has received inquires from interested educators in Asian, European, South American, and African countries. Languages of instruction will differ; many will be new to Reading Recovery. Experiences with US Hispanic and French Canadian educational communities have given Trainers confidence to welcome the linguistic and systemic challenges inherent in these enquiries. As they problem-solve the best procedures for initiating Reading Recovery in new education systems, they know they are well-equipped by powerful guidelines 'within which to shape expectations and policies' (Clay, 1997, p. 662).

Each new venture will demand reflective and reasoned thinking. Local needs must be accommodated within a successful replication of Reading Recovery's implementation model, thereby providing children and teachers with high-quality teaching and training. This work will exemplify the dynamic dimensions of change and will offer new research opportunities. The foci will include ongoing monitoring of children's progress, the training and practices of teachers, issues regarding the quality of the implementation, and the longitudinal progress of children.

Reaching out to speakers of other languages

Offering Reading Recovery in a language other than English requires extensive preparation and research. The process is exacting and can be protracted. It is not one of direct translation because assessment and instructional materials must reflect appropriate cultural and linguistic decisions in the new language setting. To date, international Trainers and other educators have worked on several languages (including

Maori,[3] Spanish, French, Danish, and Irish), and Marie Clay's model of redevelopment has directed their efforts.

The initial step in the reconstruction process is to redevelop the assessment tasks of *An Observation Survey of Early Literacy Achievement* (Clay, 2002, 2006) and to trial them in order to establish indices of reliability and validity. The first redevelopment project was with Spanish, and the results of that undertaking now provide direction for the reconstruction process (Rodriguez, 2007) and for the field testing to examine statistical properties of the assessments.

Marie Clay worked with Trainers to supervise the challenging reconstruction of Reading Recovery texts into other languages, making Reading Recovery available for children in Spanish (in the United States) and in French (in Canada). Because Descubriendo la Lectura, Reading Recovery in Spanish, is used in the United States with bilingual teachers who read English well, only the Observation Survey tasks, directions, and Reading Recovery teaching procedures have been redeveloped in Spanish. For Intervention préventive en lecture-écriture, Reading Recovery in French, Canadian Reading Recovery educators have not only redeveloped the Observation Survey in French, but are currently preparing French editions of Marie Clay's (2005a, 2005b) *Literacy Lessons Designed for Individuals, Part One and Part Two (Leçons de Littératie Individualisées, Tome 1 et Tome 2)*. Both implementations have published evaluation data in their annual national reports, confirming the effectiveness of the venture and its design, and providing blueprints for future developments.

The theoretical underpinnings of these developments are the same as for every Reading Recovery implementation, as are teacher training procedures and requirements for teaching individual children. The proven success of that fundamental design has led to the creation of procedures for future reconstructions of Reading Recovery in other languages. One is currently under way in Denmark.

When offering guidance to nations on the implementation of Reading Recovery in another language, Trainers work with educators in the new setting and collect information to gain understandings of both the context and the education system's literacy perspectives. One aspect of the process is a review of literature familiar to the new participants. This is especially necessary because they may be unfamiliar with the theoretical perspectives upon which Reading Recovery is built. Bridges must be built to link the new concepts to existing ones. Clarifying questions may include:

---

3 See Rau (1998).

- What literacy research informs educators in this national context and accounts for their theoretical perspectives of early literacy and expectations for young learners?

- What does this research literature suggest regarding both early literacy instruction and assessment?

- What are the implications of this literature for the training courses?

The study of Reading Recovery implementations in new languages leads to new and interesting questions regarding a child's literacy processing. For example, Marie Clay (1997) identified possible future research questions in relation to learning to read in Spanish:

- What is the role of the syllable in Spanish literacy acquisition?

- Does the linguistic discovery of onset and rime apply to Spanish?

- How can teachers help beginning readers cope with many long words in their first books?

Other languages and cultures will motivate additional questions, and future directions of Reading Recovery will embark on development of understandings of literacy processing across languages.

Another example of the international interest in Marie Clay's assessment of literacy processing behaviours is the redevelopment of Concepts About Print into other languages (Clay, 1989). Currently available in several languages, Concepts About Print was most recently (2008) published in Greek (Task for the Evaluation of the Knowledge of Print). Additional requests for redevelopments of this assessment in other languages are anticipated. They represent another area of important research activity that will include development and validation efforts.

Literacy Lessons for individuals with extraordinary needs

A new and exciting research and development focus for international Trainers involves possibilities for using Marie Clay's text *Literacy Lessons Designed for Individuals* (2005a, 2005b) to offer effective one-to-one teaching to a wider set of children having difficulty in literacy learning. The theory outlined in the text provides a generic framework applicable to a range of tutoring circumstances. In addition to Reading Recovery, it may have relevance in such situations as instruction for special education children. Marie Clay proposed a trademark for the intervention Literacy

Lessons based on her literacy processing theory, the Reading Recovery model of teacher training and ongoing professional development, and a commitment to the integrity of the intervention through accountability, evaluation of data, and research.

Literacy Lessons (LL) will incorporate the following distinctive features:

- individually designed and individually delivered instruction for children,

- a recognized course for qualified teachers with ongoing professional development,

- ongoing data collection, research and evaluation, and

- establishment of an infrastructure and standards to sustain the implementation and maintain quality control.

To address the important, careful work needed to complete this design process and ensure its research-based excellence, Trainers have begun to explore new applications of Clay's Literacy Lessons. These initial efforts will include defining the possibilities for Literacy Lessons beyond Reading Recovery, developing and trialling any modifications, preparing standards for implementing Literacy Lessons modifications, identifying research questions and initiating research studies, and communicating about new developments across the international network.

In recent years, Tutors/Teacher Leaders in some Reading Recovery centres in Australia, New Zealand, the United Kingdom, and the United States have trained Reading Recovery teachers who are also experienced teachers of deaf children. The opportunity prompted studies in Victoria, Australia to investigate the adaptive procedures used for teaching deaf children (Charlesworth, Charlesworth, Raban, & Rickards, 2006). In the United States, exploratory trials of instruction taught by either deaf or hearing teachers have been examining the potential of Reading Recovery/ Literacy Lessons for deaf children and documenting related, teacher training issues (Fullerton, 2008). In addition, a number of training sites in the United States have begun working with special education teachers in the theory and procedural implications of Literacy Lessons. More specific and detailed studies of these efforts are forthcoming. The goal is to establish a well-documented, redesigned intervention that ensures the highest effectiveness for special populations of children requiring individual instruction to address extraordinary literacy difficulties.

At the cutting edge: research into complex issues

Collaborative international research

Rich benefits arise from ongoing international collaborations. The global Reading Recovery network and other researchers exploring literacy-related issues around the world can explore literacy issues together. Exchanges can probe new challenges and promote further development of existing theoretical explanations. Marie Clay engaged in such activity continuously through both her research efforts and her study of related theorists and researchers. She posed new questions, applied alternative research procedures, and discovered evidence and explanations that challenged commonly held assumptions. She gave the world complex understandings in relation to early literacy development; and just as importantly, she identified many lingering questions that will now lead to future explorations. The continuing investigation of Reading Recovery, addressing issues of learning, teaching, and implementation, will create an exciting way forward.

Sustaining high quality implementations

Ongoing research by Reading Recovery Trainers and their colleagues will continue to explore issues of effective implementation (in the full range of international settings and languages) and seek evidence of success, including examination of sustained effects for children over time. Related issues of teacher effectiveness and professional development will likewise be explored, and some attention may be given to investigating those children who do not experience accelerated progress in order to further understand the needs of these learners and the implications for the teachers who must respond to their needs. The results of these efforts will be instructive in the self-monitoring of Reading Recovery's effectiveness and will assure current and future stakeholders of the power of this early intervention to reduce the number of children with reading and writing difficulties.

Deepening and extending theoretical understanding

While maintaining its focus on implementation issues, Trainers will continue the quest for deeper understandings of the theoretical base of Reading Recovery. Marie Clay attributed the documented success of Reading Recovery teachers with at-risk learners to their theoretical perspective, which entails a *processing view* of children's literacy progress (Clay, 2001, pp. 41–43). But currently there is neither a research-based explanation of the components of this complex theory, nor any detailed description of specific shifts in the learner's processing over time. In

301

Change Over Time in Children's Literacy Development, Marie Clay (2001) suggests a range of research questions about several changes observed in children's processing. A partial list includes examination of children's changes over time (a) in self-correction behaviours, (b) from single-word and single-letter processing to using parts of words in clusters/chunks/syllables/roots, (c) in the ability to process multi-syllabic words, (d) from word by word reading to smooth phrasing with intonation, and (e) in the speed of reading.

Ongoing research efforts are needed to extend theories of early literacy learning and early intervention. Studies will focus on how children gradually build processing strategies as they increase their ability to read and write. Marie Clay has left her successors a rich mine of enquiry (Clay, 2001, 2003). She challenged them to explore specific processes in children's literacy learning, the reciprocal benefits of early reading and writing, the nature and benefits of individual instruction, the notion of Reading Recovery as prevention, and a myriad of other questions to which answers are needed (see Appendix for a representative set of questions).

This partial list opens boundless horizons for ongoing scientific enquiry. Marie Clay's original work stands as an exemplar of descriptive, developmental research. However, for directing the construction of new knowledge, her research methodologies and tools are as important as the challenging questions. Her unique methodology allowed her to detail how effective readers process text, how literacy processing changes over time for children engaged in reading and writing continuous texts, and how teacher interactions scaffold the child's learning and processing. Her observation tools, i.e., the tasks comprising the Observation Survey, were designed to capture processing behaviours and to inform instruction, an alternative to the more prevalent use of traditional measures (see Chapter 3). Ongoing applications of her productive, unusual approaches to studying reading and writing behaviours will be replicated to continue the fruitful description of both learners and the important processes of theory development.

Future directions in research of Reading Recovery will involve the international cohort of Trainers working with international researchers to address relevant questions. The informative procedures they will follow will be much in the tradition of Marie Clay's original investigations. This important work will be informed and enriched by research in a wide range of related areas such as developmental psychology, neuroscience, and cognitive psychology. The results will advance our understandings and ultimately enhance the teaching of children.

What is possible?

The richness of Reading Recovery's history of development, research, and success suggests an exciting future vision of what is possible when societies embrace this proven early intervention. Consider the impact of the following possibilities for children and societies:

- Early literacy intervention will be embraced by educators and policy makers and will be available to children in all education systems.

- Intervention specialists will provide powerful teaching for all children deserving of individual instruction in literacy.

- Reading Recovery teachers will bring a high percentage of the lowest achievers to average levels of proficiency in reading and writing and identify the small number of children for whom specialist attention may be needed. That specialist help will be available and accessible. Both outcomes will yield positive outcomes for children and their schools.

- Ongoing research of a range of issues regarding complex processing will clarify and enhance both theoretical perspectives and instructional procedures.

- Monitoring and research will continue to inform and direct the redesign process.

- Marie Clay's quest for what is possible will lead to new discoveries and have a profound affect on our societies.

- Boundless horizons will open on a full range of literacy research areas, enticing further explorations in support of children and teachers.

A shining future

Boundless Horizons traces the influence and contributions of Marie Clay across approximately 45 years of research, design, evaluation, and redesign of her early intervention for struggling readers and writers (1963–2008). Ever present in her thinking and her work were attention to new questions and response to ongoing change. She made reasoned decisions based on research evidence, both established and emerging, and her ability to transcend disciplines and apply complex theory with clarity was profound. As the evidence accumulated and her thinking evolved, her new texts offered revised applications and procedures. Her commitment to successful redesign, or *change processes*, resulted in a dynamic, evolving literacy intervention for young children who were experiencing temporary difficulty early in their schooling.

This chapter relates how Marie Clay generously engaged others in her work and the important steps she took to ensure that leadership, research, implementation efforts, trademark responsibilities, and authority for her intellectual property were transferred to others. Her vision for the future extended to the international stage and to the importance of securing international collaboration in the support of research and implementation issues. By supporting and encouraging the international Trainers in establishing the International Reading Recovery Trainers Organization and by creating the Marie Clay Literacy Trust, she helped to create structures that provide sustainable leadership and the basis for ongoing research and development.

The International Reading Recovery Trainers Organization is charged with maintaining the integrity of Reading Recovery and supporting implementations around the world. The responsibilities also extend to any new developments pertaining to *Literacy Lessons Designed for Individuals*, i.e., the application of Reading Recovery teaching procedures to new populations of learners. Trainers' activities will include attention to problem-solving, development, research exploration, and guiding the redevelopments of Reading Recovery and/or Literacy Lessons in new nations and in languages other than English. The International Reading Recovery Trainers Organization has the appropriate structures and systems in place for ensuring the integrity of Reading Recovery/Literacy Lessons and for directing the successful redesigns of Marie Clay's early intervention.

International Reading Recovery Trainers, alongside the professional community of teachers, Tutors/Teacher Leaders, administrators, other educators, and policy makers worldwide, offer a unique synergy that results from combining research, development, mentoring, and redesign (Wilson & Daviss, 1994). This synergy forecasts a dynamic, evolving, creative, and yet secure future for Reading Recovery and Literacy Lessons designed for and delivered to individual children throughout the world.

Andy Hargreaves (2006) suggests that the 'most effective legacies . . . are found in purposes, principles, practices, and people' (p. 41). Countless educators have benefited from Marie Clay's remarkable legacy. As all continue to work together to sustain her heritage, they will ensure access to Reading Recovery/Literacy Lessons for all children who need an individual, literacy intervention in any country. The future holds exciting possibilities, shining with promise. The way forward is clear, and the horizons are indeed boundless.

References

Charlesworth. A., Charlesworth. R., Raban, B., & Rickards, F. (2006). Teaching children with hearing loss in Reading Recovery. *Literacy Teaching and Learning: An International Journal of Early Reading and Writing, 11*(1), 21–50.

Clay, M. M. (1989). Concepts about print: In English and other languages. *The Reading Teacher, 42*(4), 268–277.

Clay, M. M. (1993). *Reading Recovery: A guidebook for teachers-in-training.* Auckland: Heinemann.

Clay, M. M. (1994). Reading Recovery: The wider implications of an educational innovation. *Literacy, Teaching and Learning: An International Journal of Early Literacy, 1*(1), 121–141.

Clay, M. M. (1997). International perspectives on the Reading Recovery program. In J. Flood, S. B. Heath, & D. Lapp (Eds.), *Handbook of research on teaching literacy through the communicative and visual arts* (pp. 655–667*).* New York: Macmillan Librarian Reference USA (a project of the International Reading Association).

Clay, M. M. (2001). *Change over time in children's literacy development.* Auckland: Heinemann.

Clay, M. M. (2002, 2006). *An observation survey of early literacy achievement* (2nd ed.). Auckland: Heinemann.

Clay, M. M. (2003). Afterword. In S. Forbes & C. Briggs (Eds.), *Research in Reading Recovery, volume two* (pp. 297–303). Auckland: Heinemann.

Clay, M. M. (2005a). *Literacy lessons designed for individuals, Part One.* Auckland: Heinemann.

Clay, M. M. (2005b). *Literacy lessons designed for individuals, Part Two.* Portsmouth, NH: Heinemann.

Fullerton, S. (2008). The development of literacy lessons with children who are deaf. *Journal of Reading Recovery, 8*(1), 34–42.

Hargreaves, A. (2006). From recovery to sustainability. *Journal of Reading Recovery, 5*(2), 39–44.

Hargreaves, A., & Fink, D. (2006). *Sustainable leadership.* San Francisco: Jossey Bass.

Hobsbaum, A. (1997). Reading Recovery in England. In S. L. Swartz & A. F. Klein (Eds.), *Research in Reading Recovery* (pp. 132–147). Portsmouth, NH: Heinemann.

Kelly, P., Gómez-Bellengé, F. X., Chen, J., & Schulz, M. (2008). Learner outcomes for English language learner low readers in an early intervention. *TESOL Quarterly, 42*(2), 135–160.

Neal, J., & Kelly, P.R. (1999). The success of Reading Recovery for English language learners and Descubiendo la Lectura for bilingual students in California. *Literacy, Teaching and Learning: An International Journal of Early Literacy*, 4(2), 81–108.

Rau, C. (1998). *He Mātai Āta Titiro Ki Te Tūtukitanga Mātātupu Pānui, Tuhi.* The Maori reconstruction of *An observation survey of early literacy achievement.* Ngaruawahia: Kia Ata Mai Educational Trust.

Rodgers, E. M., Gómez-Bellengé, F. X., Wang, C. (2004, April). *Closing the literacy achievement gap with early intervention.* Paper presented at the annual meeting of the American Educational Research Association in San Diego, CA.

Rodgers, E. M., Gómez-Bellengé, F. X., Wang, C., & Schultz, M. M. (2005, April). *Predicting the literacy achievement of struggling readers: Does intervening early make a difference?* Paper presented at the annual meeting of the American Educational Research Association in Montreal, Quebec.

Rodriguez, Y. (2007). A journey with Marie Clay: Translating An Observation Survey of Early Literacy Achievement. *Journal of Reading Recovery*, 7(1), 123–125.

Rowe, K. J. (1997). Factors affecting students' progress in reading: Key findings from a longitudinal study. In S. L. Swartz & A. F. Klein (Eds.), *Research in Reading Recovery* (pp. 53–101). Portsmouth, NH: Heinemann.

Smith, P. (1994). Reading Recovery and children with English as a second language. *New Zealand Journal of Educational Studies*, 29(2), 141–159.

Wilson, K. G., & Daviss, B. (1994). *Redesigning education: A Nobel Prize winner reveals what must be done to reform American education.* New York: Henry Holt.

Appendix

The following questions for research were suggested by Marie Clay. They are but a sample of her many enquiries into learning, teaching, and implementing Reading Recovery (Clay, 2001, 2003). Some of the questions are stated in her words while others are paraphrased from her work.

- How does a learner learn to work on the different kinds of information in the text? Separately, at first; and then in some integrated way?

- How does a reader learn to search, cross-check, make links, make decisions and evaluate those decisions while working across print?

- How and when does a learner initiate problem-solving from context and meaning at several levels? From oral language knowledge? From analogy with known words? From breaking the word apart in some way? From using letter-sound knowledge?

- What makes the learner cluster letters and work on chunks of words?

- Does the learner learn to deal with these possibilities one before the other or at one and the same time?

- How does the learner avoid the dominance of any type of information and keep the processing flexible?

- How does the use of phonological knowledge change over time?

- How can learners extend their own working systems? What mediates the changes? What is it that teachers need to support?

- What special demands does the reading and writing of continuous text place on learners?

- How is self-correction explained? What does the close study of self-correction behaviour reveal?

- What are the strategic processes of children learning to write?

- How does silent reading develop over time?

- How should initial knowledge be acquired and organized to facilitate the flexibility needed for a wide range of future applications?

- How can learners sustain flexibility across the systems?

- What are the implications of a complex theory of literacy processing for the study of older readers?

- What makes early literacy intervention so effective? What are we doing right?

- What makes Reading Recovery preventive in contrast to instruction designed to add new items of knowledge?

- How do children use knowledge gained in reading in their writing and vice versa?

- For what kinds of learning is individual instruction particularly powerful?

- Can we design research that will track how the sequence of changes differs (varies) from child to child? Can we demonstrate that there are different paths to common outcomes?

- What does the transition from Reading Recovery look like 1 year after the intervention? And 2 years after? What does classroom learning the year after Reading Recovery look like for all children and what does the subsequent learning of discontinued children look like? What does the self-extending system look like?

Contributors

Billie Askew	Texas Woman's University, Professor Emerita
Ann Ballantyne	New York University, Formerly National Reading Recovery New Zealand
Christine Boocock	National Reading Recovery, Faculty of Education, The University of Auckland
Sue Burroughs-Lange	European Centre for Reading Recovery, University of London Institute of Education
Marie M. Clay	3rd January 1926 – 13th April 2007
Julia Douëtil	European Centre for Reading Recovery, University of London Institute of Education
Mary Anne Doyle	University of Connecticut Chair, IRRTO Executive Board
Francisco Gómez-Bellengé	The Ohio State University
Irene Huggins	Brandon University, Western Canadian Institute of Reading Recovery
Sue McDowall	New Zealand Council for Educational Research
Robert M. Schwartz	Oakland University, Michigan
Janet Scull	University of Melbourne
Bryan Tuck	Retired Reader in Education, Auckland College of Education, incorporated within Faculty of Education, The University of Auckland
Barbara Watson	Former National Director, Reading Recovery New Zealand Trustee, Marie Clay Literacy Trust

Acknowledgements

Sincere thanks go to an international group of literacy leaders and researchers who collaborated to make possible this volume about Marie Clay's search for the possible in children's literacy. We owe a debt of gratitude to the chapter authors around the globe who provided unique perspectives of Marie's contributions, placing her research and her accomplishments into an international and historical context.

Our appreciation extends to all members of the International Reading Recovery Trainers Organization (IRRTO) for their support and their contribution to ongoing research and study, providing direction for change and growth in Reading Recovery through international collaboration and investigation.

We also wish to acknowledge the following reviewers who gave of their time to read and provide feedback to the editors and the contributing authors:

Roger Beard, Lydia Berger, Christine Boocock, Mary Anne Doyle, Jann Farmer-Hailey, Angela Hobsbaum, Irene Huggins, Patricia Kelly, Blair Koefoed, Eva Konstantellou, Carol A. Lyons, Barbara MacGilchrist, Claire Marshall, Allyson Matczuk, Shirley Nalder, Bridie Raban, Jeni Riley, Emily Rodgers, Maribeth Schmitt, Janet Scull, Dianne Stuart, Bryan Tuck, and Janice Van Dyke.

Their input is greatly valued.

Rosalie Lockwood merits recognition for her support to the editors throughout the process. Her skill as a wordsmith is exceptional.

A special acknowledgement goes to our publisher, Graham McEwan, Marie Clay's long-time publisher and now Chair of the Marie Clay Literacy Trust. His commitment to the importance and the integrity of her work continues, unabated.

And finally, without the daily efforts of each and every individual who participates in some way in this remarkable early literacy intervention, such a volume would not have been possible.